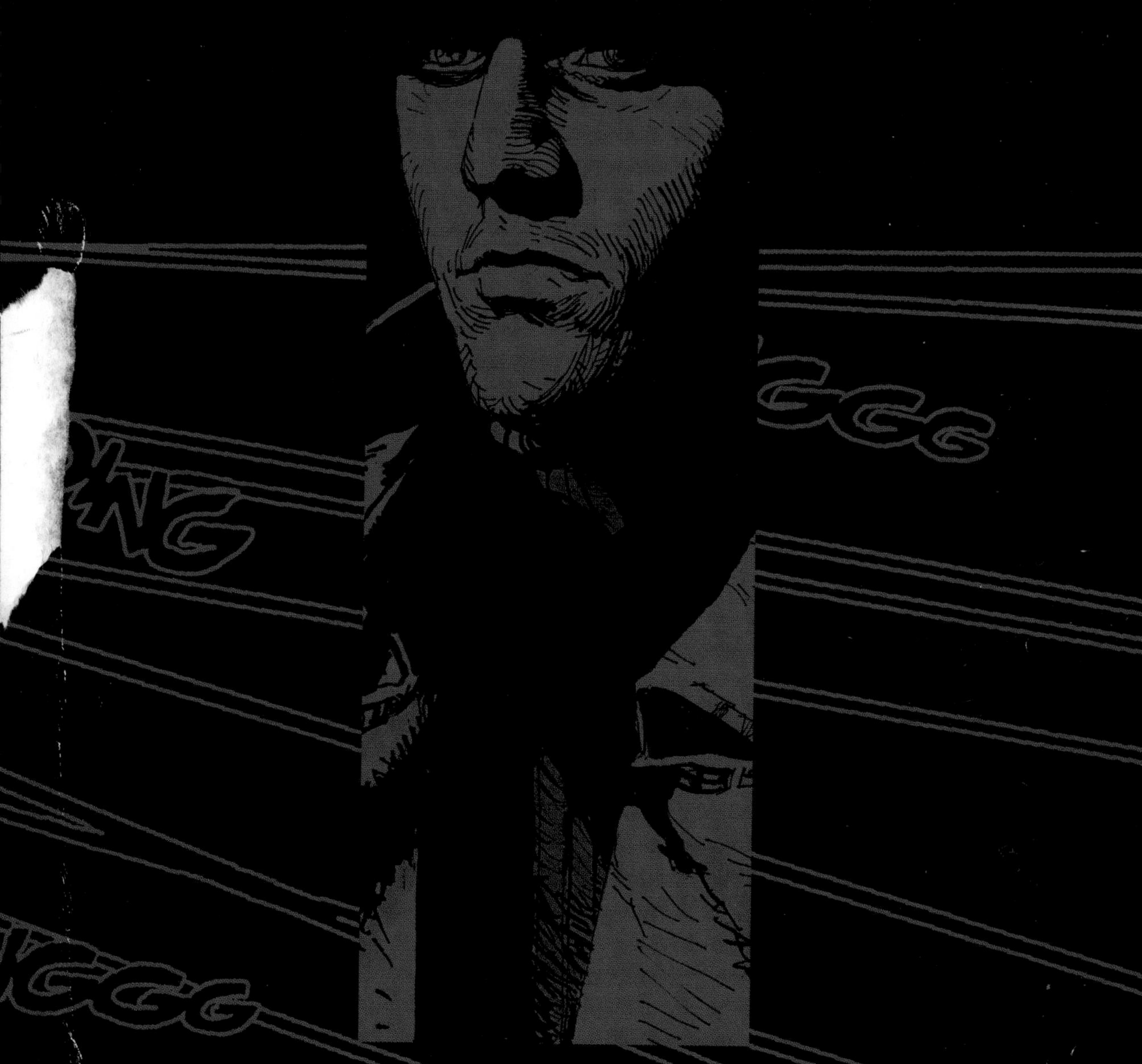

BUTTON MAN

KILLER KILLER

BUTTON MAN CREATED BY JOHN WAGNER AND ARTHUR RANSON

BUTTON MAN

KILLER KILLER

JOHN WAGNER
Writer

ARTHUR RANSON
Artist

KEVIN WALKER
Cover Artist

Creative Director and CEO: Jason Kingsley
Chief Technical Officer: Chris Kingsley
2000 AD Editor in Chief: Matt Smith
Graphic Design: Simon Parr & Luke Preece
Marketing and PR: Keith Richardson
Repro Assistant: Kathryn Symes

Graphic Novels Editor: Jonathan Oliver
Original Commissioning Editor: Andy Diggle

Published by Rebellion, Riverside House, Osney Mead, Oxford, UK. OX2 0ES
www.rebellion.co.uk

ISBN: 978-1-906735-09-8
Printed in Malta by Gutenberg Press
Manufactured in the EU by LPPS Ltd., Wellingborough, NN8 3PJ, UK.
First published: June 2009
10 9 8 7 6 5 4 3 2 1

Printed on FSC Accredited Paper

A CIP catalogue record for this book is available from the British Library.

For information on other *2000 AD* graphic novels, or if you have any comments on this book, please email books@2000ADonline.com

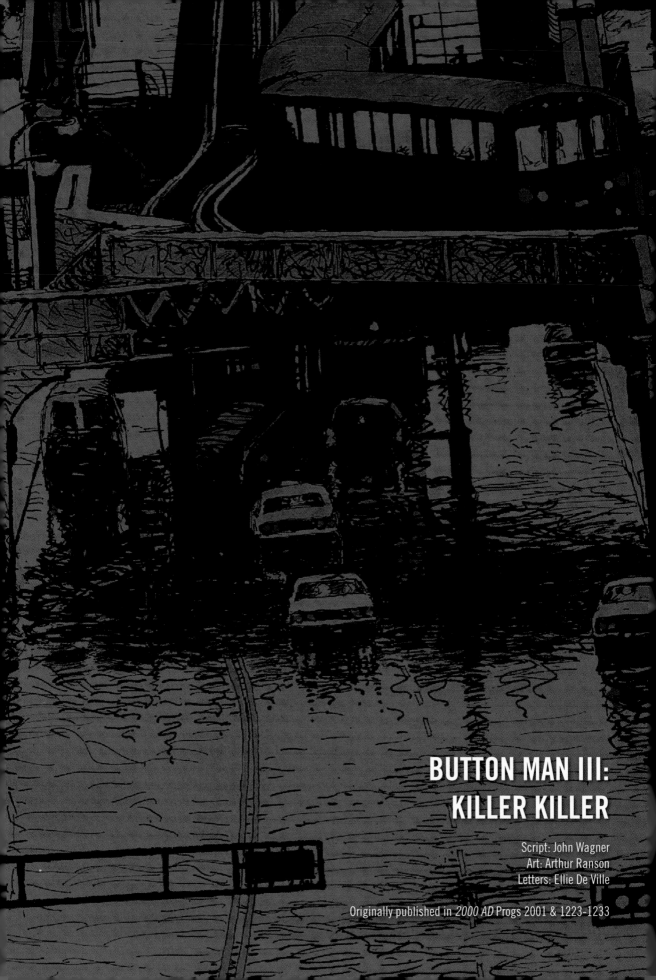

BUTTON MAN III:
KILLER KILLER

Script: John Wagner
Art: Arthur Ranson
Letters: Ellie De Ville

Originally published in *2000 AD* Progs 2001 & 1223-1233

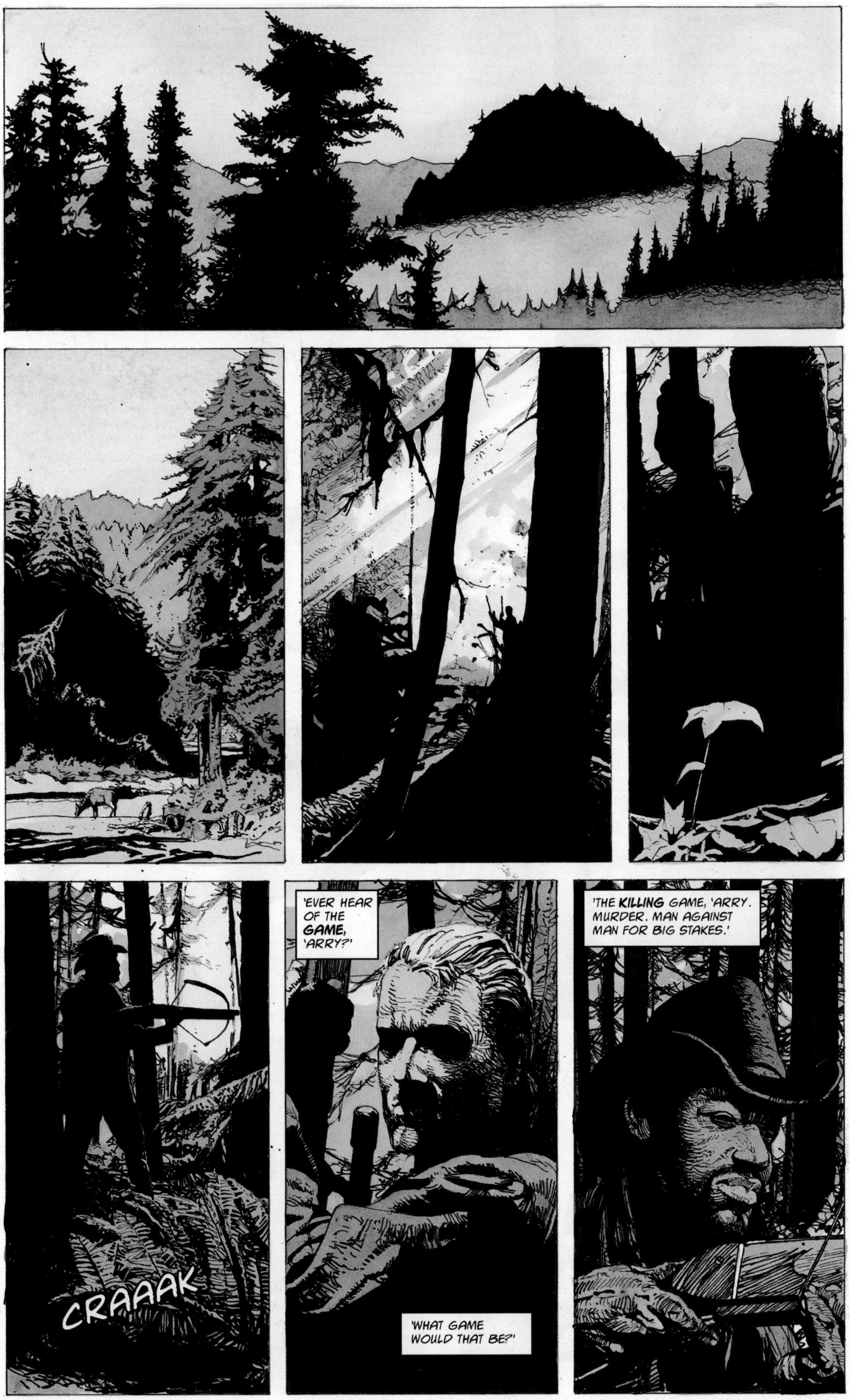
CRAAAK
'EVER HEAR OF THE **GAME**, 'ARRY?'
'WHAT GAME WOULD THAT BE?'
'THE **KILLING** GAME, 'ARRY. MURDER. MAN AGAINST MAN FOR BIG STAKES.'

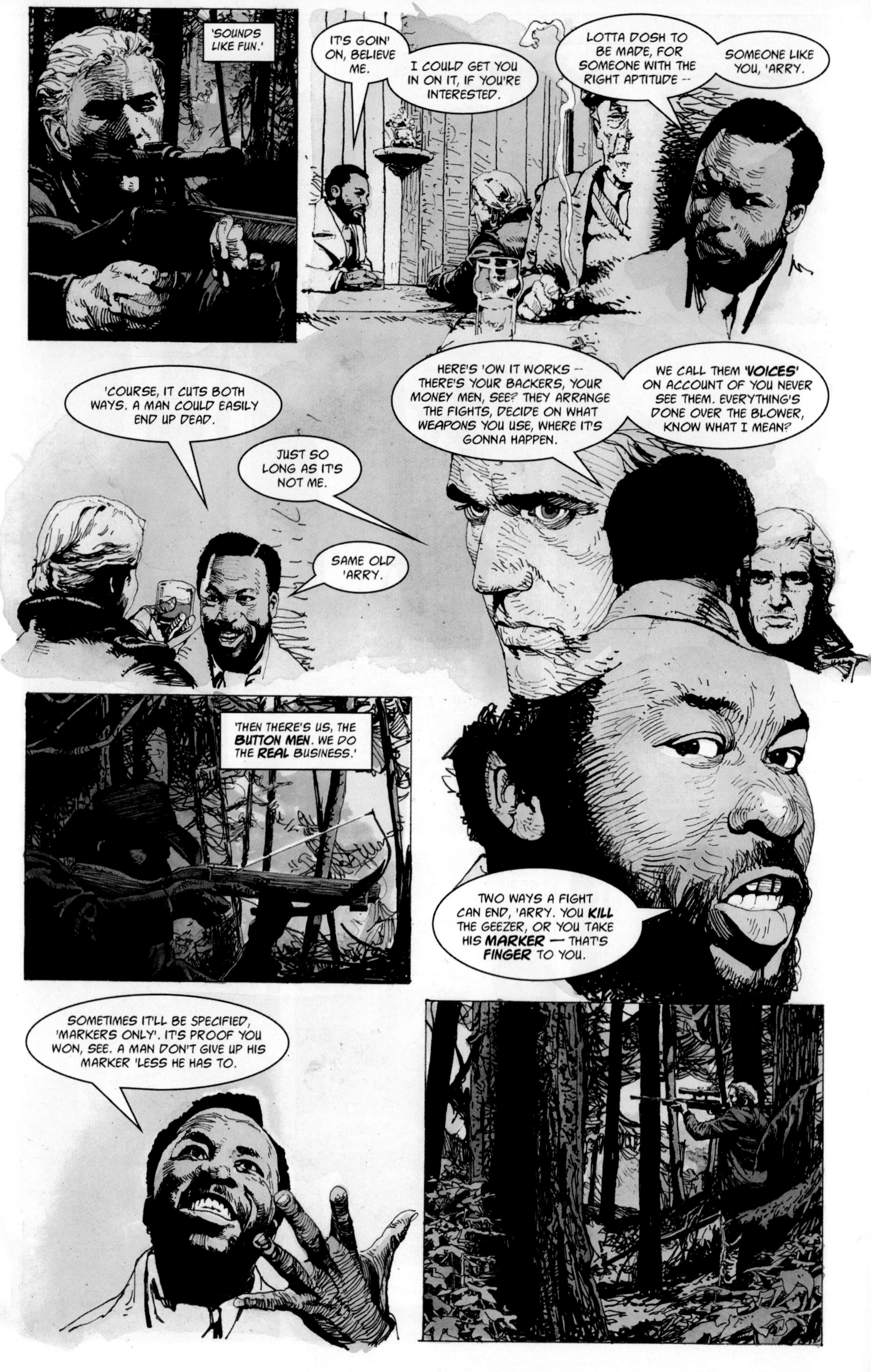
'SOUNDS LIKE FUN.'
IT'S GOIN' ON, BELIEVE ME.
I COULD GET YOU IN ON IT, IF YOU'RE INTERESTED.
LOTTA DOSH TO BE MADE, FOR SOMEONE WITH THE RIGHT APTITUDE --
SOMEONE LIKE YOU, 'ARRY.
'COURSE, IT CUTS BOTH WAYS. A MAN COULD EASILY END UP DEAD.
JUST SO LONG AS IT'S NOT ME.
SAME OLD 'ARRY.
HERE'S 'OW IT WORKS -- THERE'S YOUR BACKERS, YOUR MONEY MEN, SEE? THEY ARRANGE THE FIGHTS, DECIDE ON WHAT WEAPONS YOU USE, WHERE IT'S GONNA HAPPEN.
WE CALL THEM 'VOICES' ON ACCOUNT OF YOU NEVER SEE THEM. EVERYTHING'S DONE OVER THE BLOWER, KNOW WHAT I MEAN?
'THEN THERE'S US, THE BUTTON MEN. WE DO THE REAL BUSINESS.'
TWO WAYS A FIGHT CAN END, 'ARRY. YOU KILL THE GEEZER, OR YOU TAKE HIS MARKER — THAT'S FINGER TO YOU.
SOMETIMES IT'LL BE SPECIFIED, 'MARKERS ONLY'. IT'S PROOF YOU WON, SEE. A MAN DON'T GIVE UP HIS MARKER 'LESS HE HAS TO.

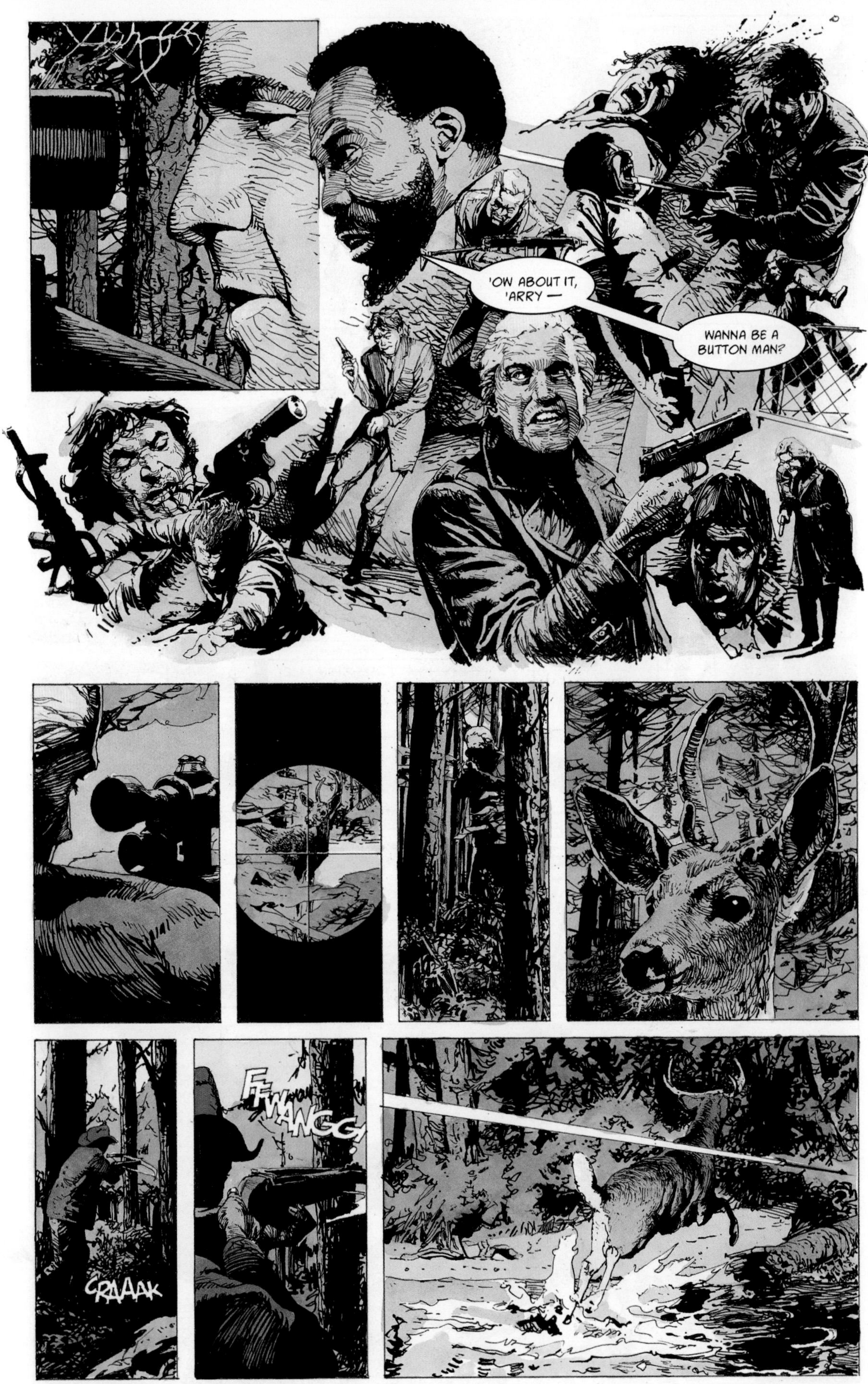
'OW ABOUT IT, 'ARRY —
WANNA BE A BUTTON MAN?
FFWANGG!
CRAAAK

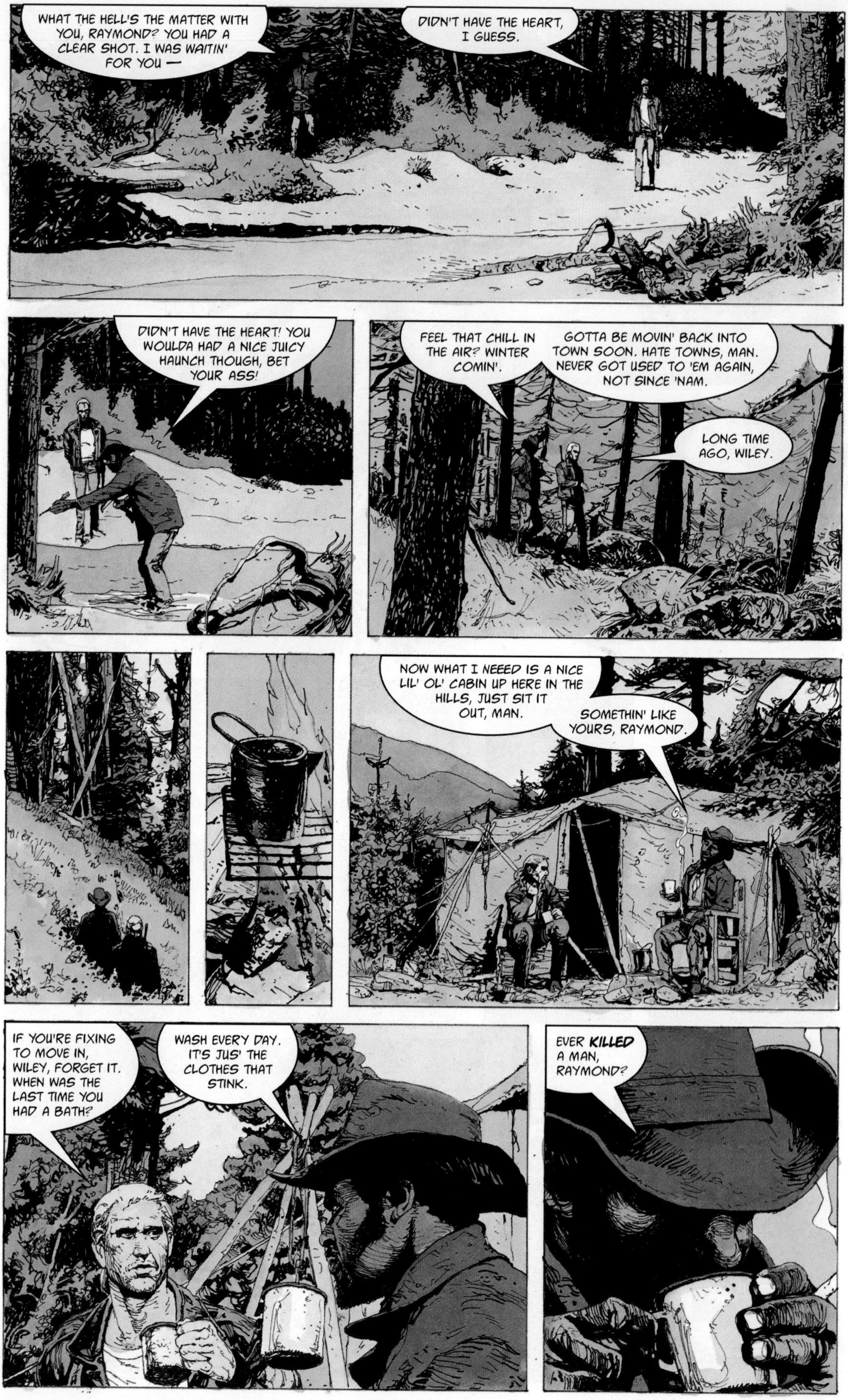
WHAT THE HELL'S THE MATTER WITH YOU, RAYMOND? YOU HAD A CLEAR SHOT. I WAS WAITIN' FOR YOU —
DIDN'T HAVE THE HEART, I GUESS.
DIDN'T HAVE THE HEART! YOU WOULDA HAD A NICE JUICY HAUNCH THOUGH, BET YOUR ASS!
FEEL THAT CHILL IN THE AIR? WINTER COMIN'.
GOTTA BE MOVIN' BACK INTO TOWN SOON. HATE TOWNS, MAN. NEVER GOT USED TO 'EM AGAIN, NOT SINCE 'NAM.
LONG TIME AGO, WILEY.
NOW WHAT I NEEED IS A NICE LIL' OL' CABIN UP HERE IN THE HILLS, JUST SIT IT OUT, MAN.
SOMETHIN' LIKE YOURS, RAYMOND.
IF YOU'RE FIXING TO MOVE IN, WILEY, FORGET IT. WHEN WAS THE LAST TIME YOU HAD A BATH?
WASH EVERY DAY. IT'S JUS' THE CLOTHES THAT STINK.
EVER **KILLED** A MAN, RAYMOND?

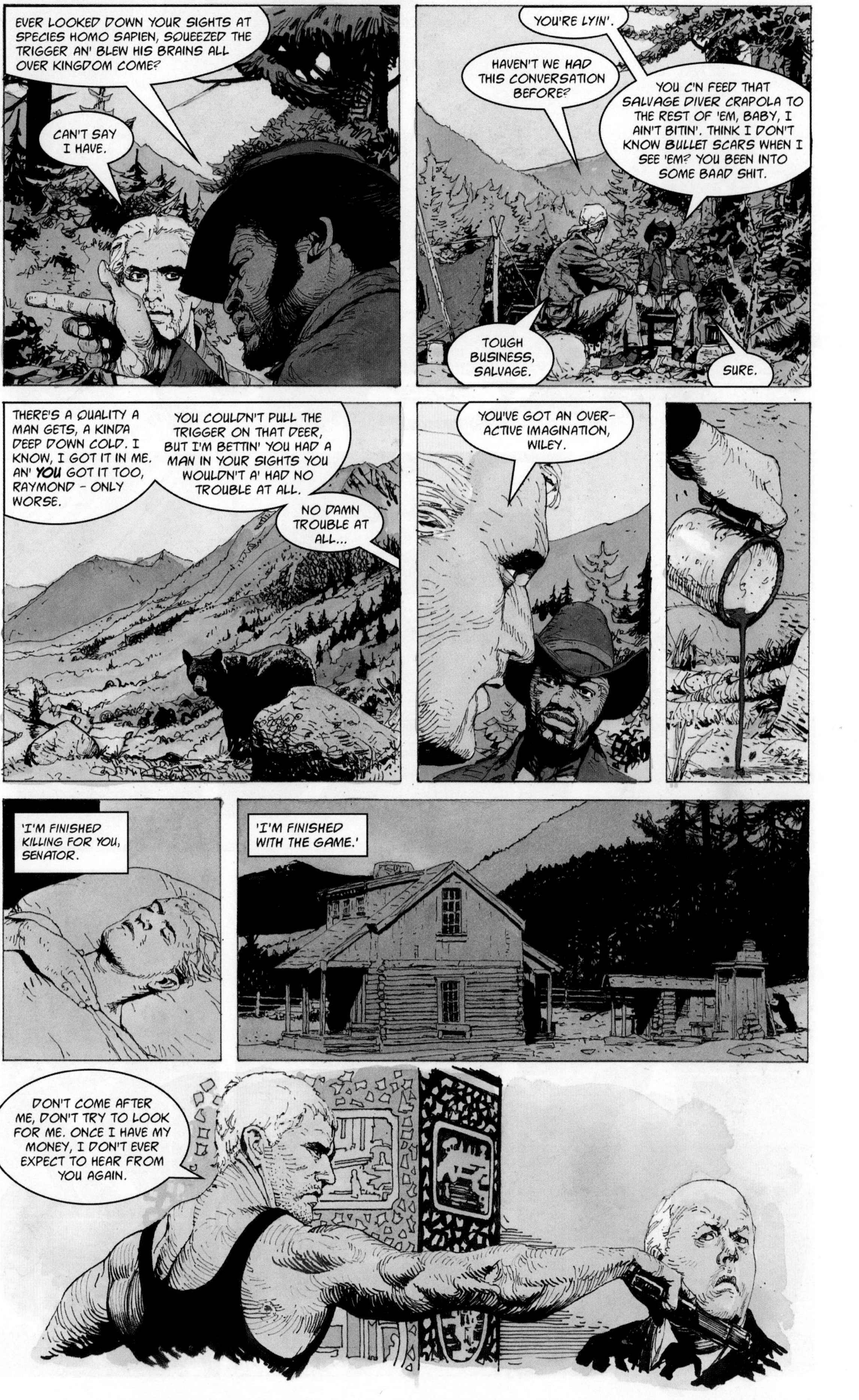
EVER LOOKED DOWN YOUR SIGHTS AT SPECIES HOMO SAPIEN, SQUEEZED THE TRIGGER AN' BLEW HIS BRAINS ALL OVER KINGDOM COME?
CAN'T SAY I HAVE.
YOU'RE LYIN'.
HAVEN'T WE HAD THIS CONVERSATION BEFORE?
YOU C'N FEED THAT SALVAGE DIVER CRAPOLA TO THE REST OF 'EM, BABY, I AIN'T BITIN'. THINK I DON'T KNOW BULLET SCARS WHEN I SEE 'EM? YOU BEEN INTO SOME BAAD SHIT.
TOUGH BUSINESS, SALVAGE.
SURE.
THERE'S A QUALITY A MAN GETS, A KINDA DEEP DOWN COLD. I KNOW, I GOT IT IN ME. AN' YOU GOT IT TOO, RAYMOND - ONLY WORSE.
YOU COULDN'T PULL THE TRIGGER ON THAT DEER, BUT I'M BETTIN' YOU HAD A MAN IN YOUR SIGHTS YOU WOULDN'T A' HAD NO TROUBLE AT ALL.
NO DAMN TROUBLE AT ALL...
YOU'VE GOT AN OVER-ACTIVE IMAGINATION, WILEY.
'I'M FINISHED KILLING FOR YOU, SENATOR.
'I'M FINISHED WITH THE GAME.'
DON'T COME AFTER ME, DON'T TRY TO LOOK FOR ME. ONCE I HAVE MY MONEY, I DON'T EVER EXPECT TO HEAR FROM YOU AGAIN.

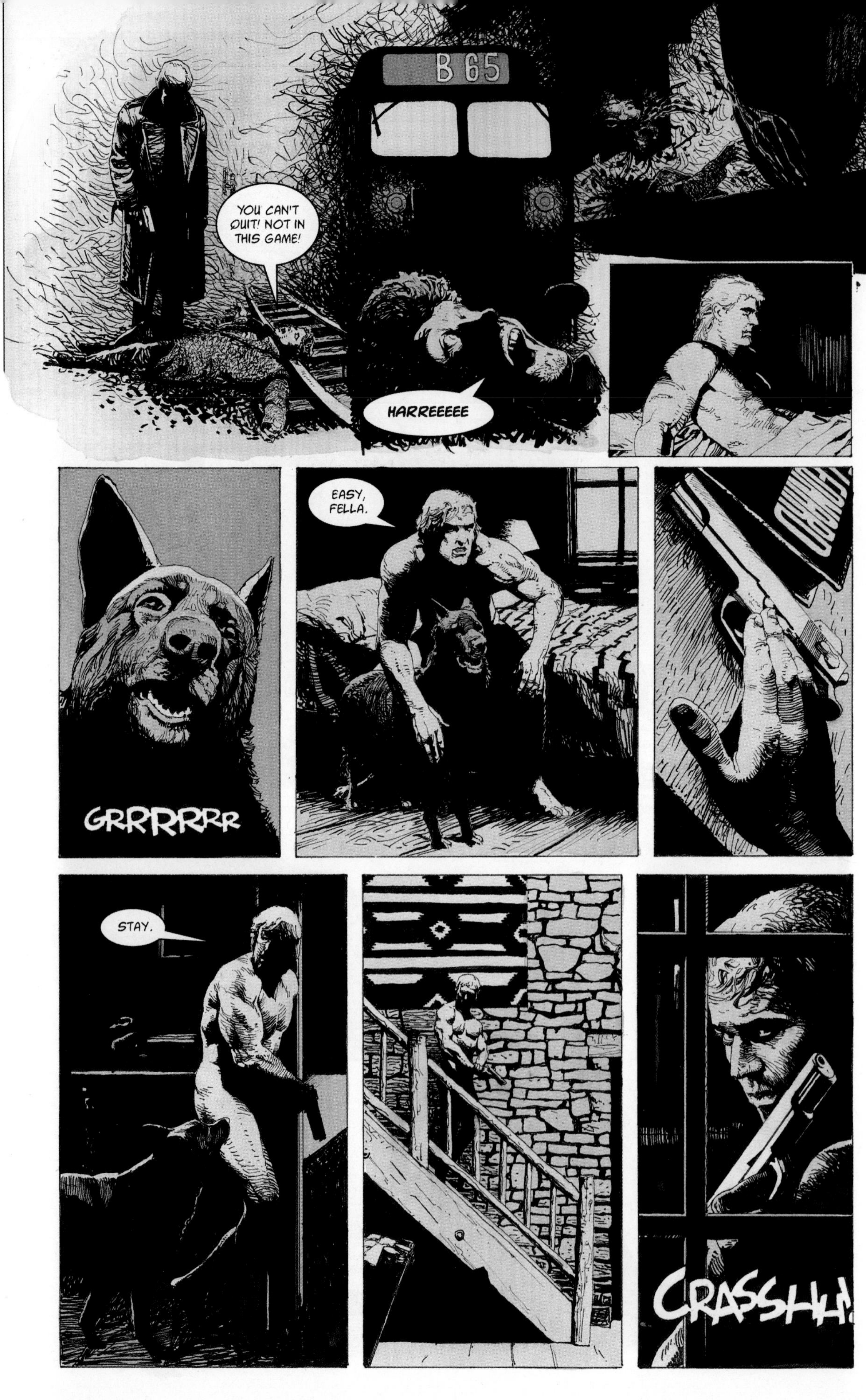
YOU CAN'T QUIT! NOT IN THIS GAME!
B 65
HARREEEEE
GRRRRRR
EASY, FELLA.
STAY.
CRASSHH!

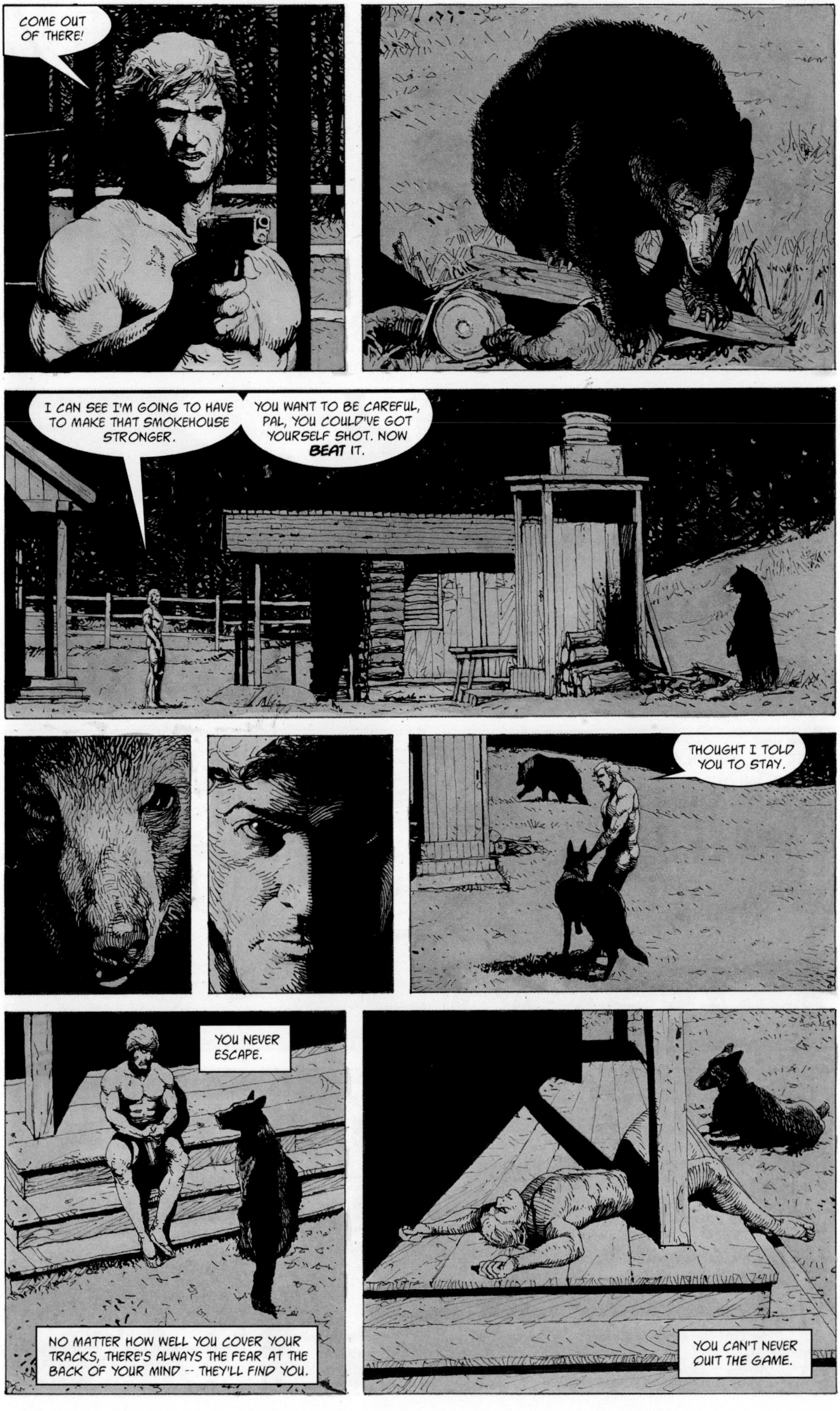

COME OUT OF THERE!
I CAN SEE I'M GOING TO HAVE TO MAKE THAT SMOKEHOUSE STRONGER.
YOU WANT TO BE CAREFUL, PAL, YOU COULD'VE GOT YOURSELF SHOT. NOW BEAT IT.
THOUGHT I TOLD YOU TO STAY.
YOU NEVER ESCAPE.
NO MATTER HOW WELL YOU COVER YOUR TRACKS, THERE'S ALWAYS THE FEAR AT THE BACK OF YOUR MIND -- THEY'LL FIND YOU.
YOU CAN'T NEVER QUIT THE GAME.

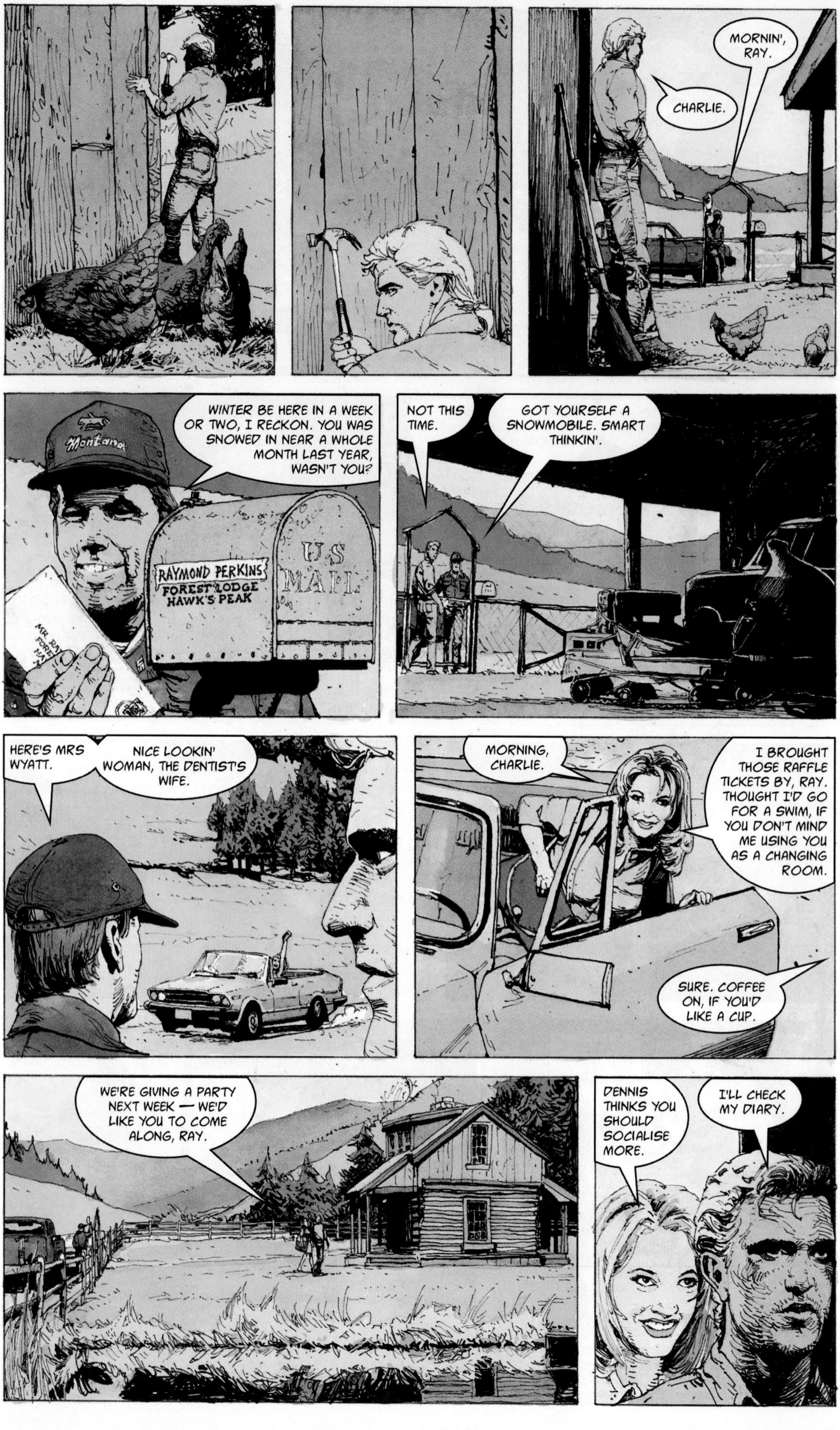
MORNIN', RAY.
CHARLIE.
WINTER BE HERE IN A WEEK OR TWO, I RECKON. YOU WAS SNOWED IN NEAR A WHOLE MONTH LAST YEAR, WASN'T YOU?
RAYMOND PERKINS
FOREST LODGE
HAWK'S PEAK
US MAIL
NOT THIS TIME.
GOT YOURSELF A SNOWMOBILE. SMART THINKIN'.
HERE'S MRS WYATT.
NICE LOOKIN' WOMAN, THE DENTIST'S WIFE.
MORNING, CHARLIE.
I BROUGHT THOSE RAFFLE TICKETS BY, RAY. THOUGHT I'D GO FOR A SWIM, IF YOU DON'T MIND ME USING YOU AS A CHANGING ROOM.
SURE. COFFEE ON, IF YOU'D LIKE A CUP.
WE'RE GIVING A PARTY NEXT WEEK — WE'D LIKE YOU TO COME ALONG, RAY.
DENNIS THINKS YOU SHOULD SOCIALISE MORE.
I'LL CHECK MY DIARY.

LAKE'S GETTING DAMNED COLD.

I'LL JUST HAVE TO COME UP WITH ANOTHER EXCUSE.

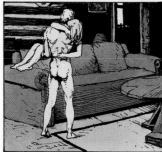

I NEED A SWIM NOW.

HAVE THAT COFFEE.

DENNIS KNOWS.

CLIK

ABOUT US?

NO, BUT HE KNOWS SOMETHING'S GOING ON.

GOING TO TELL HIM?

WOULD YOU MIND?

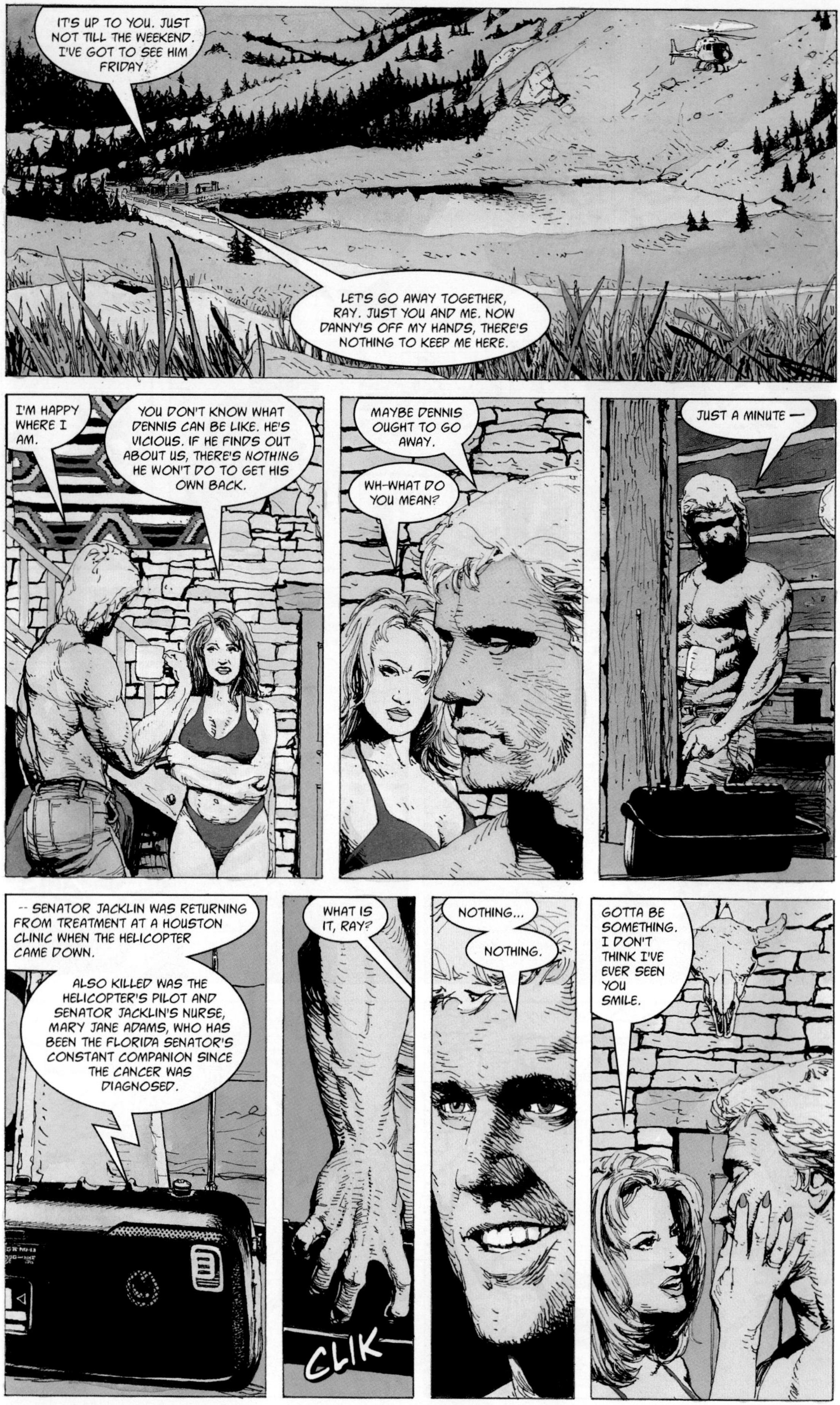
IT'S UP TO YOU. JUST NOT TILL THE WEEKEND. I'VE GOT TO SEE HIM FRIDAY.
LET'S GO AWAY TOGETHER, RAY. JUST YOU AND ME. NOW DANNY'S OFF MY HANDS, THERE'S NOTHING TO KEEP ME HERE.
I'M HAPPY WHERE I AM.
YOU DON'T KNOW WHAT DENNIS CAN BE LIKE. HE'S VICIOUS. IF HE FINDS OUT ABOUT US, THERE'S NOTHING HE WON'T DO TO GET HIS OWN BACK.
MAYBE DENNIS OUGHT TO GO AWAY.
WH-WHAT DO YOU MEAN?
JUST A MINUTE —
-- SENATOR JACKLIN WAS RETURNING FROM TREATMENT AT A HOUSTON CLINIC WHEN THE HELICOPTER CAME DOWN.
ALSO KILLED WAS THE HELICOPTER'S PILOT AND SENATOR JACKLIN'S NURSE, MARY JANE ADAMS, WHO HAS BEEN THE FLORIDA SENATOR'S CONSTANT COMPANION SINCE THE CANCER WAS DIAGNOSED.
WHAT IS IT, RAY?
CLIK
NOTHING...
NOTHING.
GOTTA BE SOMETHING. I DON'T THINK I'VE EVER SEEN YOU SMILE.

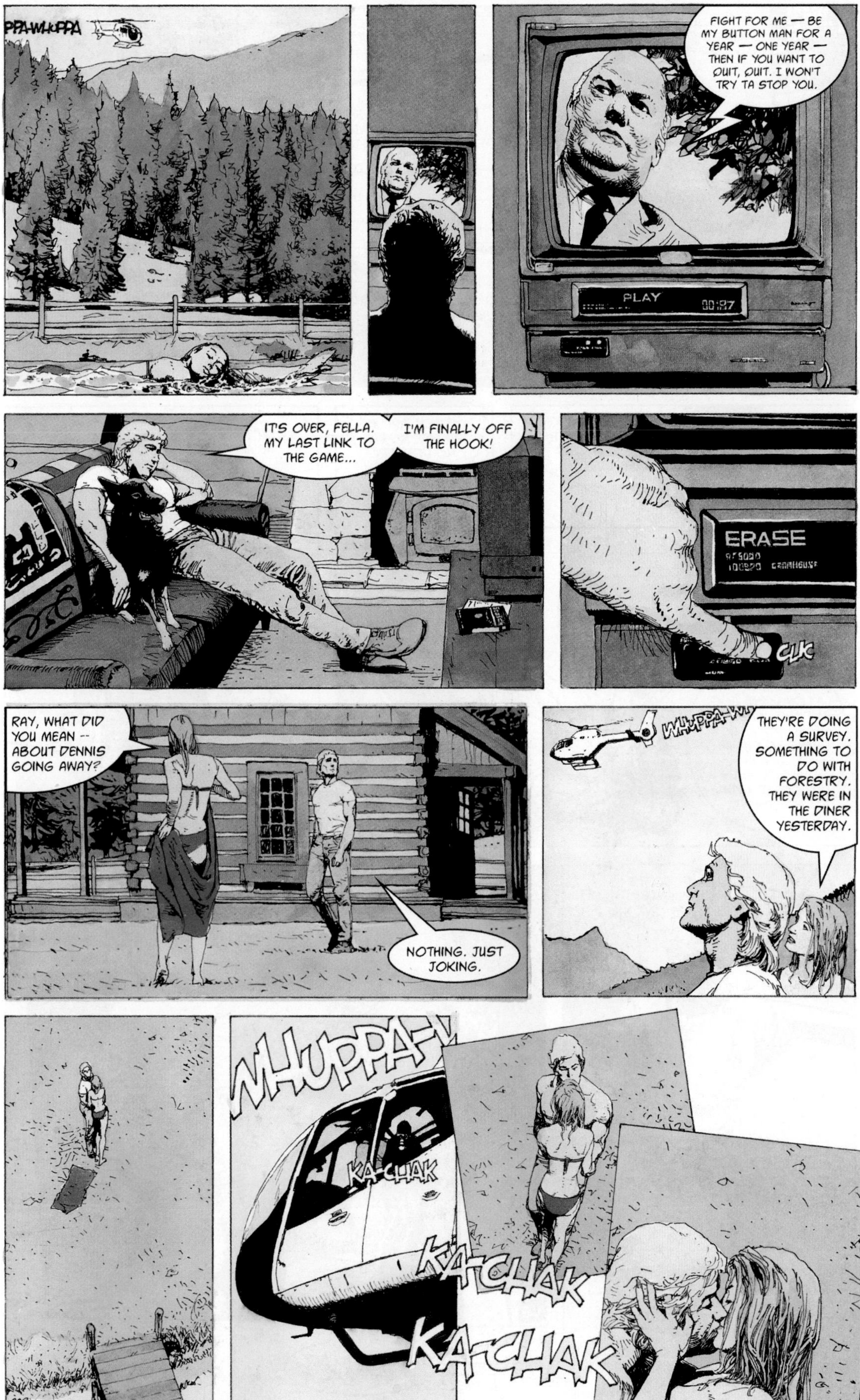
PPA-WHUPPA
FIGHT FOR ME — BE MY BUTTON MAN FOR A YEAR — ONE YEAR — THEN IF YOU WANT TO QUIT, QUIT. I WON'T TRY TA STOP YOU.
PLAY
IT'S OVER, FELLA. MY LAST LINK TO THE GAME...
I'M FINALLY OFF THE HOOK!
ERASE
CLIK
RAY, WHAT DID YOU MEAN -- ABOUT DENNIS GOING AWAY?
NOTHING. JUST JOKING.
WHUPPA-WH
THEY'RE DOING A SURVEY. SOMETHING TO DO WITH FORESTRY. THEY WERE IN THE DINER YESTERDAY.
WHUPPA
KA-CHAK
KA-CHAK
KA-CHAK

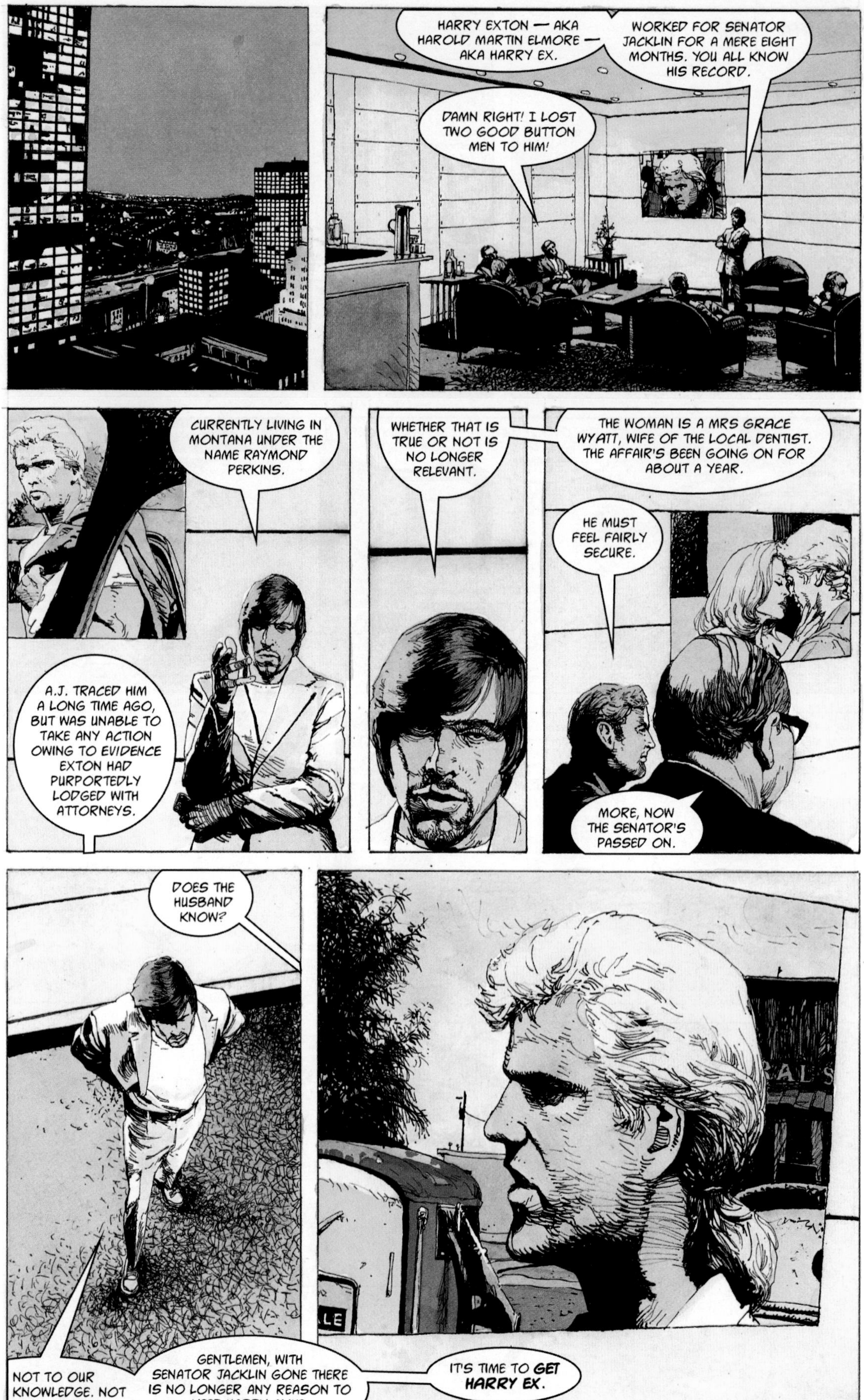

HARRY EXTON — AKA HAROLD MARTIN ELMORE — AKA HARRY EX.
WORKED FOR SENATOR JACKLIN FOR A MERE EIGHT MONTHS. YOU ALL KNOW HIS RECORD.
DAMN RIGHT! I LOST TWO GOOD BUTTON MEN TO HIM!
CURRENTLY LIVING IN MONTANA UNDER THE NAME RAYMOND PERKINS.
A.J. TRACED HIM A LONG TIME AGO, BUT WAS UNABLE TO TAKE ANY ACTION OWING TO EVIDENCE EXTON HAD PURPORTEDLY LODGED WITH ATTORNEYS.
WHETHER THAT IS TRUE OR NOT IS NO LONGER RELEVANT.
THE WOMAN IS A MRS GRACE WYATT, WIFE OF THE LOCAL DENTIST. THE AFFAIR'S BEEN GOING ON FOR ABOUT A YEAR.
HE MUST FEEL FAIRLY SECURE.
MORE, NOW THE SENATOR'S PASSED ON.
DOES THE HUSBAND KNOW?
NOT TO OUR KNOWLEDGE. NOT YET, AT LEAST.
GENTLEMEN, WITH SENATOR JACKLIN GONE THERE IS NO LONGER ANY REASON TO KEEP HARRY ALIVE.
IT'S TIME TO **GET HARRY EX.**

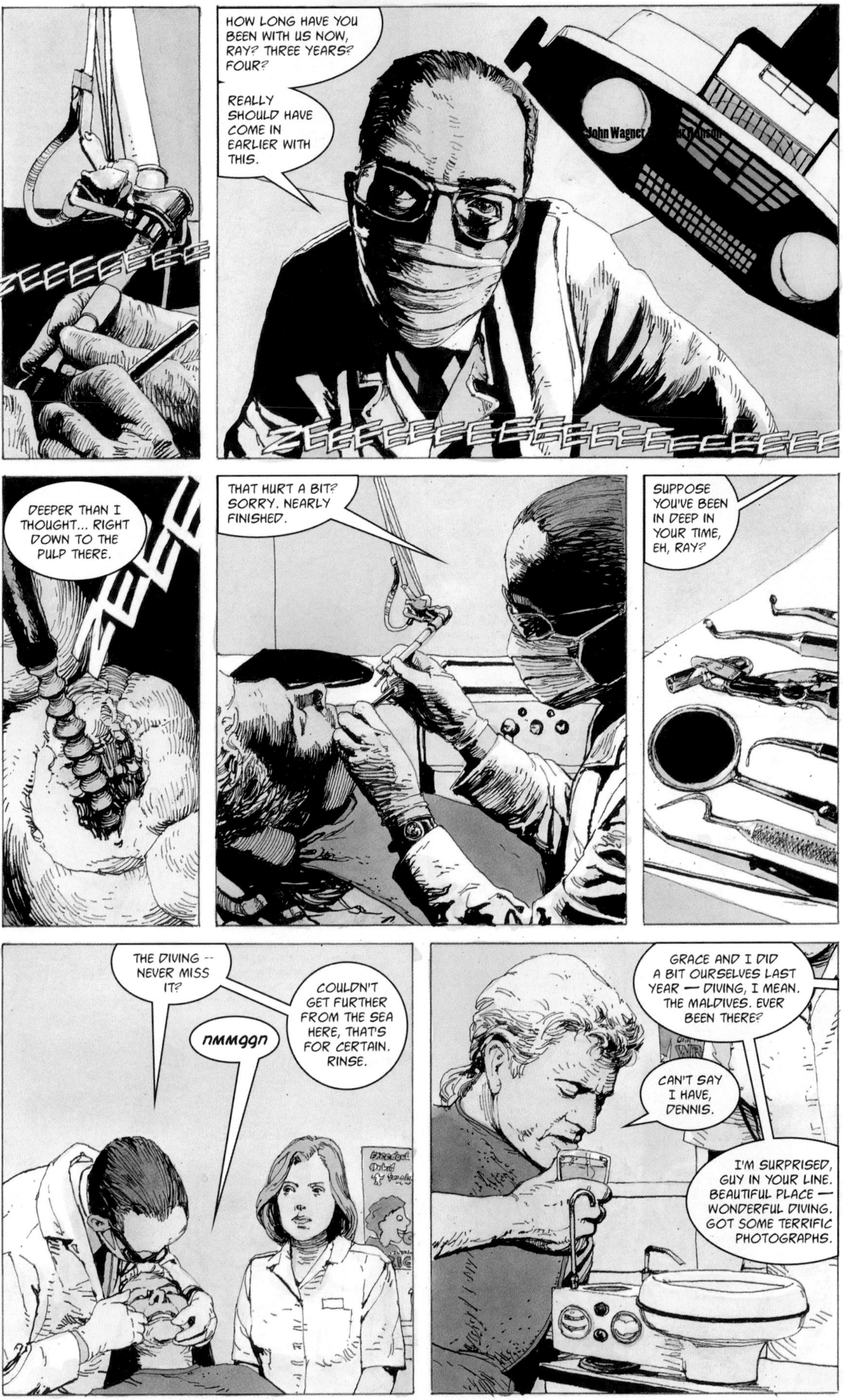
ZEEEEEEEE
HOW LONG HAVE YOU BEEN WITH US NOW, RAY? THREE YEARS? FOUR?
REALLY SHOULD HAVE COME IN EARLIER WITH THIS.
John Wagner
ZEEEEEEEEEEEEEEEEEEEEEE
DEEPER THAN I THOUGHT... RIGHT DOWN TO THE PULP THERE.
ZEEE
THAT HURT A BIT? SORRY. NEARLY FINISHED.
SUPPOSE YOU'VE BEEN IN DEEP IN YOUR TIME, EH, RAY?
THE DIVING -- NEVER MISS IT?
nmmggn
COULDN'T GET FURTHER FROM THE SEA HERE, THAT'S FOR CERTAIN. RINSE.
GRACE AND I DID A BIT OURSELVES LAST YEAR — DIVING, I MEAN. THE MALDIVES. EVER BEEN THERE?
CAN'T SAY I HAVE, DENNIS.
I'M SURPRISED, GUY IN YOUR LINE. BEAUTIFUL PLACE — WONDERFUL DIVING. GOT SOME TERRIFIC PHOTOGRAPHS.

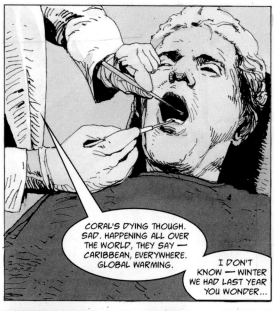

CORAL'S DYING THOUGH. SAD. HAPPENING ALL OVER THE WORLD, THEY SAY — CARIBBEAN, EVERYWHERE. GLOBAL WARMING.

I DON'T KNOW — WINTER WE HAD LAST YEAR YOU WONDER...

JANE, GO INTO MY DESK DRAWER — TOP RIGHT, I THINK. WANT TO SHOW RAY THOSE SNAPS.

IT'S ALL RIGHT, I CAN HANDLE THE FILLING.

GOOD LOOKING WOMAN, DON'T YOU THINK — GRACE — FOR HER AGE...?

STILL TAKES A GOOD PHOTOGRAPH. KEPT HER FIGURE. TOO MANY LET THEMSELVES GO...

SHE STOPPED BY YOUR CABIN THE OTHER DAY.

rrrnn

STOPS BY A LOT. YOU MUST BE SEEING MORE OF HER THAN I DO THESE DAYS.

HANDY, WITH THE LAKE. LIKES SWIMMING, GRACE. ALWAYS LIKED THE WATER.

I'M SORRY, DOCTOR WYATT, I COULDN'T FIND THEM ANYWHERE.

REALLY? MUST HAVE TAKEN THEM HOME. PITY. ANOTHER TIME.

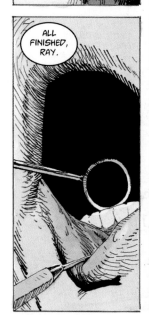

ALL FINISHED, RAY.

TRY NOT TO BITE ON THAT TODAY. NOTHING HARD FOR A DAY OR TWO.

AND HEY — DON'T LEAVE IT SO LONG NEXT TIME.

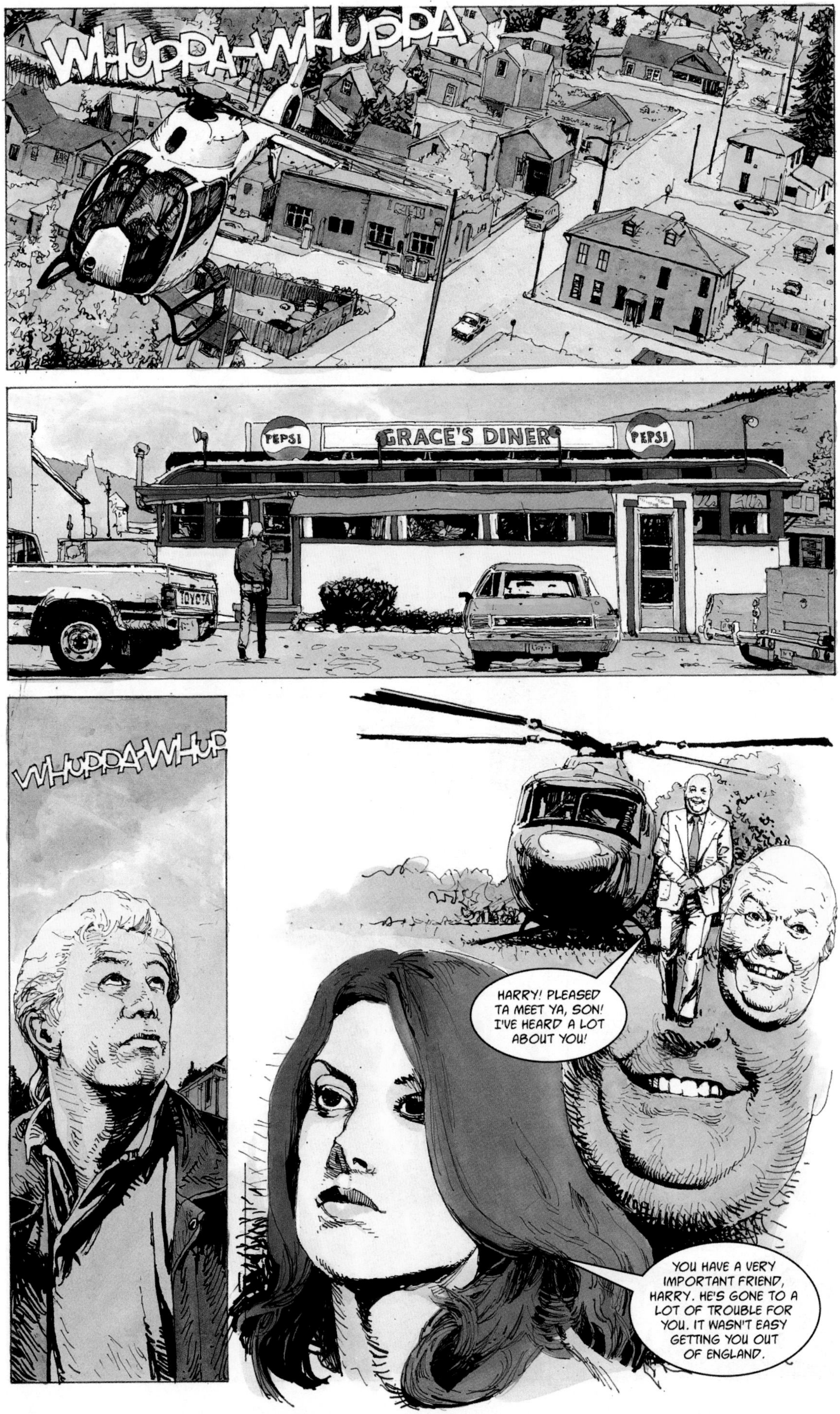
WHUPPA-WHUPPA
GRACE'S DINER
PEPSI
PEPSI
TOYOTA
WHUPPA-WHUP
HARRY! PLEASED TA MEET YA, SON! I'VE HEARD A LOT ABOUT YOU!
YOU HAVE A VERY IMPORTANT FRIEND, HARRY. HE'S GONE TO A LOT OF TROUBLE FOR YOU. IT WASN'T EASY GETTING YOU OUT OF ENGLAND.

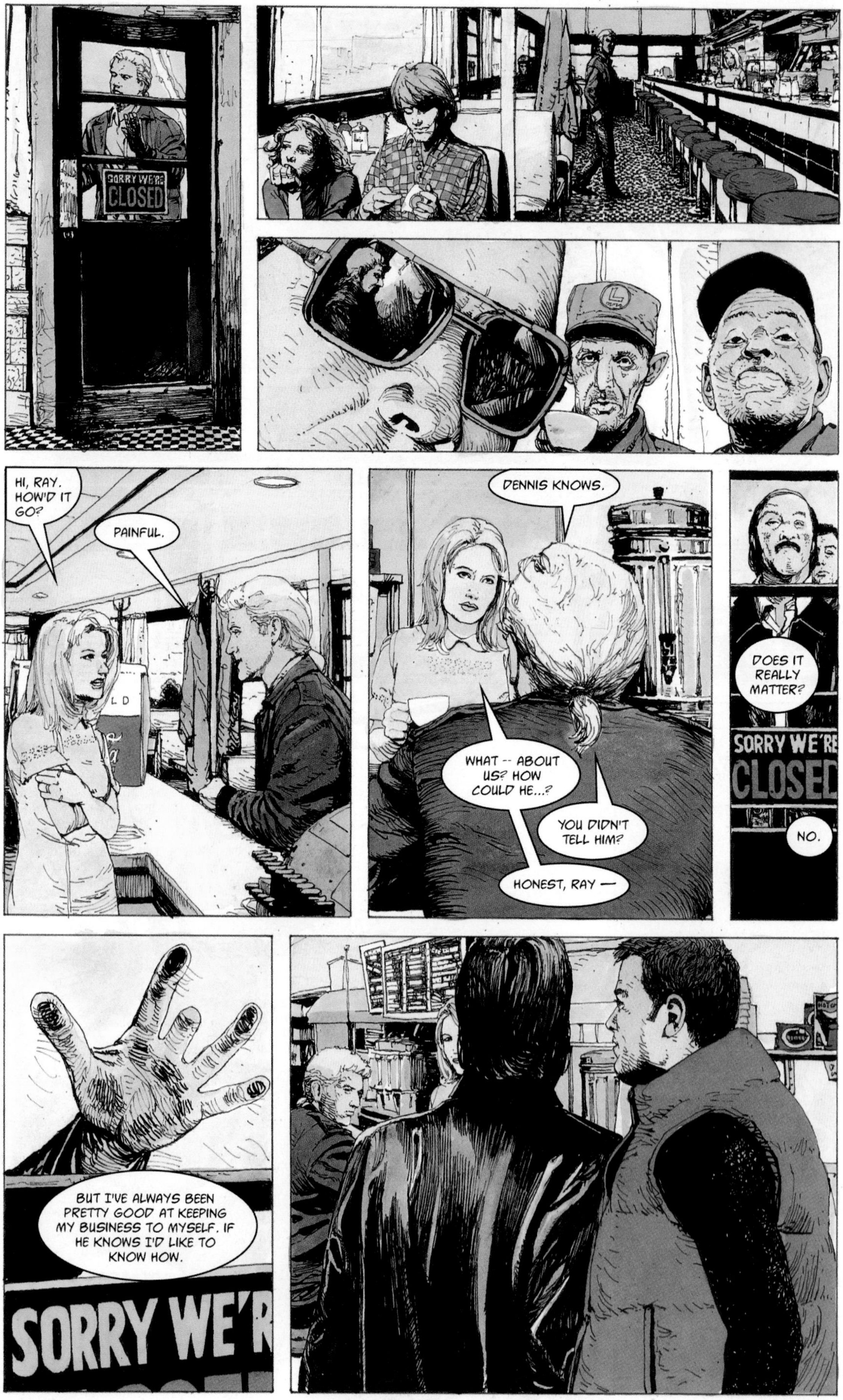
SORRY WE'RE CLOSED
HI, RAY. HOW'D IT GO?
PAINFUL.
DENNIS KNOWS.
WHAT -- ABOUT US? HOW COULD HE...?
YOU DIDN'T TELL HIM?
HONEST, RAY —
DOES IT REALLY MATTER?
SORRY WE'RE CLOSED
NO.
BUT I'VE ALWAYS BEEN PRETTY GOOD AT KEEPING MY BUSINESS TO MYSELF. IF HE KNOWS I'D LIKE TO KNOW HOW.
SORRY WE'R

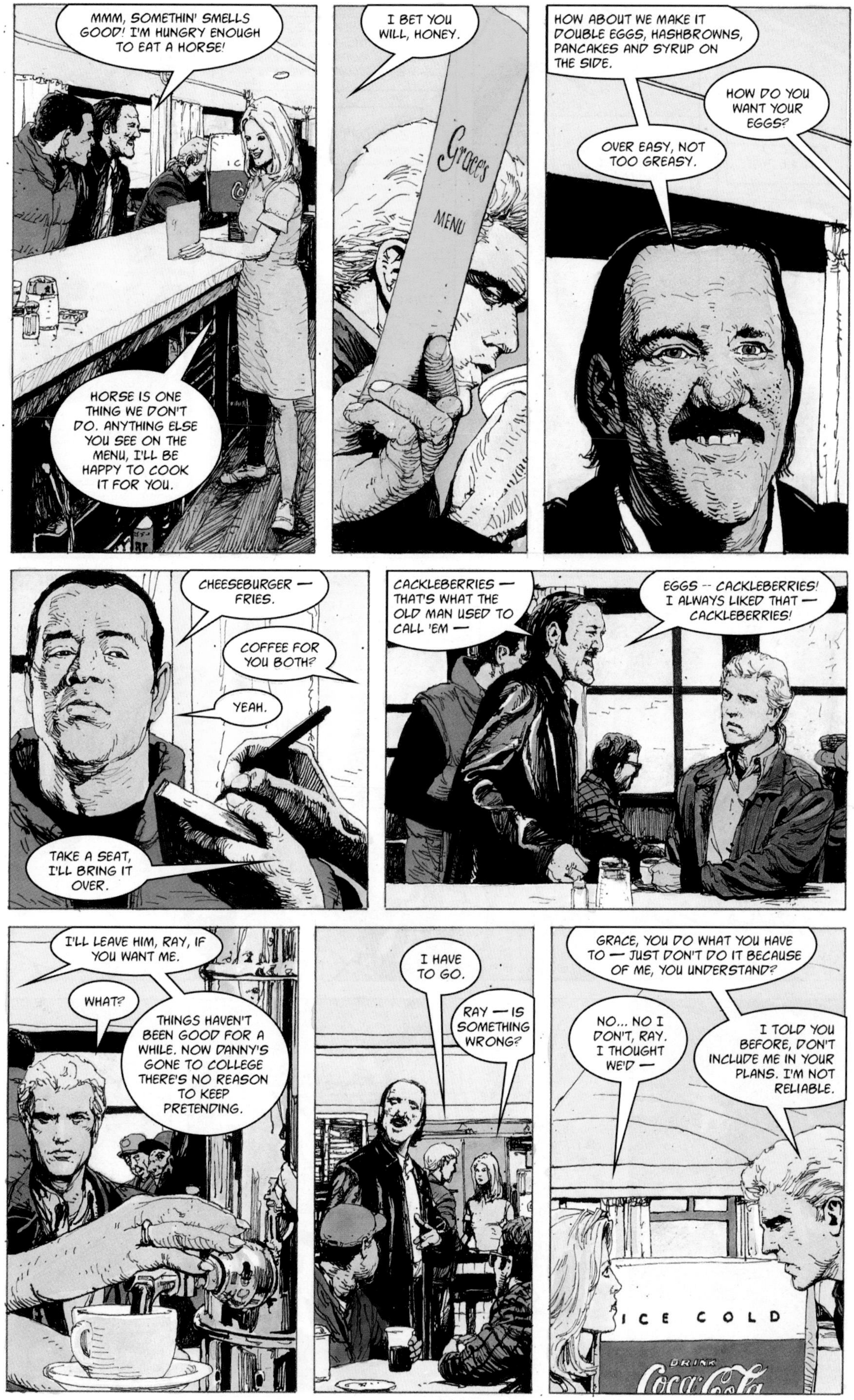

MMM, SOMETHIN' SMELLS GOOD! I'M HUNGRY ENOUGH TO EAT A HORSE!
HORSE IS ONE THING WE DON'T DO. ANYTHING ELSE YOU SEE ON THE MENU, I'LL BE HAPPY TO COOK IT FOR YOU.
I BET YOU WILL, HONEY.
Grace's
MENU
HOW ABOUT WE MAKE IT DOUBLE EGGS, HASHBROWNS, PANCAKES AND SYRUP ON THE SIDE.
HOW DO YOU WANT YOUR EGGS?
OVER EASY, NOT TOO GREASY.
CHEESEBURGER — FRIES.
COFFEE FOR YOU BOTH?
YEAH.
TAKE A SEAT, I'LL BRING IT OVER.
CACKLEBERRIES — THAT'S WHAT THE OLD MAN USED TO CALL 'EM —
EGGS -- CACKLEBERRIES! I ALWAYS LIKED THAT — CACKLEBERRIES!
I'LL LEAVE HIM, RAY, IF YOU WANT ME.
WHAT?
THINGS HAVEN'T BEEN GOOD FOR A WHILE. NOW DANNY'S GONE TO COLLEGE THERE'S NO REASON TO KEEP PRETENDING.
I HAVE TO GO.
RAY — IS SOMETHING WRONG?
GRACE, YOU DO WHAT YOU HAVE TO — JUST DON'T DO IT BECAUSE OF ME, YOU UNDERSTAND?
NO... NO I DON'T, RAY. I THOUGHT WE'D —
I TOLD YOU BEFORE, DON'T INCLUDE ME IN YOUR PLANS. I'M NOT RELIABLE.
ICE COLD
DRINK
Coca-Cola

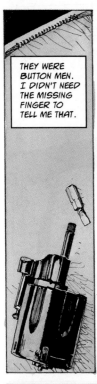

THEY WERE BUTTON MEN. I DIDN'T NEED THE MISSING FINGER TO TELL ME THAT.
I TRIED TO CONVINCE MYSELF IT WAS TOTAL COINCIDENCE — THEY COULDN'T KNOW ABOUT ME.
THEY WERE HERE FOR A CONTEST. THIS WAS JUST ANOTHER ROUND IN THE KILLING GAME. I DIDN'T COME INTO IT.
THEY COULDN'T KNOW.
BRINGGG BRINGGG
WINCHESTE
38mm REVOLV
PRO LOAD
10mm AUTO
180 GR. JHP
BRINGGG BRINGG
RAY — IT'S GRACE. YOU WERE RIGHT. DENNIS DOES KNOW.
I DIDN'T TELL HIM, I SWEAR I DIDN'T TELL HIM. RAY, CAN I COME OVER?
THIS ISN'T A GOOD TIME, GRACE.
CRAKC!
SCASSH!
SKATUMM
RARF RARF!
RAY — ?

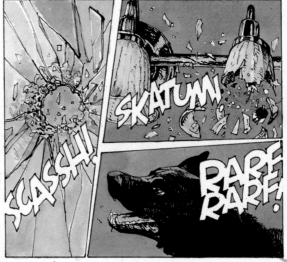

CRAKE!

SKASSH! KA-RANGGGG!

THUM!

THE FIRST SHOT BLEW AWAY ANY LINGERING ILLUSIONS I MIGHT HAVE HAD. GUNMEN DON'T ARRIVE ON YOUR DOORSTEP BY ACCIDENT —

CRA-AK CRAKE!

NOT WHEN YOU'RE CARRYING AROUND MY KIND OF HISTORY.

THUMP! SPANGG!

CLIC

YOU CAN'T QUIT! NOT IN THIS GAME!

FOOL THAT I WAS TO HAVE CONVINCED MYSELF DIFFERENT.

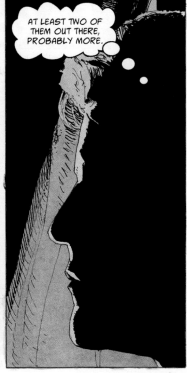

AT LEAST TWO OF THEM OUT THERE, PROBABLY MORE.

GET TRAPPED IN THE CABIN AND I COULD GET DEAD PRETTY QUICK.

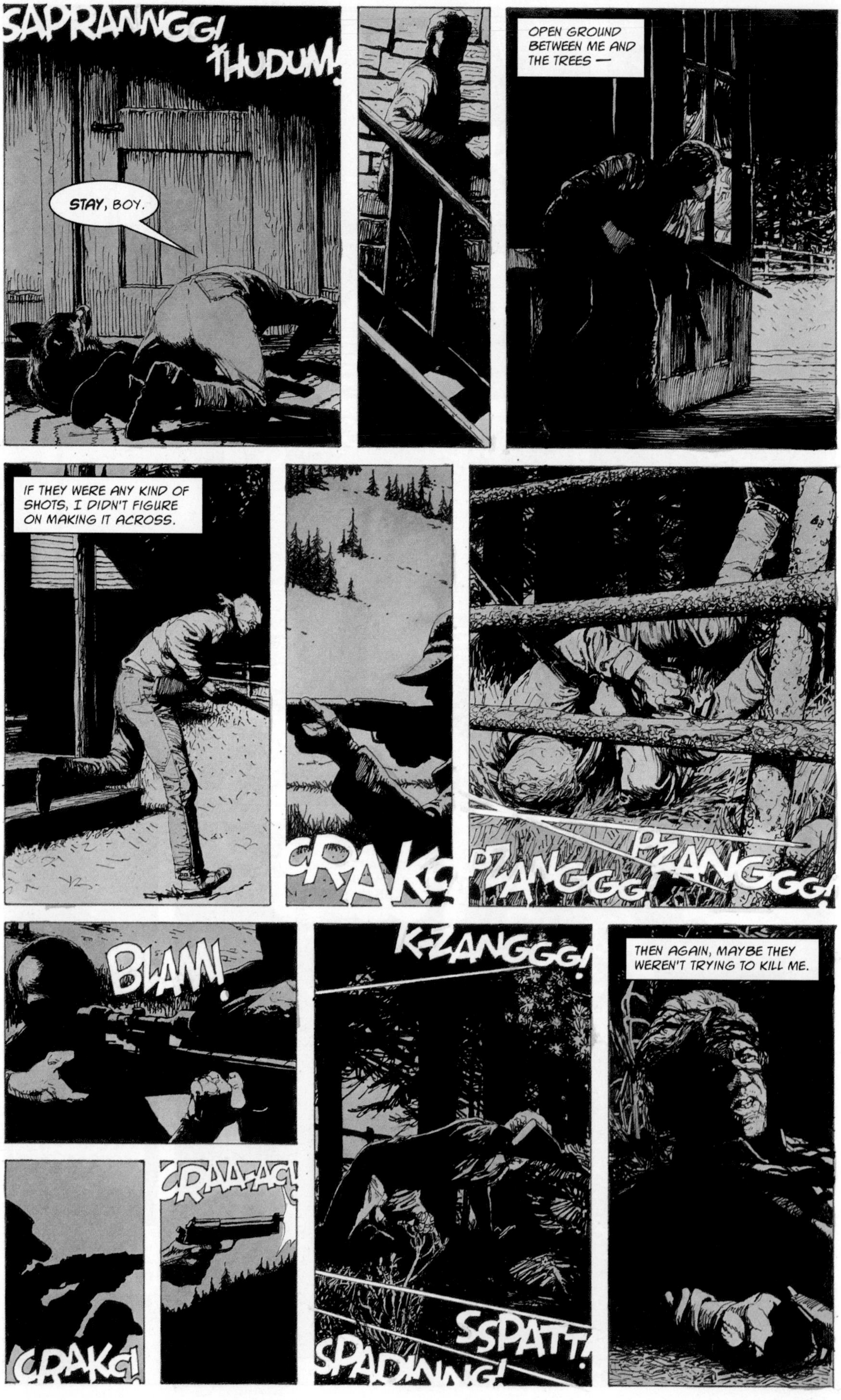
SAPRANNGG!
THUDUM!
STAY, BOY.
OPEN GROUND BETWEEN ME AND THE TREES —
IF THEY WERE ANY KIND OF SHOTS, I DIDN'T FIGURE ON MAKING IT ACROSS.
CRAKG!
PZANGGG!
PZANGGG!
BLAM!
CRAKG!
CRAA-AC!
K-ZANGGG!
SSPATT!
SPADINNG!
THEN AGAIN, MAYBE THEY WEREN'T TRYING TO KILL ME.

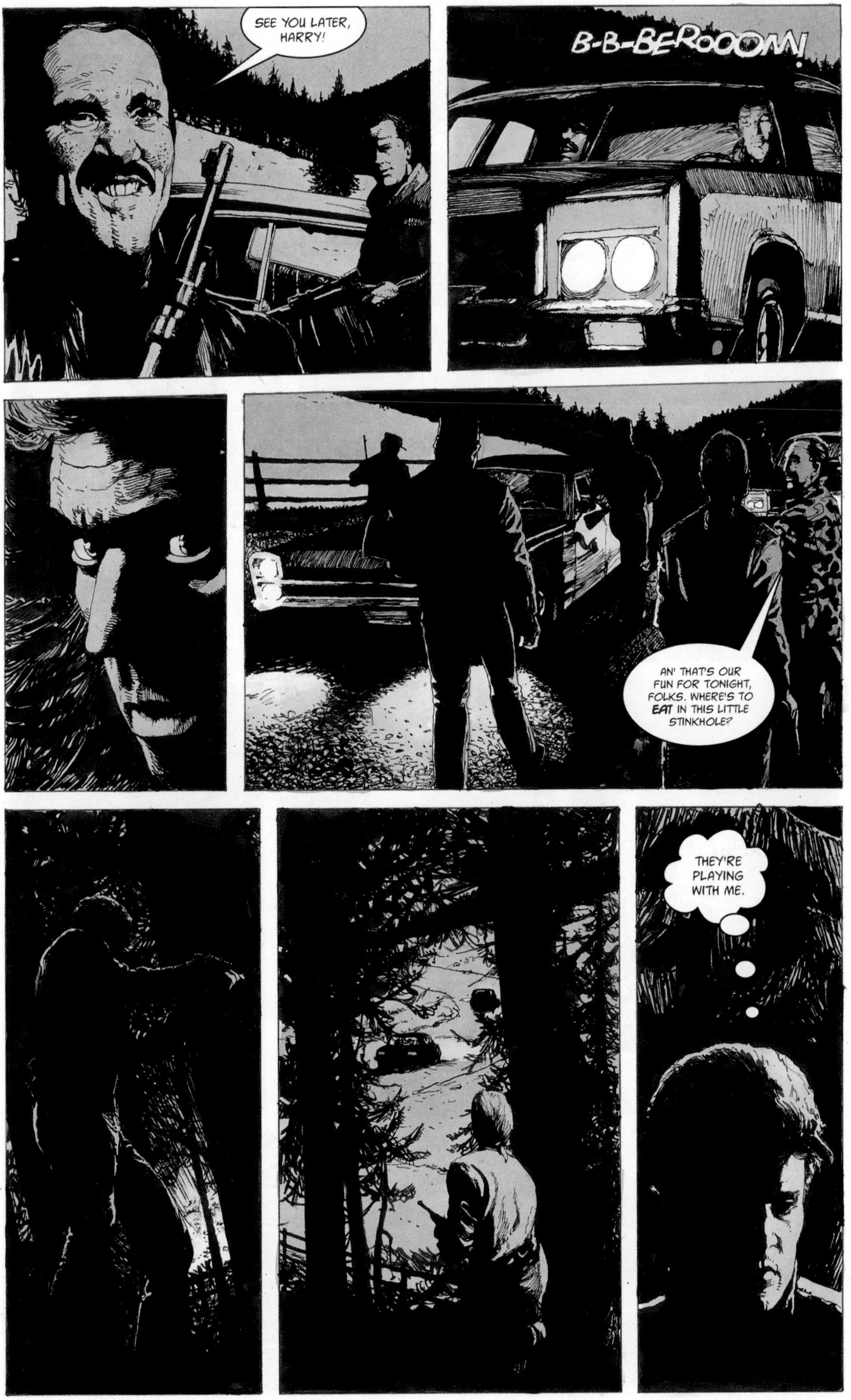
SEE YOU LATER, HARRY!
B-B-BEROOOM!
AN' THAT'S OUR FUN FOR TONIGHT, FOLKS. WHERE'S TO EAT IN THIS LITTLE STINKHOLE?
THEY'RE PLAYING WITH ME.

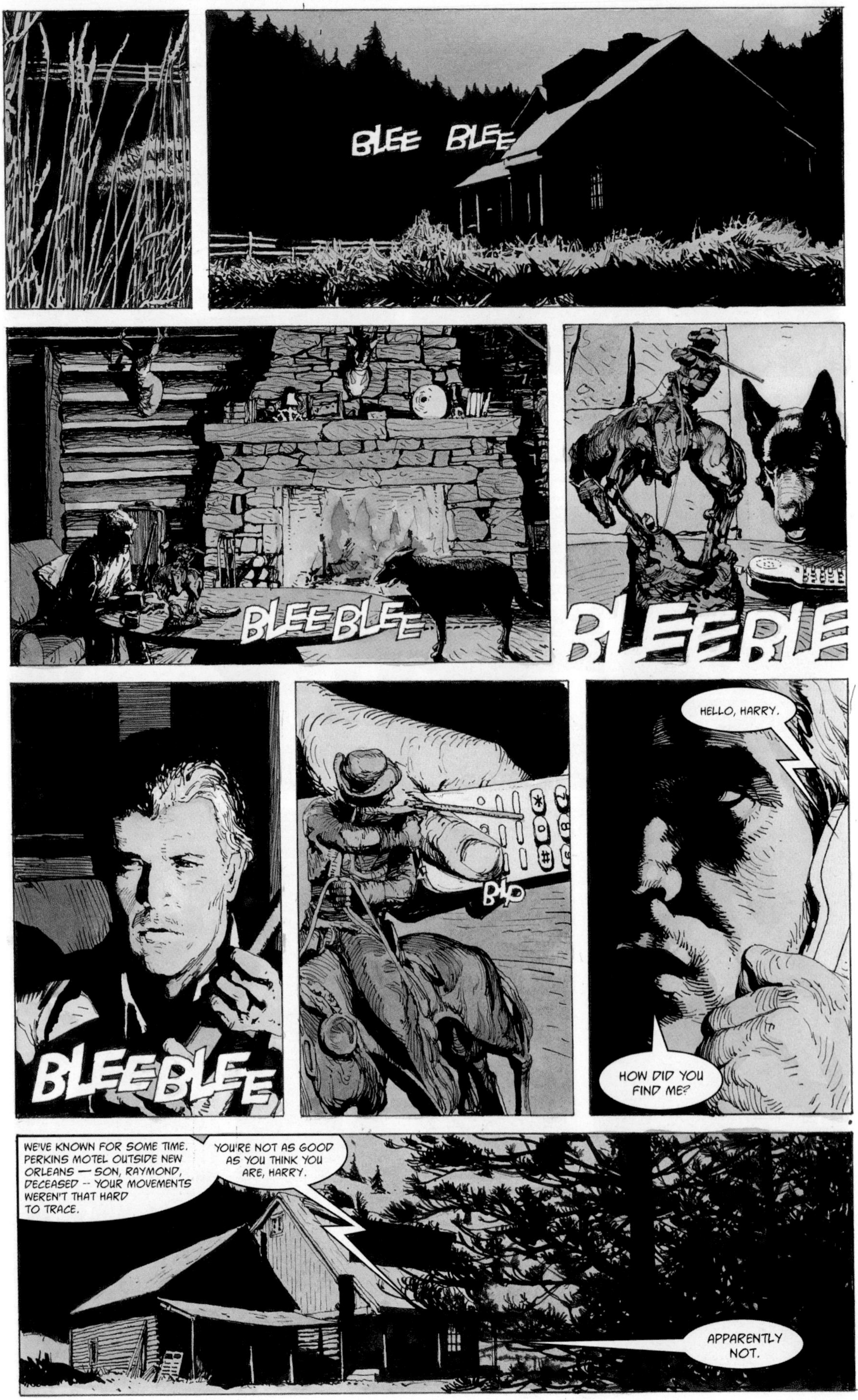
BLEE BLEE
BLEEBLEE
BLEEBLEE
BLEEBLEE
BIP
HELLO, HARRY.
HOW DID YOU FIND ME?
WE'VE KNOWN FOR SOME TIME. PERKINS MOTEL OUTSIDE NEW ORLEANS — SON, RAYMOND, DECEASED -- YOUR MOVEMENTS WEREN'T THAT HARD TO TRACE.
YOU'RE NOT AS GOOD AS YOU THINK YOU ARE, HARRY.
APPARENTLY NOT.

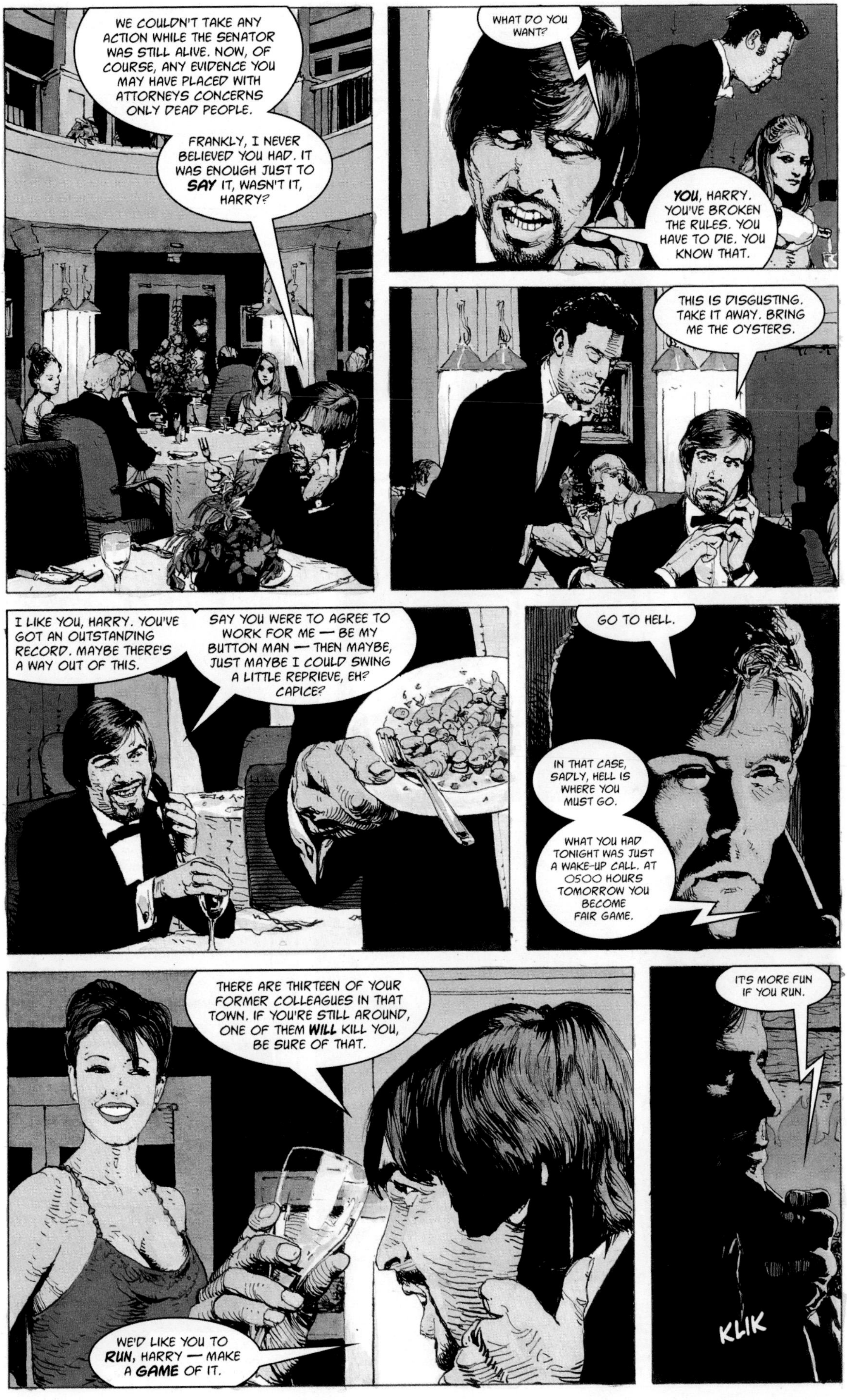
WE COULDN'T TAKE ANY ACTION WHILE THE SENATOR WAS STILL ALIVE. NOW, OF COURSE, ANY EVIDENCE YOU MAY HAVE PLACED WITH ATTORNEYS CONCERNS ONLY DEAD PEOPLE.
FRANKLY, I NEVER BELIEVED YOU HAD. IT WAS ENOUGH JUST TO SAY IT, WASN'T IT, HARRY?
WHAT DO YOU WANT?
YOU, HARRY. YOU'VE BROKEN THE RULES. YOU HAVE TO DIE. YOU KNOW THAT.
THIS IS DISGUSTING. TAKE IT AWAY. BRING ME THE OYSTERS.
I LIKE YOU, HARRY. YOU'VE GOT AN OUTSTANDING RECORD. MAYBE THERE'S A WAY OUT OF THIS.
SAY YOU WERE TO AGREE TO WORK FOR ME — BE MY BUTTON MAN — THEN MAYBE, JUST MAYBE I COULD SWING A LITTLE REPRIEVE, EH? CAPICE?
GO TO HELL.
IN THAT CASE, SADLY, HELL IS WHERE YOU MUST GO.
WHAT YOU HAD TONIGHT WAS JUST A WAKE-UP CALL. AT 0500 HOURS TOMORROW YOU BECOME FAIR GAME.
THERE ARE THIRTEEN OF YOUR FORMER COLLEAGUES IN THAT TOWN. IF YOU'RE STILL AROUND, ONE OF THEM WILL KILL YOU, BE SURE OF THAT.
WE'D LIKE YOU TO RUN, HARRY — MAKE A GAME OF IT.
IT'S MORE FUN IF YOU RUN.
KLIK

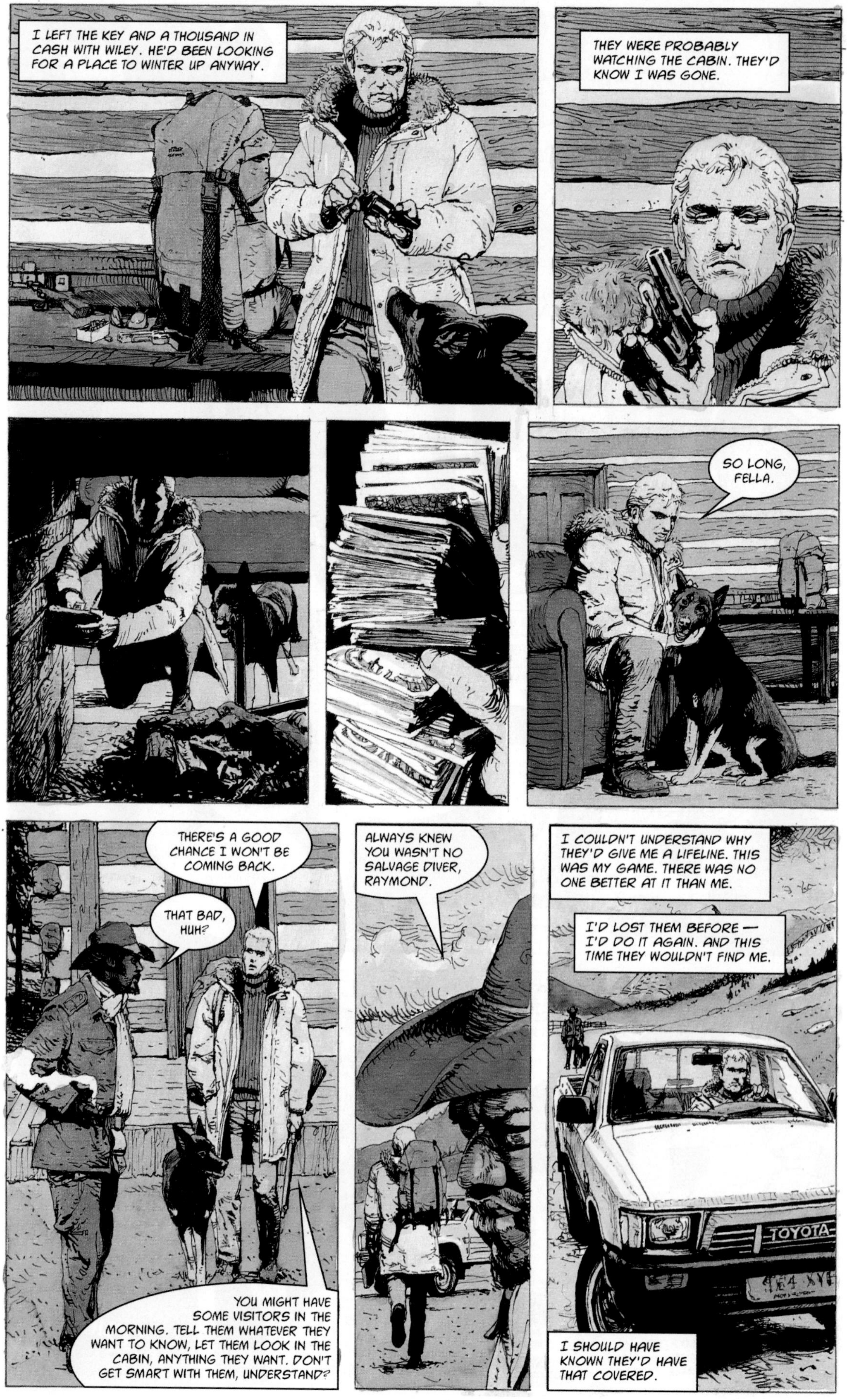
I LEFT THE KEY AND A THOUSAND IN CASH WITH WILEY. HE'D BEEN LOOKING FOR A PLACE TO WINTER UP ANYWAY.
THEY WERE PROBABLY WATCHING THE CABIN. THEY'D KNOW I WAS GONE.
SO LONG, FELLA.
THERE'S A GOOD CHANCE I WON'T BE COMING BACK.
THAT BAD, HUH?
YOU MIGHT HAVE SOME VISITORS IN THE MORNING. TELL THEM WHATEVER THEY WANT TO KNOW, LET THEM LOOK IN THE CABIN, ANYTHING THEY WANT. DON'T GET SMART WITH THEM, UNDERSTAND?
ALWAYS KNEW YOU WASN'T NO SALVAGE DIVER, RAYMOND.
I COULDN'T UNDERSTAND WHY THEY'D GIVE ME A LIFELINE. THIS WAS MY GAME. THERE WAS NO ONE BETTER AT IT THAN ME.
I'D LOST THEM BEFORE — I'D DO IT AGAIN. AND THIS TIME THEY WOULDN'T FIND ME.
TOYOTA
I SHOULD HAVE KNOWN THEY'D HAVE THAT COVERED.

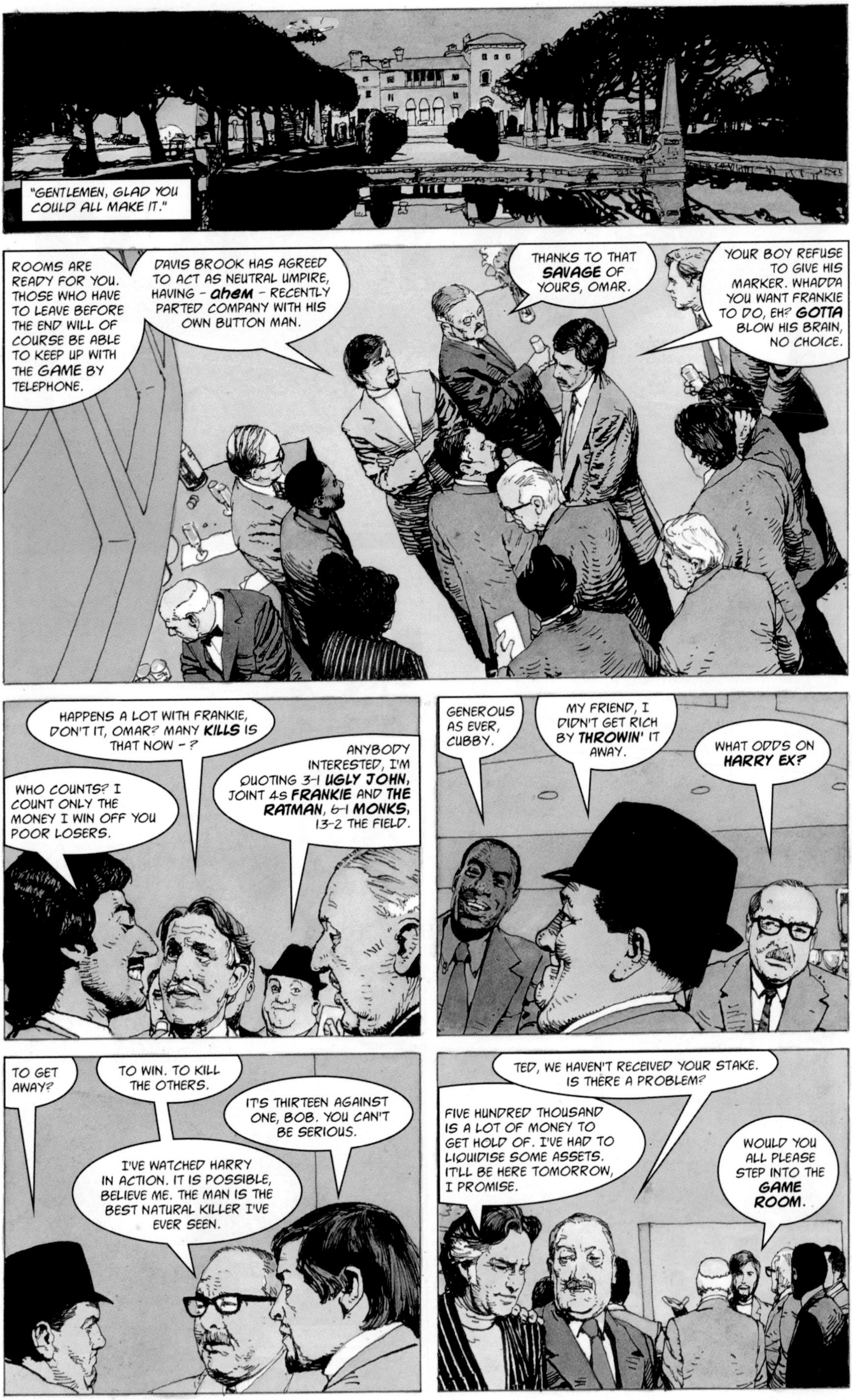
"GENTLEMEN, GLAD YOU COULD ALL MAKE IT."
ROOMS ARE READY FOR YOU. THOSE WHO HAVE TO LEAVE BEFORE THE END WILL OF COURSE BE ABLE TO KEEP UP WITH THE GAME BY TELEPHONE.
DAVIS BROOK HAS AGREED TO ACT AS NEUTRAL UMPIRE, HAVING - ahem - RECENTLY PARTED COMPANY WITH HIS OWN BUTTON MAN.
THANKS TO THAT SAVAGE OF YOURS, OMAR.
YOUR BOY REFUSE TO GIVE HIS MARKER. WHADDA YOU WANT FRANKIE TO DO, EH? GOTTA BLOW HIS BRAIN, NO CHOICE.
HAPPENS A LOT WITH FRANKIE, DON'T IT, OMAR? MANY KILLS IS THAT NOW -?
WHO COUNTS? I COUNT ONLY THE MONEY I WIN OFF YOU POOR LOSERS.
ANYBODY INTERESTED, I'M QUOTING 3-1 UGLY JOHN, JOINT 4s FRANKIE AND THE RATMAN, 6-1 MONKS, 13-2 THE FIELD.
GENEROUS AS EVER, CUBBY.
MY FRIEND, I DIDN'T GET RICH BY THROWIN' IT AWAY.
WHAT ODDS ON HARRY EX?
TO GET AWAY?
TO WIN. TO KILL THE OTHERS.
IT'S THIRTEEN AGAINST ONE, BOB. YOU CAN'T BE SERIOUS.
I'VE WATCHED HARRY IN ACTION. IT IS POSSIBLE, BELIEVE ME. THE MAN IS THE BEST NATURAL KILLER I'VE EVER SEEN.
TED, WE HAVEN'T RECEIVED YOUR STAKE. IS THERE A PROBLEM?
FIVE HUNDRED THOUSAND IS A LOT OF MONEY TO GET HOLD OF. I'VE HAD TO LIQUIDISE SOME ASSETS. IT'LL BE HERE TOMORROW, I PROMISE.
WOULD YOU ALL PLEASE STEP INTO THE GAME ROOM.

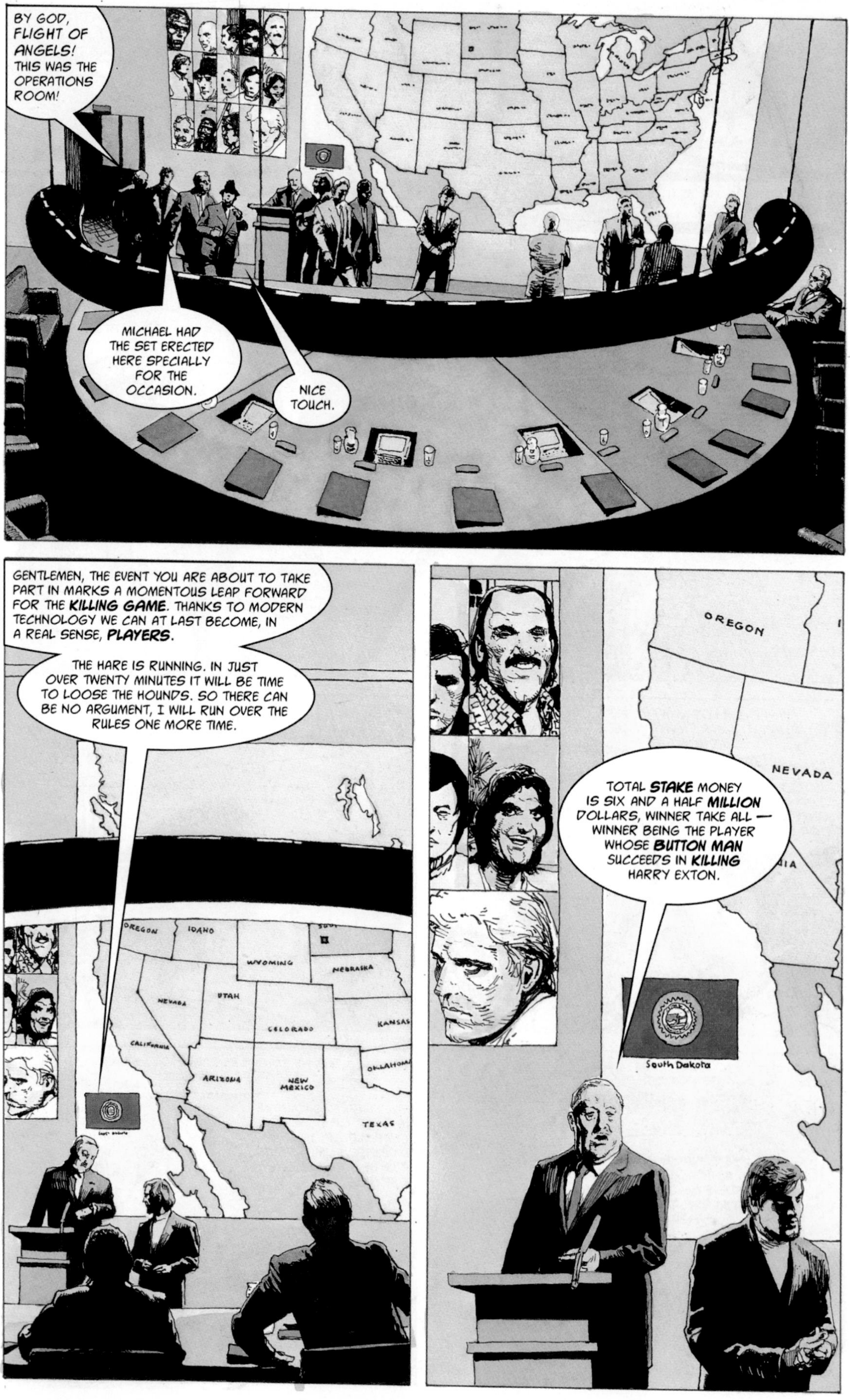
BY GOD, FLIGHT OF ANGELS! THIS WAS THE OPERATIONS ROOM!
MICHAEL HAD THE SET ERECTED HERE SPECIALLY FOR THE OCCASION.
NICE TOUCH.
GENTLEMEN, THE EVENT YOU ARE ABOUT TO TAKE PART IN MARKS A MOMENTOUS LEAP FORWARD FOR THE **KILLING GAME**. THANKS TO MODERN TECHNOLOGY WE CAN AT LAST BECOME, IN A REAL SENSE, **PLAYERS**.
THE HARE IS RUNNING. IN JUST OVER TWENTY MINUTES IT WILL BE TIME TO LOOSE THE HOUNDS. SO THERE CAN BE NO ARGUMENT, I WILL RUN OVER THE RULES ONE MORE TIME.
OREGON
IDAHO
WYOMING
NEBRASKA
UTAH
NEVADA
COLORADO
KANSAS
CALIFORNIA
ARIZONA
NEW MEXICO
OKLAHOMA
TEXAS
OREGON
NEVADA
TOTAL **STAKE** MONEY IS SIX AND A HALF **MILLION** DOLLARS, WINNER TAKE ALL — WINNER BEING THE PLAYER WHOSE **BUTTON MAN** SUCCEEDS IN **KILLING** HARRY EXTON.
South Dakota

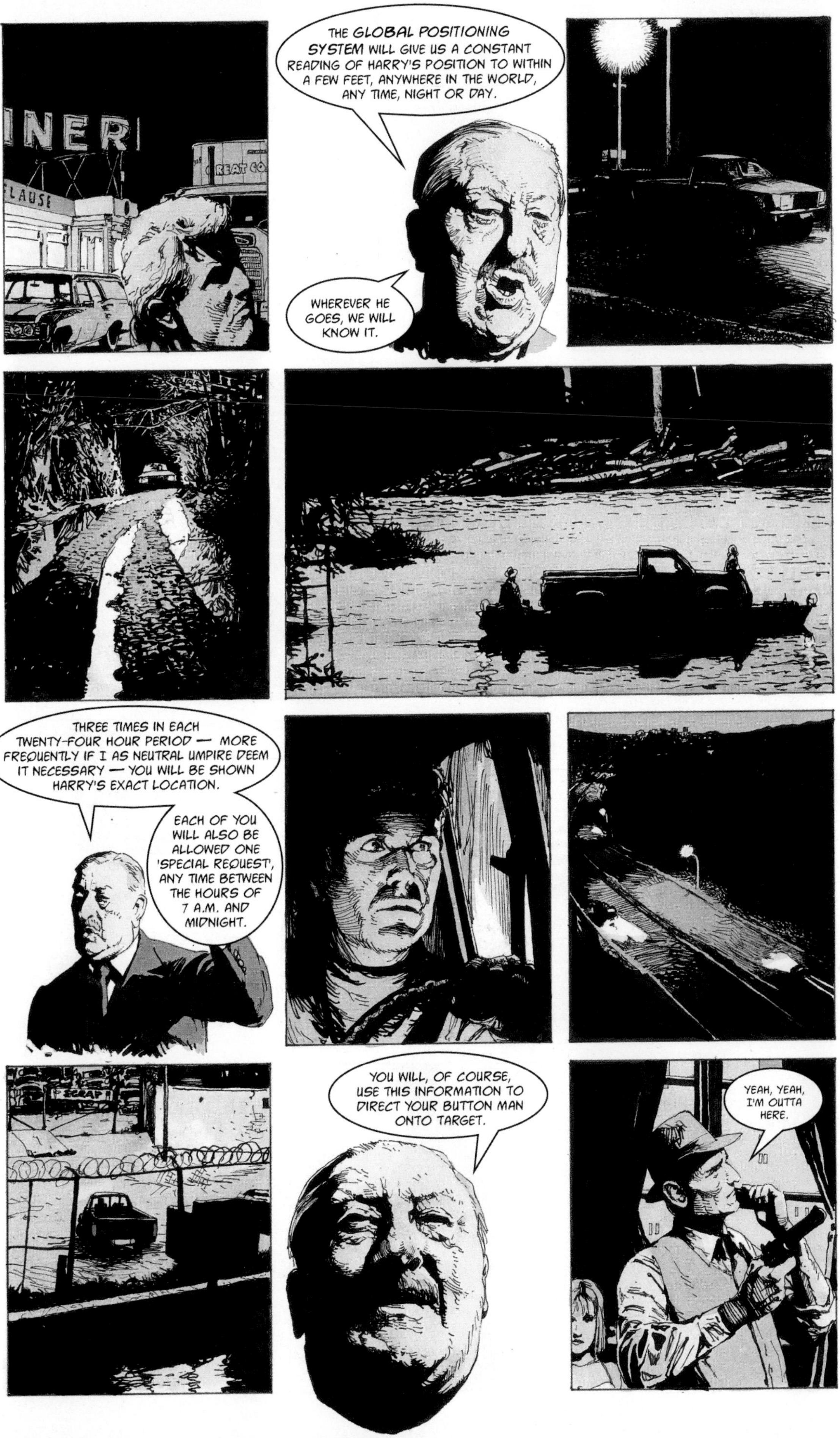
INER
FLAUSE
REAT CO
THE GLOBAL POSITIONING SYSTEM WILL GIVE US A CONSTANT READING OF HARRY'S POSITION TO WITHIN A FEW FEET, ANYWHERE IN THE WORLD, ANY TIME, NIGHT OR DAY.
WHEREVER HE GOES, WE WILL KNOW IT.
THREE TIMES IN EACH TWENTY-FOUR HOUR PERIOD — MORE FREQUENTLY IF I AS NEUTRAL UMPIRE DEEM IT NECESSARY — YOU WILL BE SHOWN HARRY'S EXACT LOCATION.
EACH OF YOU WILL ALSO BE ALLOWED ONE 'SPECIAL REQUEST', ANY TIME BETWEEN THE HOURS OF 7 A.M. AND MIDNIGHT.
SCRAP
YOU WILL, OF COURSE, USE THIS INFORMATION TO DIRECT YOUR BUTTON MAN ONTO TARGET.
YEAH, YEAH, I'M OUTTA HERE.

NO COLLUSION BETWEEN BUTTON MEN IS PERMITTED. ONLY SCHEDULED FLIGHTS MAY BE USED.

CHOICE OF WEAPONS IS ENTIRELY AT YOUR DISCRETION.

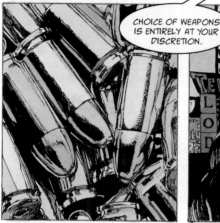

PROOF OF DEATH WILL BE BY **MARKER**. ONE FINGER, EITHER HAND. WE HAVE HARRY'S PRINTS ON FILE.

THE BODY **MUST** BE DISPOSED OF CAREFULLY. WE DO NOT WANT IT TURNING UP.

THIS IS MOST IMPORTANT. MAKE SURE YOUR BUTTON MEN UNDERSTAND THIS.

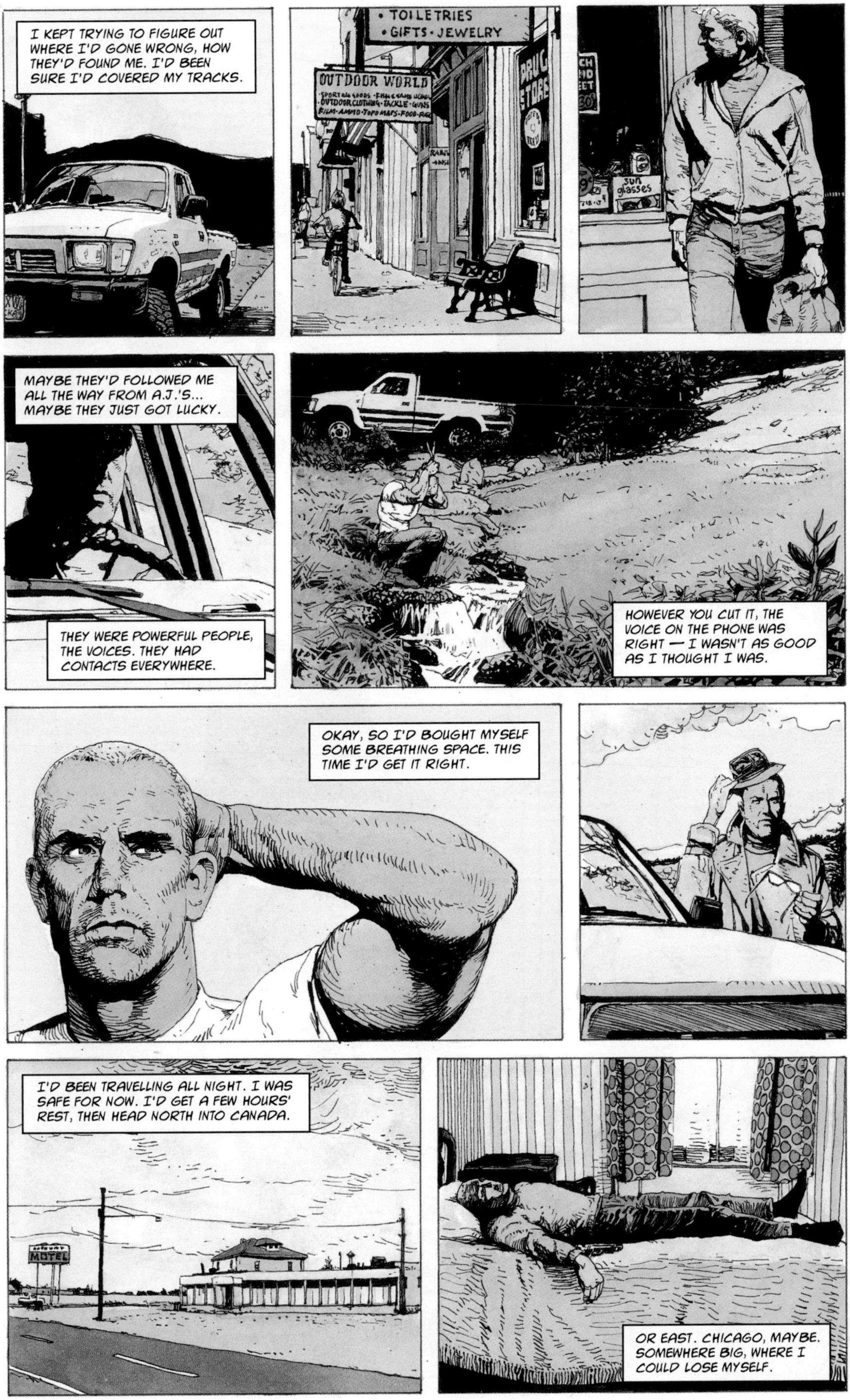
I KEPT TRYING TO FIGURE OUT WHERE I'D GONE WRONG, HOW THEY'D FOUND ME. I'D BEEN SURE I'D COVERED MY TRACKS.
• TOILETRIES • GIFTS • JEWELRY
OUTDOOR WORLD
sun glasses
MAYBE THEY'D FOLLOWED ME ALL THE WAY FROM A.J.'S... MAYBE THEY JUST GOT LUCKY.
THEY WERE POWERFUL PEOPLE, THE VOICES. THEY HAD CONTACTS EVERYWHERE.
HOWEVER YOU CUT IT, THE VOICE ON THE PHONE WAS RIGHT — I WASN'T AS GOOD AS I THOUGHT I WAS.
OKAY, SO I'D BOUGHT MYSELF SOME BREATHING SPACE. THIS TIME I'D GET IT RIGHT.
I'D BEEN TRAVELLING ALL NIGHT. I WAS SAFE FOR NOW. I'D GET A FEW HOURS' REST, THEN HEAD NORTH INTO CANADA.
MOTEL
OR EAST. CHICAGO, MAYBE. SOMEWHERE BIG, WHERE I COULD LOSE MYSELF.

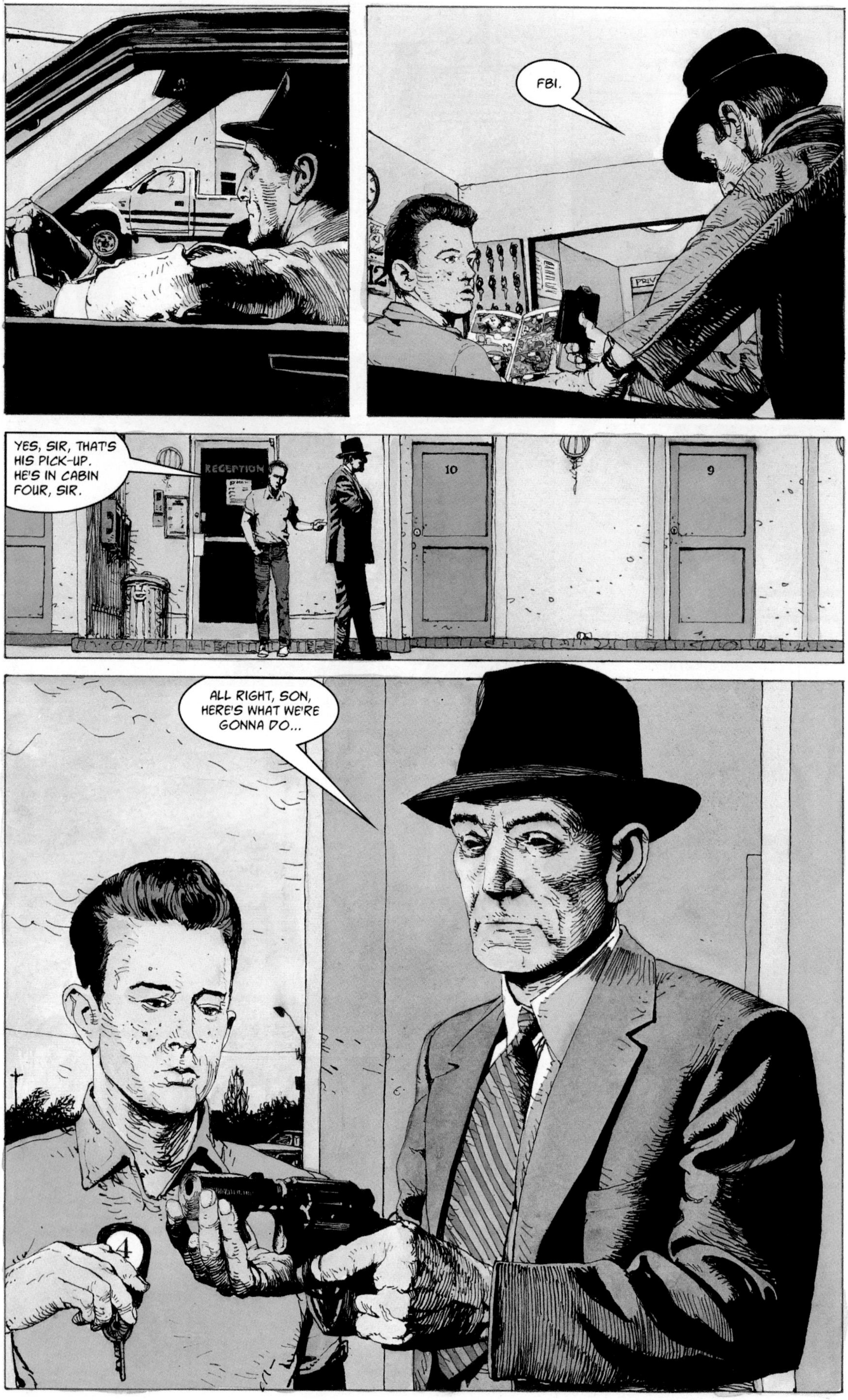
FBI.
YES, SIR, THAT'S HIS PICK-UP. HE'S IN CABIN FOUR, SIR.
RECEPTION
10
9
ALL RIGHT, SON, HERE'S WHAT WE'RE GONNA DO...

MR BIRT, THIS IS CHIP FROM RECEPTION! I GOTTA COME IN AND CHANGE YOUR LINEN. I'M COMIN' IN, MR BIRT --

CLFFF! CLFFF! CLFFF!

CLFFF!

FUP! FUP!

BLAM!

WRONG GUESS.

UNNHH!

BLAM!

OH JESUS, D-D-DON'T KILL ME, MISTER!

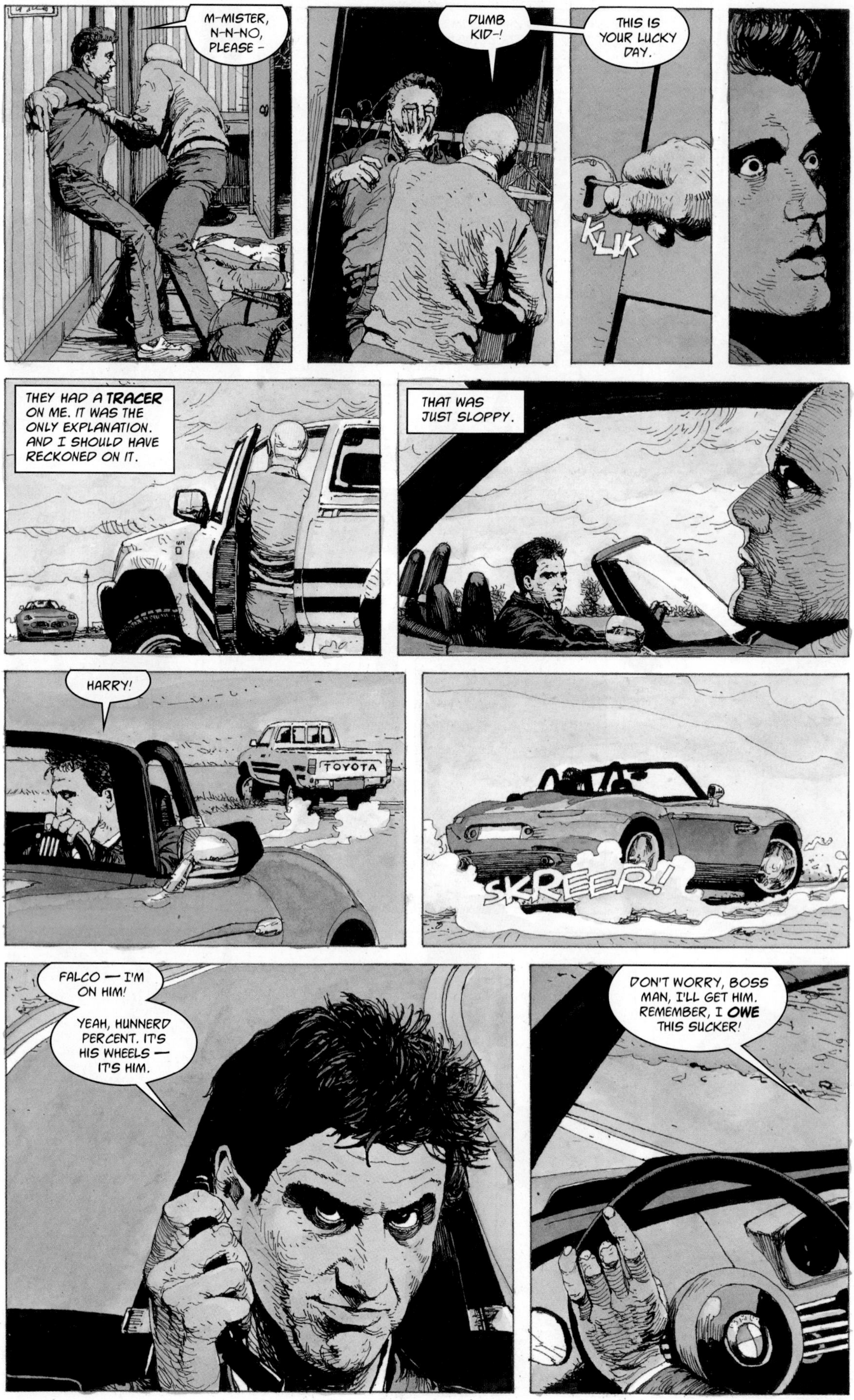
M-MISTER, N-N-NO, PLEASE -
DUMB KID-!
THIS IS YOUR LUCKY DAY.
KLIK
THEY HAD A **TRACER** ON ME. IT WAS THE ONLY EXPLANATION. AND I SHOULD HAVE RECKONED ON IT.
THAT WAS JUST SLOPPY.
HARRY!
TOYOTA
SKREEER!
FALCO — I'M ON HIM!
YEAH, HUNNERD PERCENT. IT'S HIS WHEELS — IT'S HIM.
DON'T WORRY, BOSS MAN, I'LL GET HIM. REMEMBER, I **OWE** THIS SUCKER!

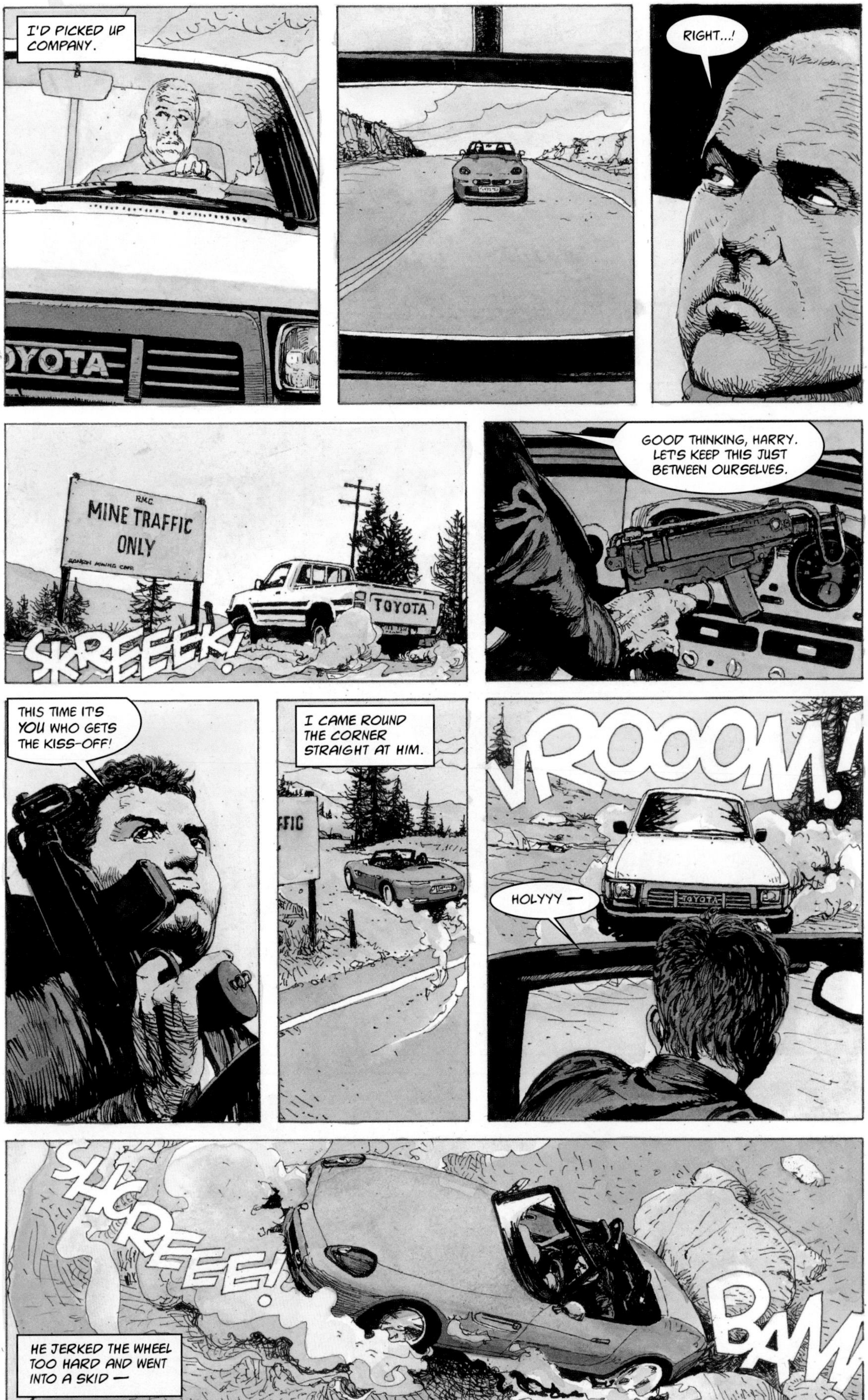
I'D PICKED UP COMPANY.
TOYOTA
RIGHT...!
R.M.C.
MINE TRAFFIC ONLY
TOYOTA
SKREEEK!
GOOD THINKING, HARRY. LET'S KEEP THIS JUST BETWEEN OURSELVES.
THIS TIME IT'S YOU WHO GETS THE KISS-OFF!
I CAME ROUND THE CORNER STRAIGHT AT HIM.
VROOOM!
HOLYYY —
SHCREEEEK
BAM
HE JERKED THE WHEEL TOO HARD AND WENT INTO A SKID —

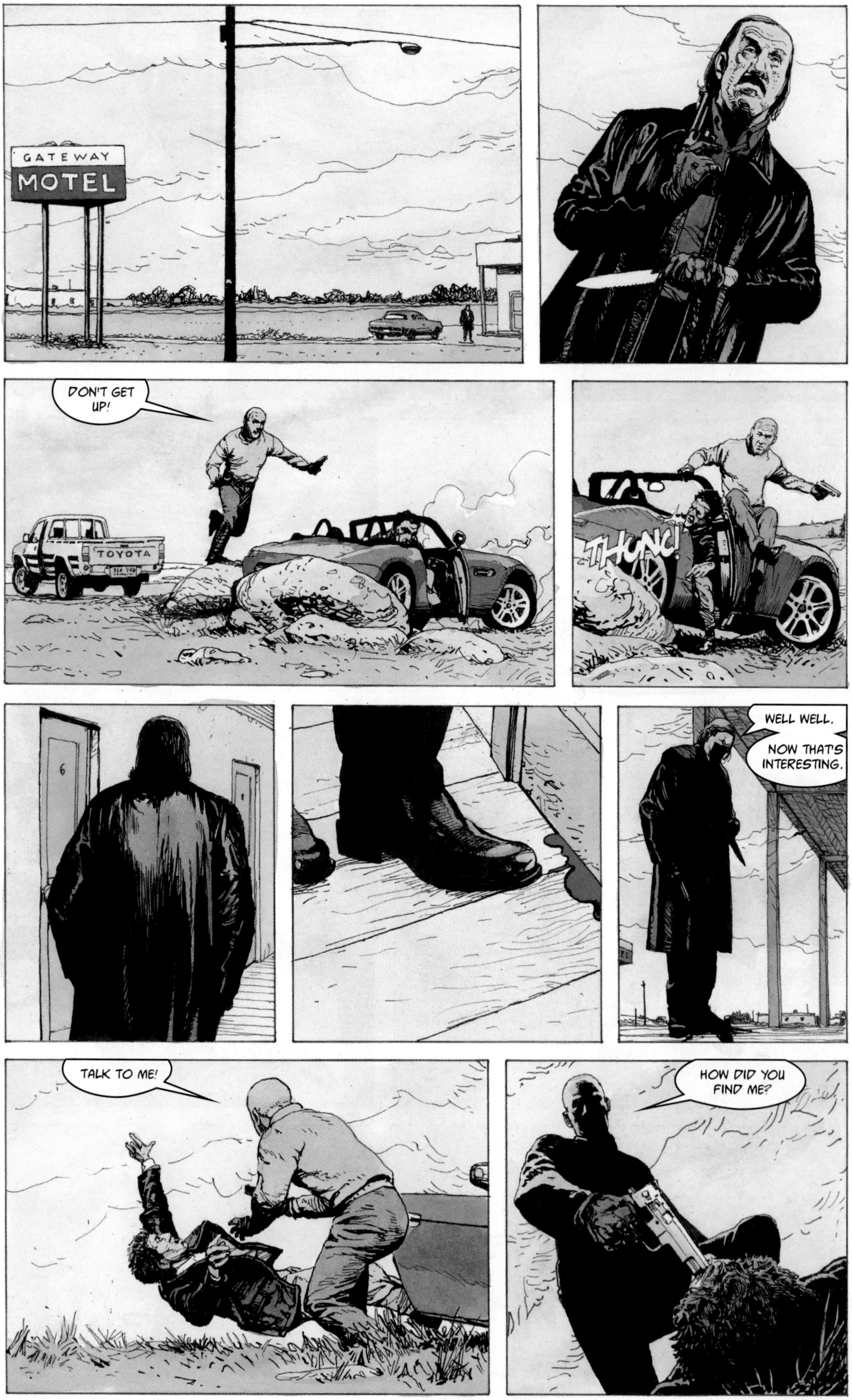
GATEWAY
MOTEL
DON'T GET UP!
TOYOTA
THUNC!
WELL WELL.
NOW THAT'S INTERESTING.
TALK TO ME!
HOW DID YOU FIND ME?

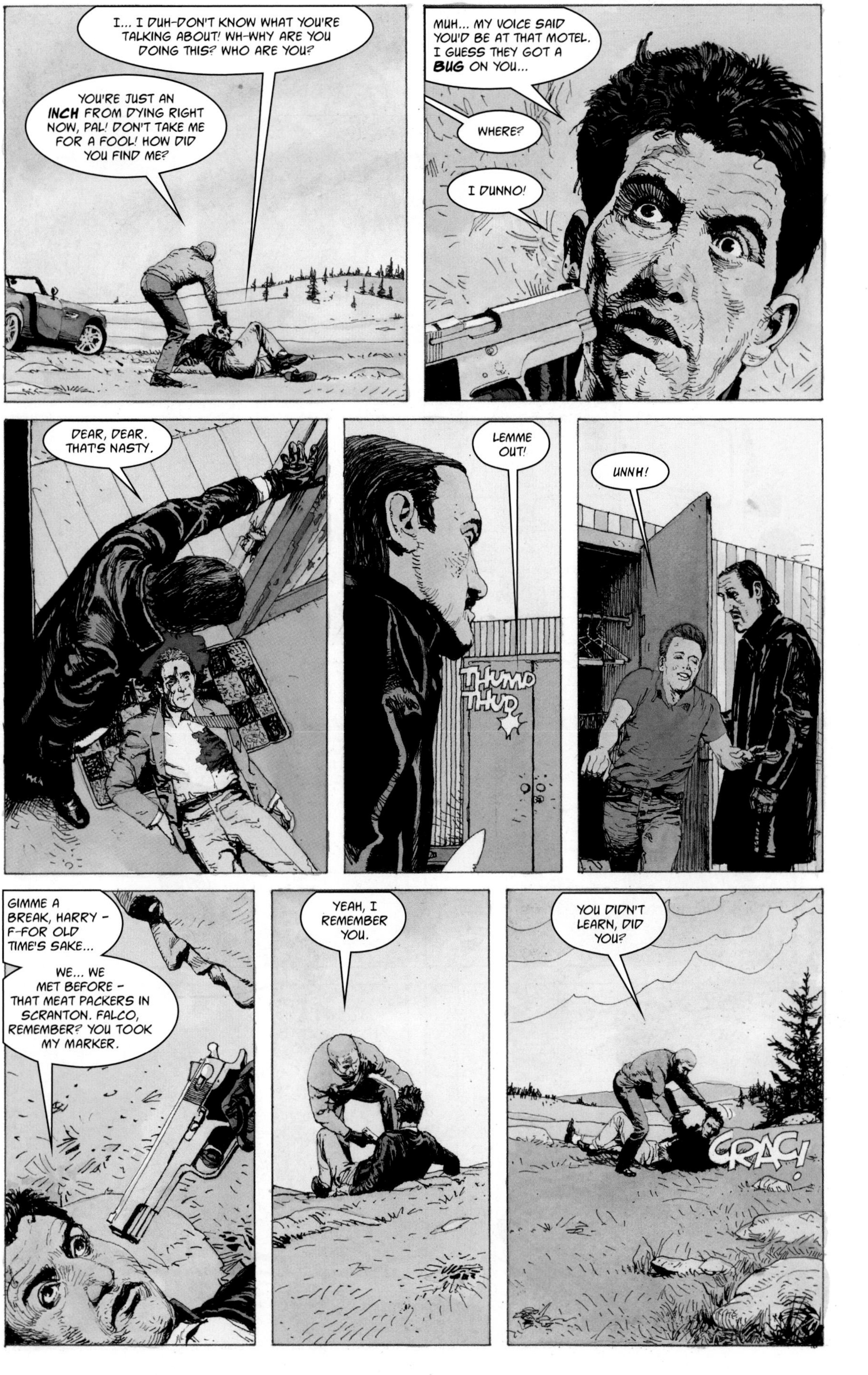
I... I DUH-DON'T KNOW WHAT YOU'RE TALKING ABOUT! WH-WHY ARE YOU DOING THIS? WHO ARE YOU?
YOU'RE JUST AN INCH FROM DYING RIGHT NOW, PAL! DON'T TAKE ME FOR A FOOL! HOW DID YOU FIND ME?
MUH... MY VOICE SAID YOU'D BE AT THAT MOTEL. I GUESS THEY GOT A BUG ON YOU...
WHERE?
I DUNNO!
DEAR, DEAR. THAT'S NASTY.
LEMME OUT!
THUMP THUD
UNNH!
GIMME A BREAK, HARRY - F-FOR OLD TIME'S SAKE...
WE... WE MET BEFORE - THAT MEAT PACKERS IN SCRANTON. FALCO, REMEMBER? YOU TOOK MY MARKER.
YEAH, I REMEMBER YOU.
YOU DIDN'T LEARN, DID YOU?
CRAC!

MAN WHO DID THIS -- BLOND, MAYBE SIX ONE, HAIR TIED UP LIKE A GIRLIE?

N-NO, SIR, SH-SHAVEHEAD.

THAT A FACT NOW? WHAT WAS HE DRIVING?

FORD PICK-UP, I THINK -- M-MAYBE IT WAS A TOYOTA. GOT ALL THE DETAILS IN THE OFFICE.

THINK YOU'D RECOGNISE ME IF YOU SAW ME AGAIN?

YES, SIR, I SURE WOULD, SIR. YOU... YOU FBI TOO?

YOU COULD SAY THAT, SON.

ONE FUCKIN' BAAAD INDIVIDUAL...

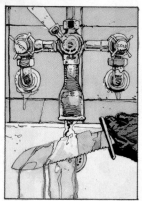

FBI -- I LIKE THAT.

THE TRACER HAD TO BE IN THE PICK-UP.

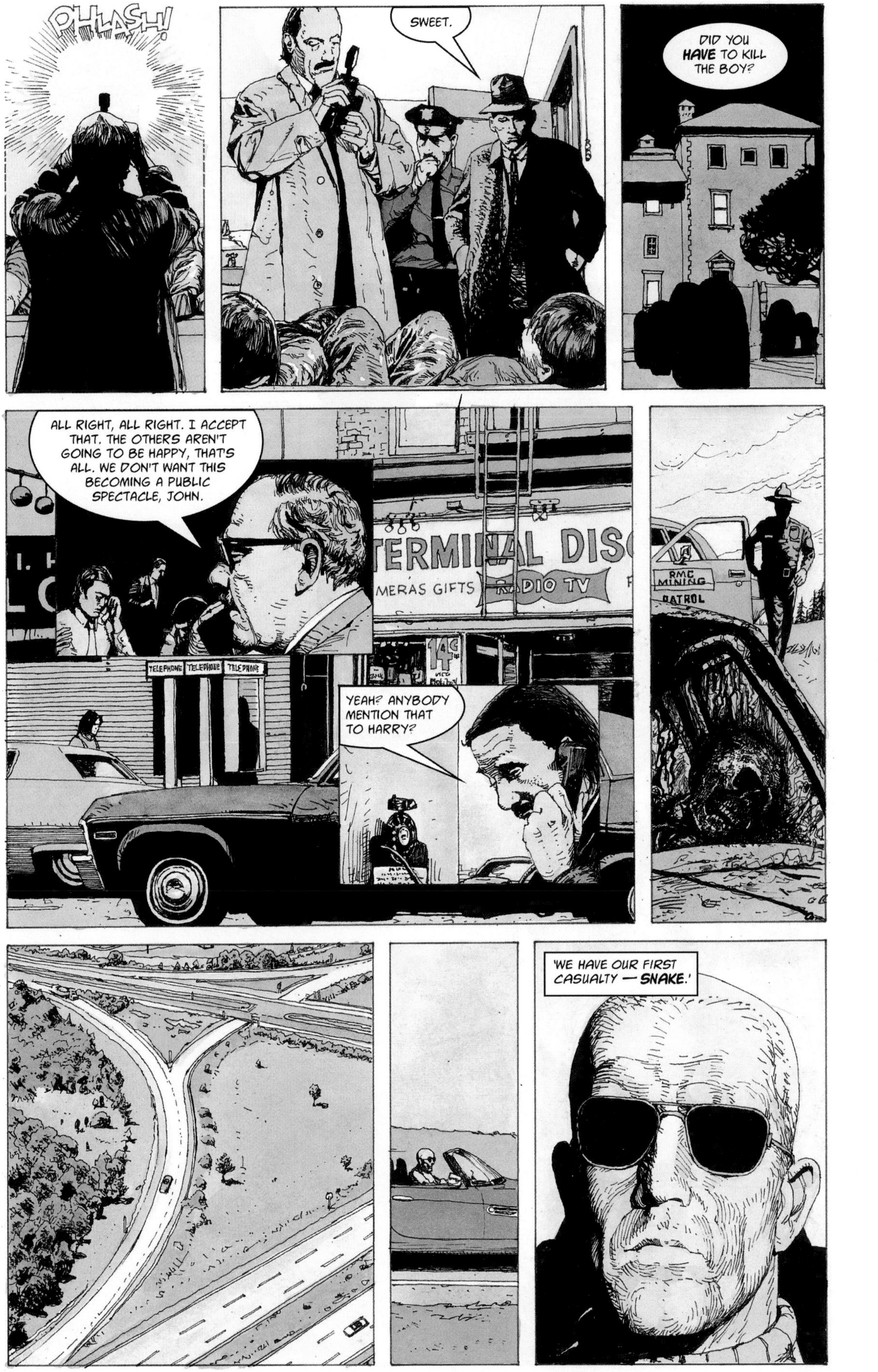
PHLASH!
SWEET.
DID YOU HAVE TO KILL THE BOY?
ALL RIGHT, ALL RIGHT. I ACCEPT THAT. THE OTHERS AREN'T GOING TO BE HAPPY, THAT'S ALL. WE DON'T WANT THIS BECOMING A PUBLIC SPECTACLE, JOHN.
TERMINAL DISC
MERAS GIFTS RADIO TV
TELEPHONE TELEPHONE TELEPHONE
YEAH? ANYBODY MENTION THAT TO HARRY?
RMC MINING PATROL
'WE HAVE OUR FIRST CASUALTY — SNAKE.'

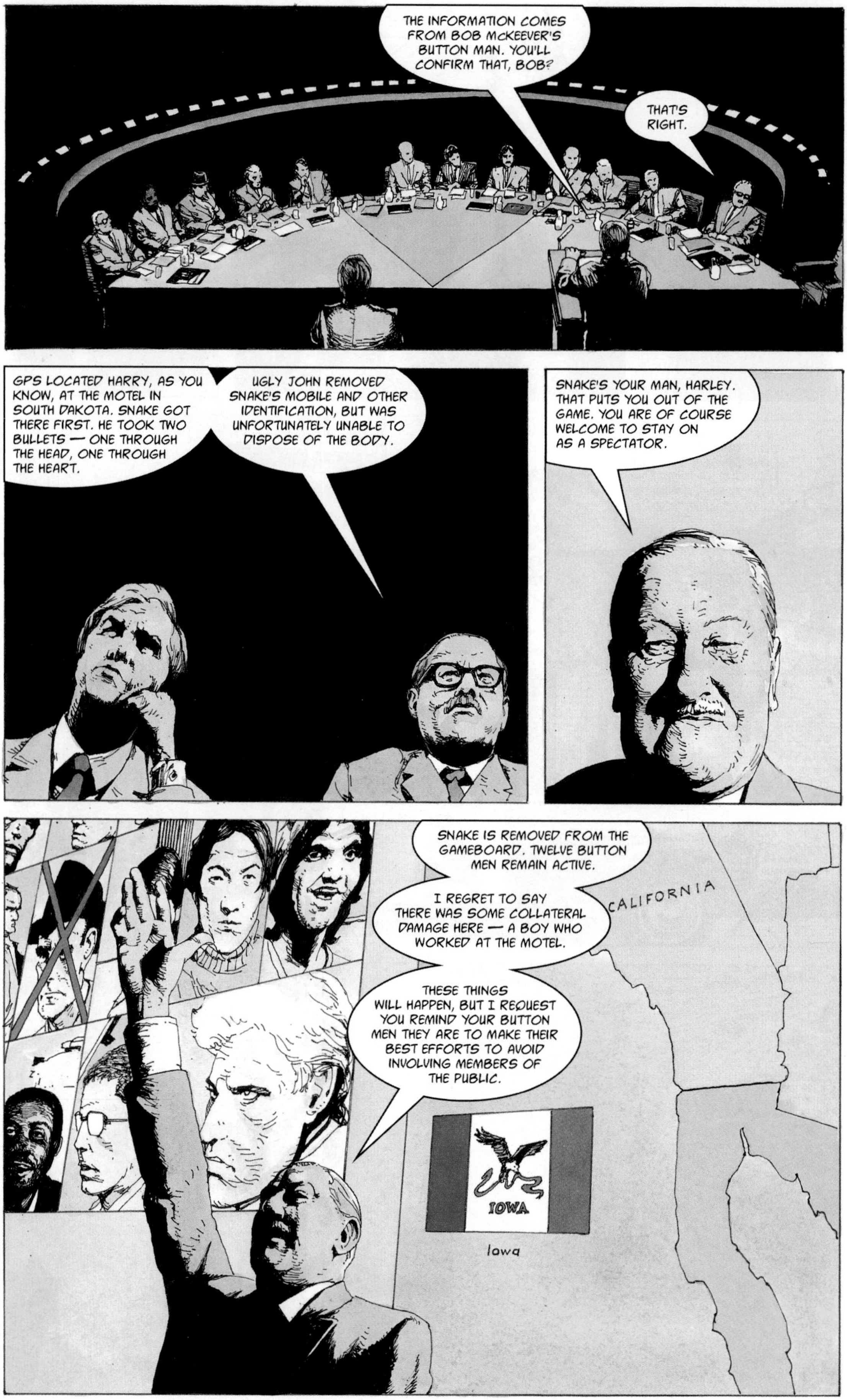
THE INFORMATION COMES FROM BOB McKEEVER'S BUTTON MAN. YOU'LL CONFIRM THAT, BOB?
THAT'S RIGHT.
GPS LOCATED HARRY, AS YOU KNOW, AT THE MOTEL IN SOUTH DAKOTA. SNAKE GOT THERE FIRST. HE TOOK TWO BULLETS — ONE THROUGH THE HEAD, ONE THROUGH THE HEART.
UGLY JOHN REMOVED SNAKE'S MOBILE AND OTHER IDENTIFICATION, BUT WAS UNFORTUNATELY UNABLE TO DISPOSE OF THE BODY.
SNAKE'S YOUR MAN, HARLEY. THAT PUTS YOU OUT OF THE GAME. YOU ARE OF COURSE WELCOME TO STAY ON AS A SPECTATOR.
SNAKE IS REMOVED FROM THE GAMEBOARD. TWELVE BUTTON MEN REMAIN ACTIVE.
I REGRET TO SAY THERE WAS SOME COLLATERAL DAMAGE HERE — A BOY WHO WORKED AT THE MOTEL.
THESE THINGS WILL HAPPEN, BUT I REQUEST YOU REMIND YOUR BUTTON MEN THEY ARE TO MAKE THEIR BEST EFFORTS TO AVOID INVOLVING MEMBERS OF THE PUBLIC.
CALIFORNIA
IOWA
Iowa

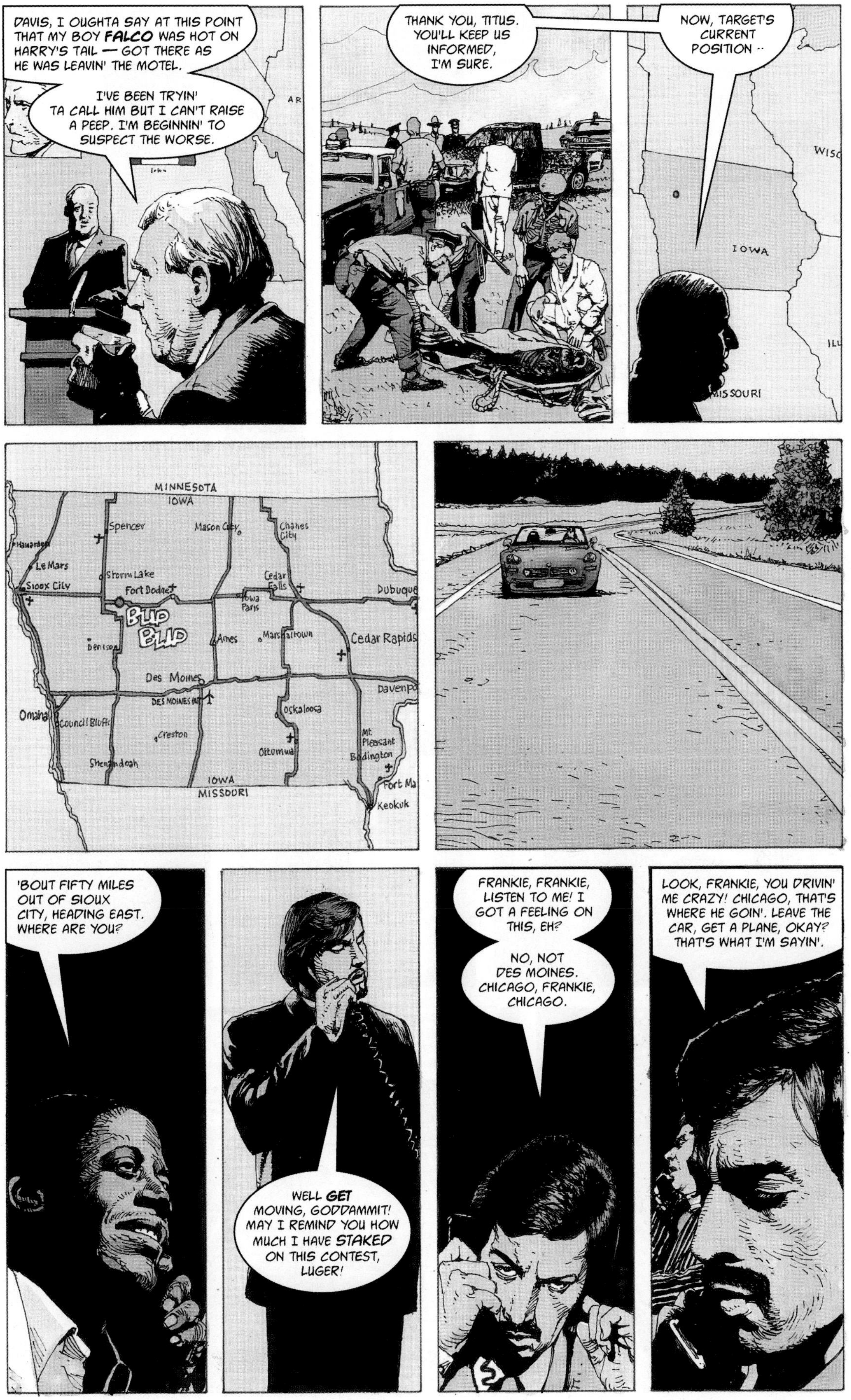
DAVIS, I OUGHTA SAY AT THIS POINT THAT MY BOY **FALCO** WAS HOT ON HARRY'S TAIL — GOT THERE AS HE WAS LEAVIN' THE MOTEL.
I'VE BEEN TRYIN' TA CALL HIM BUT I CAN'T RAISE A PEEP. I'M BEGINNIN' TO SUSPECT THE WORSE.
THANK YOU, TITUS. YOU'LL KEEP US INFORMED, I'M SURE.
NOW, TARGET'S CURRENT POSITION --
IOWA
MISSOURI
MINNESOTA
IOWA
Spencer
Mason City
Le Mars
Storm Lake
Sioux City
Fort Dodge
Cedar Falls
Dubuque
BLIP
BLIP
Ames
Marshalltown
Cedar Rapids
Des Moines
DES MOINES INT
Omaha
Council Bluffs
Oskaloosa
Creston
Ottumwa
Mt Pleasant
Shenandoah
IOWA
MISSOURI
Keokuk
'BOUT FIFTY MILES OUT OF SIOUX CITY, HEADING EAST. WHERE ARE YOU?
WELL **GET** MOVING, GODDAMMIT! MAY I REMIND YOU HOW MUCH I HAVE **STAKED** ON THIS CONTEST, LUGER!
FRANKIE, FRANKIE, LISTEN TO ME! I GOT A FEELING ON THIS, EH?
NO, NOT DES MOINES. CHICAGO, FRANKIE, CHICAGO.
LOOK, FRANKIE, YOU DRIVIN' ME CRAZY! CHICAGO, THAT'S WHERE HE GOIN'. LEAVE THE CAR, GET A PLANE, OKAY? THAT'S WHAT I'M SAYIN'.

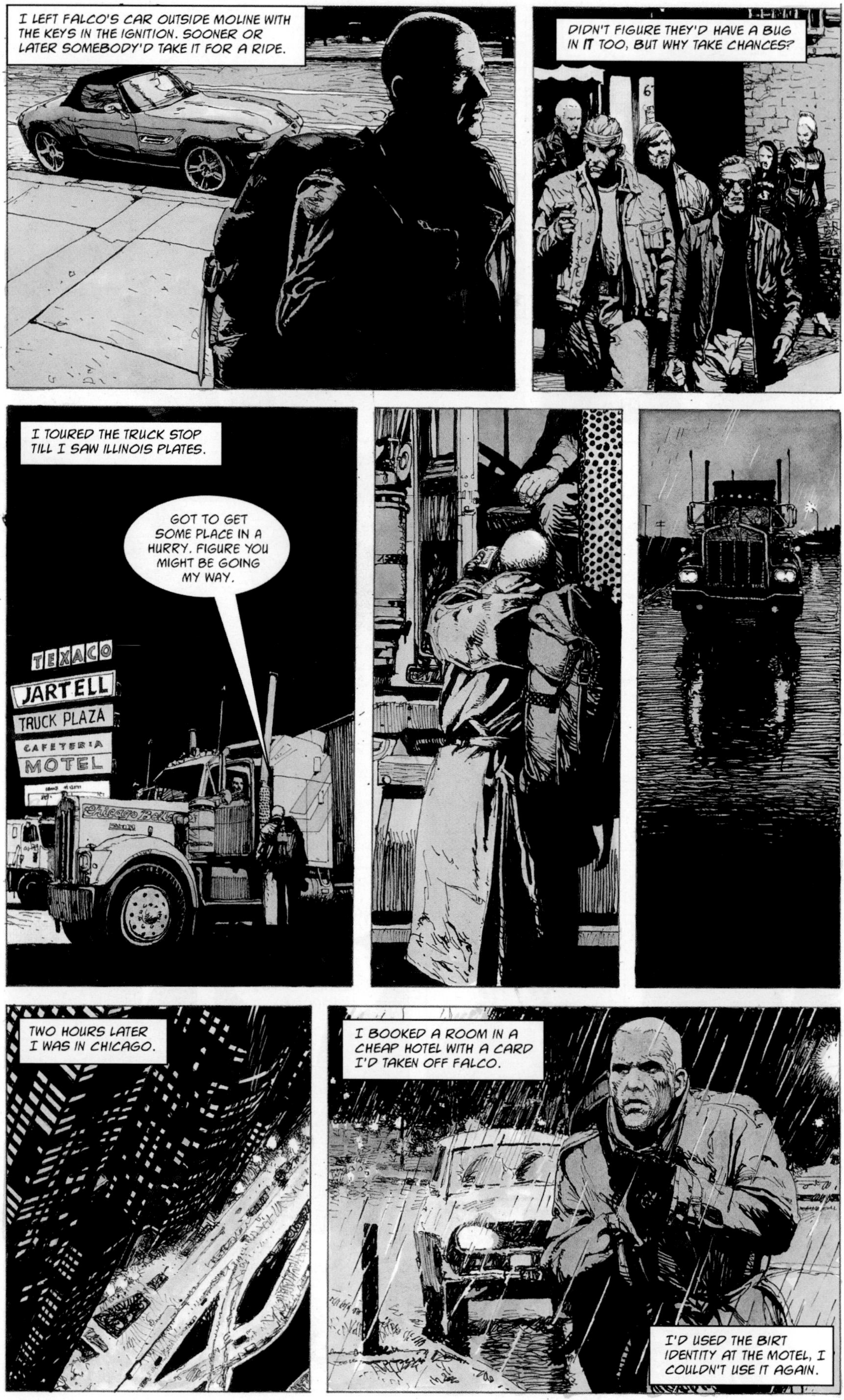
I LEFT FALCO'S CAR OUTSIDE MOLINE WITH THE KEYS IN THE IGNITION. SOONER OR LATER SOMEBODY'D TAKE IT FOR A RIDE.
DIDN'T FIGURE THEY'D HAVE A BUG IN IT TOO, BUT WHY TAKE CHANCES?
I TOURED THE TRUCK STOP TILL I SAW ILLINOIS PLATES.
GOT TO GET SOME PLACE IN A HURRY. FIGURE YOU MIGHT BE GOING MY WAY.
TEXACO
JARTELL
TRUCK PLAZA
CAFETERIA
MOTEL
TWO HOURS LATER I WAS IN CHICAGO.
I BOOKED A ROOM IN A CHEAP HOTEL WITH A CARD I'D TAKEN OFF FALCO.
I'D USED THE BIRT IDENTITY AT THE MOTEL, I COULDN'T USE IT AGAIN.

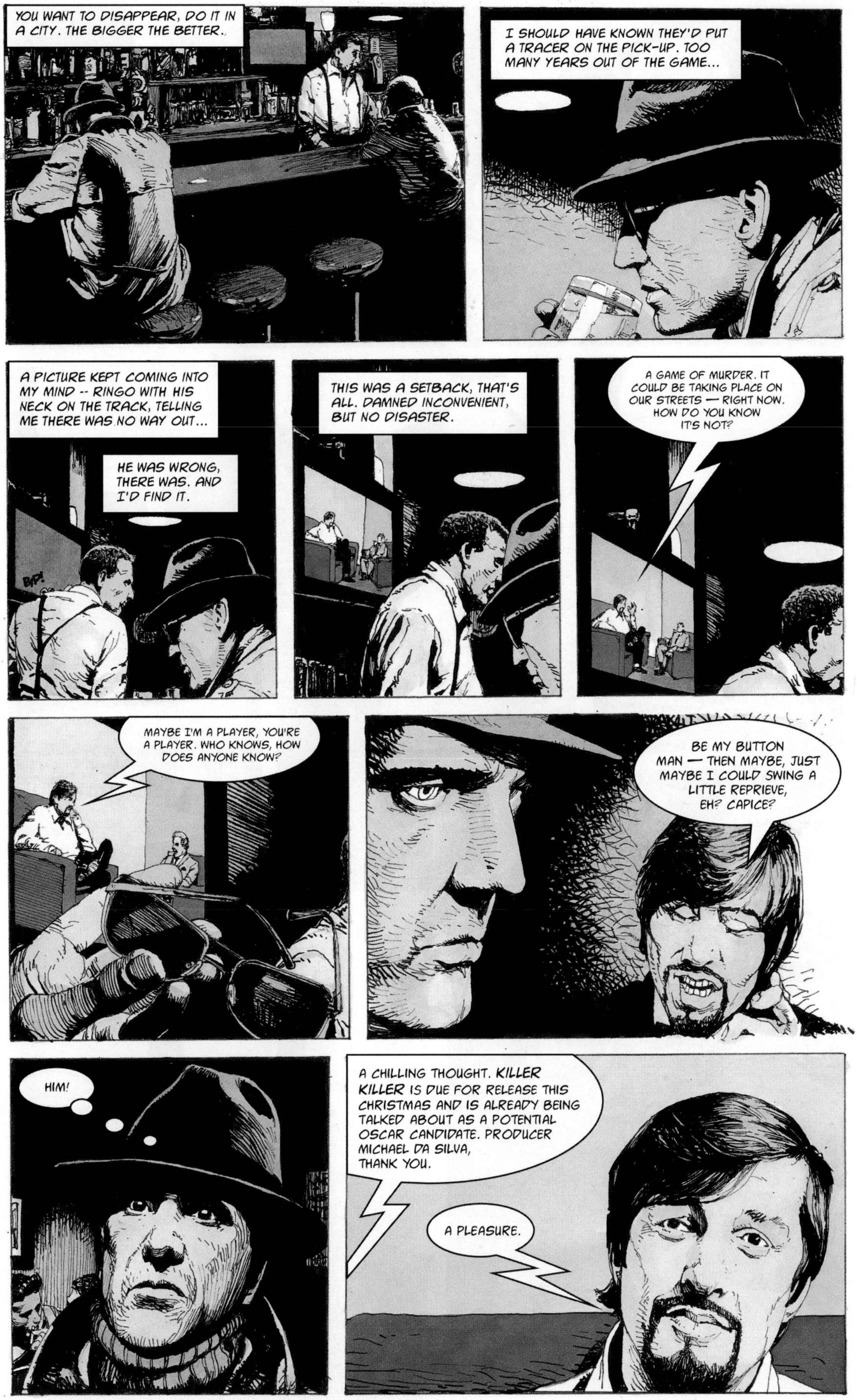
YOU WANT TO DISAPPEAR, DO IT IN A CITY. THE BIGGER THE BETTER.
I SHOULD HAVE KNOWN THEY'D PUT A TRACER ON THE PICK-UP. TOO MANY YEARS OUT OF THE GAME...
A PICTURE KEPT COMING INTO MY MIND -- RINGO WITH HIS NECK ON THE TRACK, TELLING ME THERE WAS NO WAY OUT...
HE WAS WRONG, THERE WAS. AND I'D FIND IT.
THIS WAS A SETBACK, THAT'S ALL. DAMNED INCONVENIENT, BUT NO DISASTER.
A GAME OF MURDER. IT COULD BE TAKING PLACE ON OUR STREETS — RIGHT NOW. HOW DO YOU KNOW IT'S NOT?
MAYBE I'M A PLAYER, YOU'RE A PLAYER. WHO KNOWS, HOW DOES ANYONE KNOW?
BE MY BUTTON MAN — THEN MAYBE, JUST MAYBE I COULD SWING A LITTLE REPRIEVE, EH? CAPICE?
HIM!
A CHILLING THOUGHT. KILLER KILLER IS DUE FOR RELEASE THIS CHRISTMAS AND IS ALREADY BEING TALKED ABOUT AS A POTENTIAL OSCAR CANDIDATE. PRODUCER MICHAEL DA SILVA, THANK YOU.
A PLEASURE.

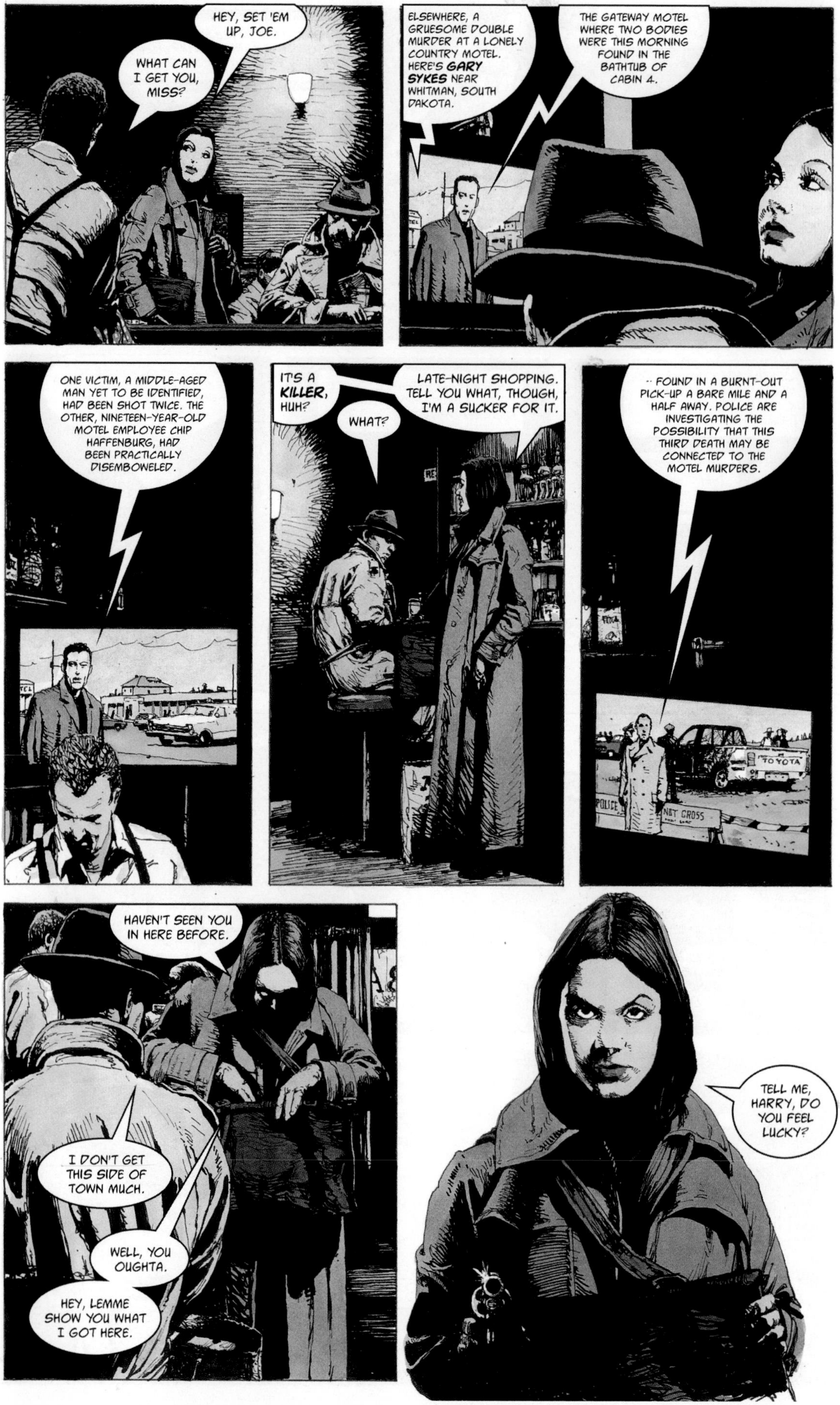
HEY, SET 'EM UP, JOE.
WHAT CAN I GET YOU, MISS?
ELSEWHERE, A GRUESOME DOUBLE MURDER AT A LONELY COUNTRY MOTEL. HERE'S GARY SYKES NEAR WHITMAN, SOUTH DAKOTA.
THE GATEWAY MOTEL WHERE TWO BODIES WERE THIS MORNING FOUND IN THE BATHTUB OF CABIN 4.
ONE VICTIM, A MIDDLE-AGED MAN YET TO BE IDENTIFIED, HAD BEEN SHOT TWICE. THE OTHER, NINETEEN-YEAR-OLD MOTEL EMPLOYEE CHIP HAFFENBURG, HAD BEEN PRACTICALLY DISEMBOWELED.
IT'S A KILLER, HUH?
LATE-NIGHT SHOPPING. TELL YOU WHAT, THOUGH, I'M A SUCKER FOR IT.
WHAT?
.. FOUND IN A BURNT-OUT PICK-UP A BARE MILE AND A HALF AWAY. POLICE ARE INVESTIGATING THE POSSIBILITY THAT THIS THIRD DEATH MAY BE CONNECTED TO THE MOTEL MURDERS.
TOYOTA
POLICE
NOT CROSS
HAVEN'T SEEN YOU IN HERE BEFORE.
I DON'T GET THIS SIDE OF TOWN MUCH.
WELL, YOU OUGHTA.
HEY, LEMME SHOW YOU WHAT I GOT HERE.
TELL ME, HARRY, DO YOU FEEL LUCKY?

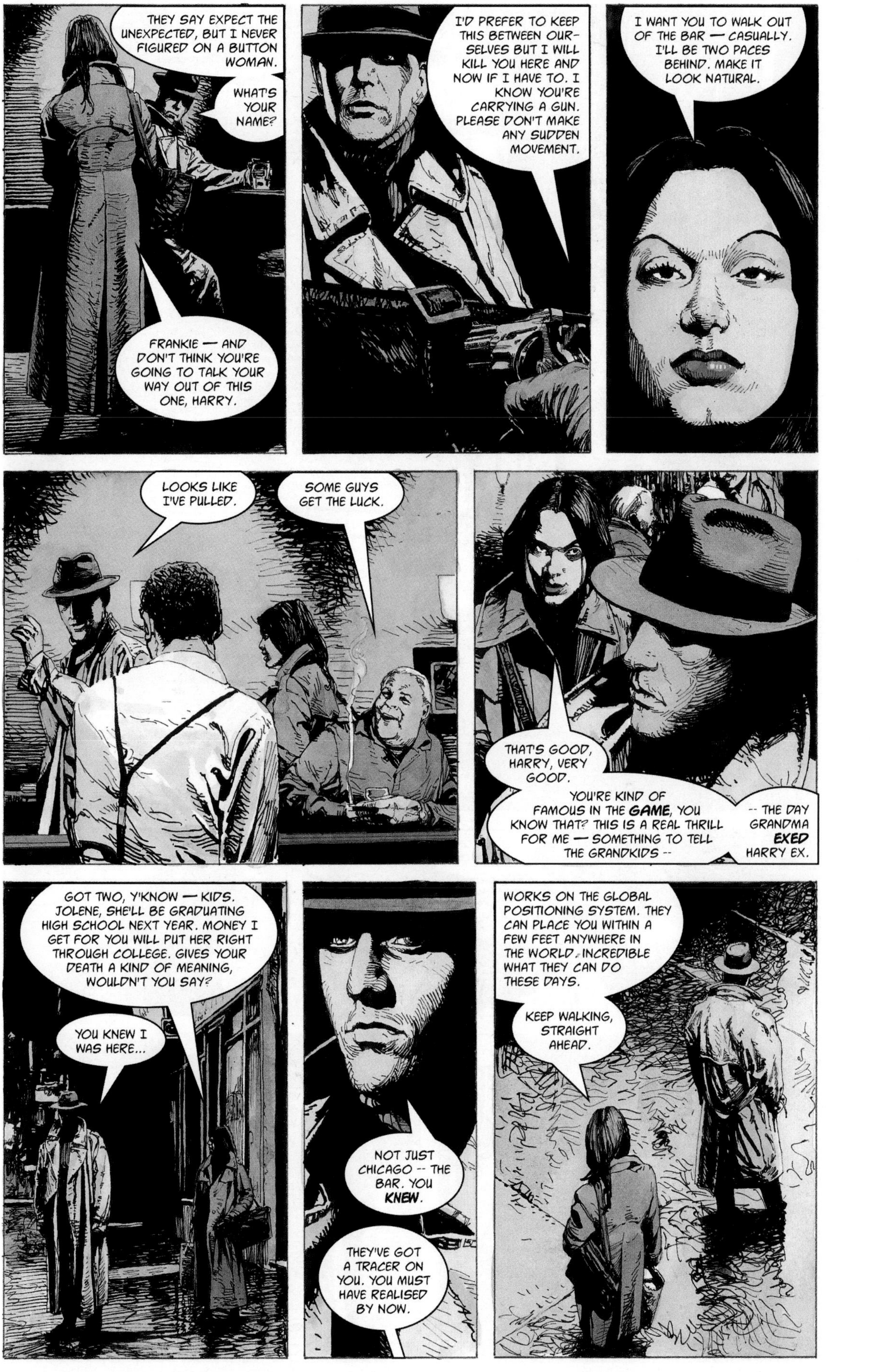
THEY SAY EXPECT THE UNEXPECTED, BUT I NEVER FIGURED ON A BUTTON WOMAN.
WHAT'S YOUR NAME?
FRANKIE — AND DON'T THINK YOU'RE GOING TO TALK YOUR WAY OUT OF THIS ONE, HARRY.
I'D PREFER TO KEEP THIS BETWEEN OURSELVES BUT I WILL KILL YOU HERE AND NOW IF I HAVE TO. I KNOW YOU'RE CARRYING A GUN. PLEASE DON'T MAKE ANY SUDDEN MOVEMENT.
I WANT YOU TO WALK OUT OF THE BAR — CASUALLY. I'LL BE TWO PACES BEHIND. MAKE IT LOOK NATURAL.
LOOKS LIKE I'VE PULLED.
SOME GUYS GET THE LUCK.
THAT'S GOOD, HARRY, VERY GOOD.
YOU'RE KIND OF FAMOUS IN THE **GAME**, YOU KNOW THAT? THIS IS A REAL THRILL FOR ME — SOMETHING TO TELL THE GRANDKIDS --
-- THE DAY GRANDMA **EXED** HARRY EX.
GOT TWO, Y'KNOW — KIDS. JOLENE, SHE'LL BE GRADUATING HIGH SCHOOL NEXT YEAR. MONEY I GET FOR YOU WILL PUT HER RIGHT THROUGH COLLEGE. GIVES YOUR DEATH A KIND OF MEANING, WOULDN'T YOU SAY?
YOU KNEW I WAS HERE...
NOT JUST CHICAGO -- THE BAR. YOU **KNEW**.
THEY'VE GOT A TRACER ON YOU. YOU MUST HAVE REALISED BY NOW.
WORKS ON THE GLOBAL POSITIONING SYSTEM. THEY CAN PLACE YOU WITHIN A FEW FEET ANYWHERE IN THE WORLD. INCREDIBLE WHAT THEY CAN DO THESE DAYS.
KEEP WALKING, STRAIGHT AHEAD.

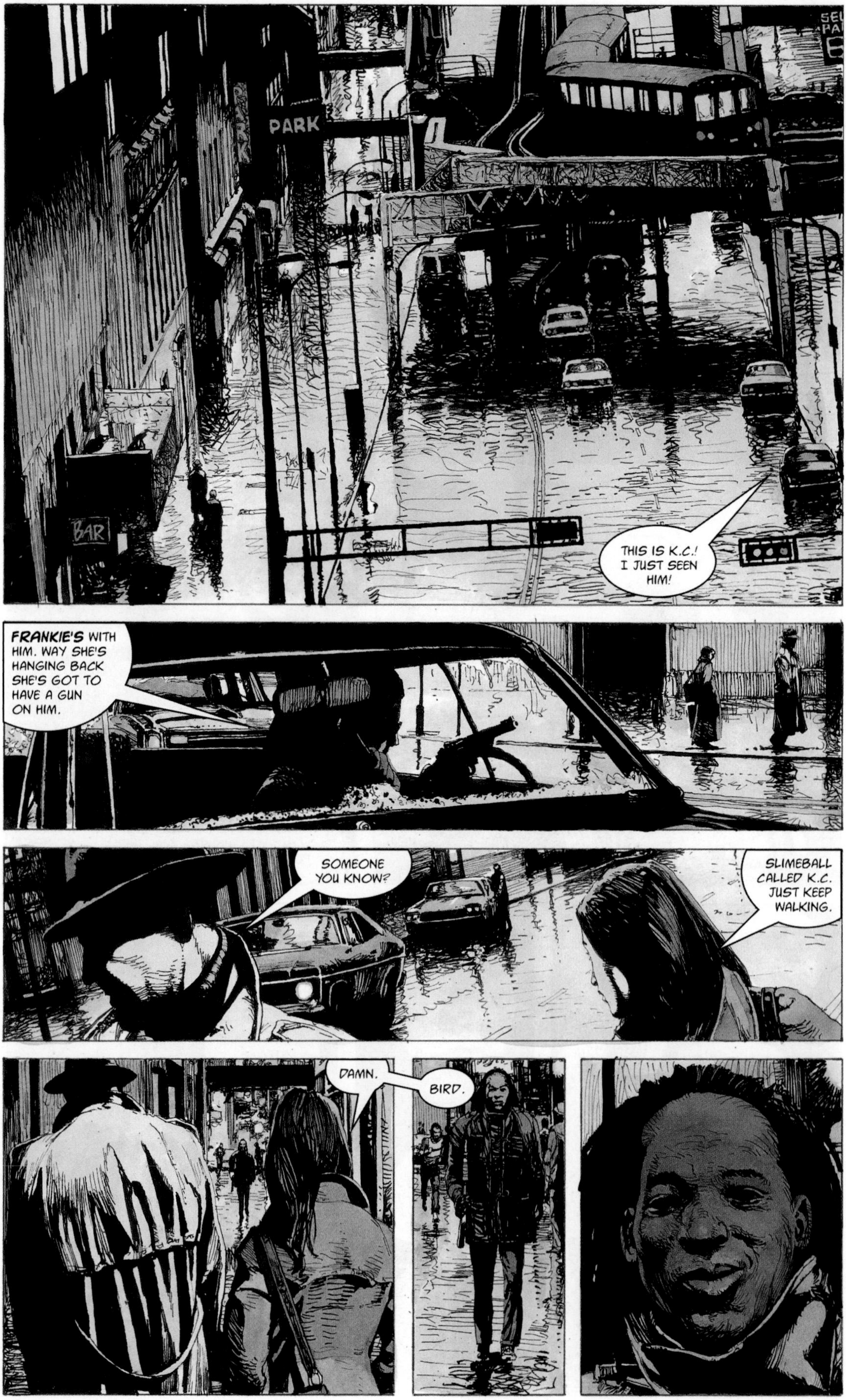
THIS IS K.C.! I JUST SEEN HIM!
FRANKIE'S WITH HIM. WAY SHE'S HANGING BACK SHE'S GOT TO HAVE A GUN ON HIM.
SOMEONE YOU KNOW?
SLIMEBALL CALLED K.C. JUST KEEP WALKING.
DAMN.
BIRD.
PARK
BAR

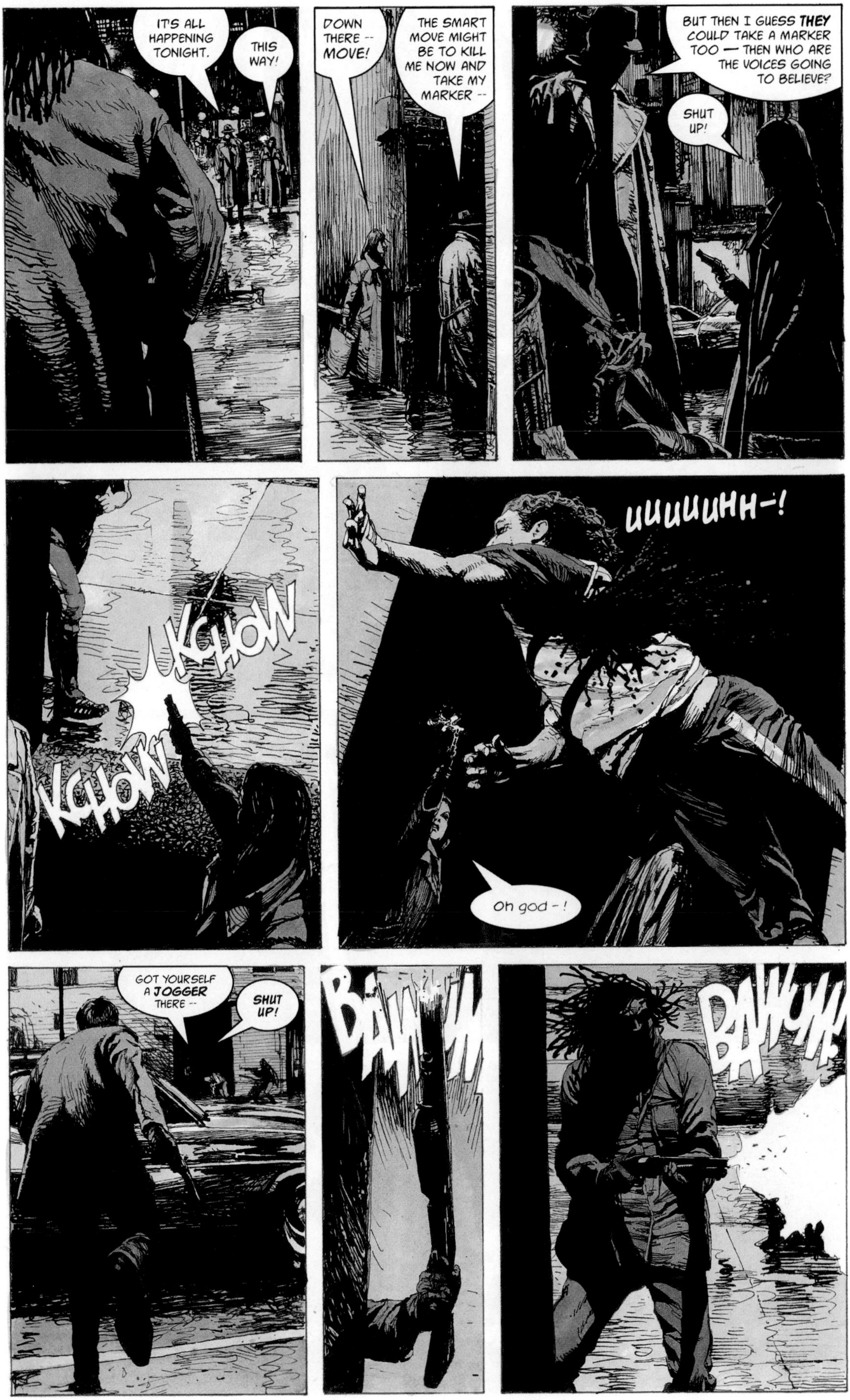
IT'S ALL HAPPENING TONIGHT.
THIS WAY!
DOWN THERE -- MOVE!
THE SMART MOVE MIGHT BE TO KILL ME NOW AND TAKE MY MARKER --
BUT THEN I GUESS THEY COULD TAKE A MARKER TOO — THEN WHO ARE THE VOICES GOING TO BELIEVE?
SHUT UP!
KCHOW
KCHOW
UUUUUHH-!
Oh god -!
GOT YOURSELF A JOGGER THERE --
SHUT UP!
BAMMM
BAMMM

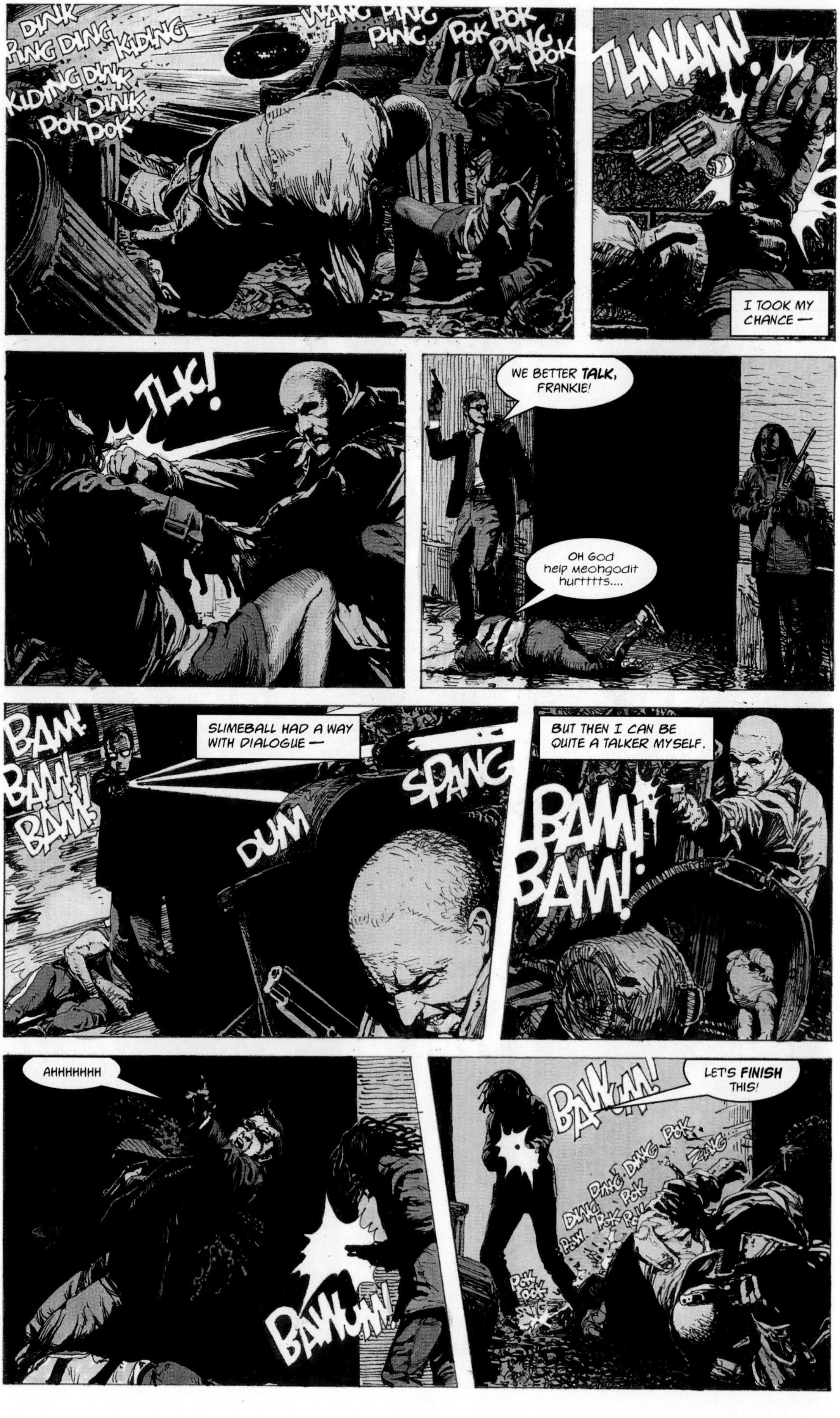
DINK
PING DING KIDING
KIDING DINK
POK DINK
POK
WANG PING
PING
POK POK
PING
POK
THWAM
I TOOK MY CHANCE —
THC!
WE BETTER TALK, FRANKIE!
OH God help meohgodit hurtttts....
BAM! BAM! BAM!
SLIMEBALL HAD A WAY WITH DIALOGUE —
SPANG
DUM
BUT THEN I CAN BE QUITE A TALKER MYSELF.
BAM! BAM!
AHHHHHHH
BAWUM!
LET'S FINISH THIS!
BAWUM!

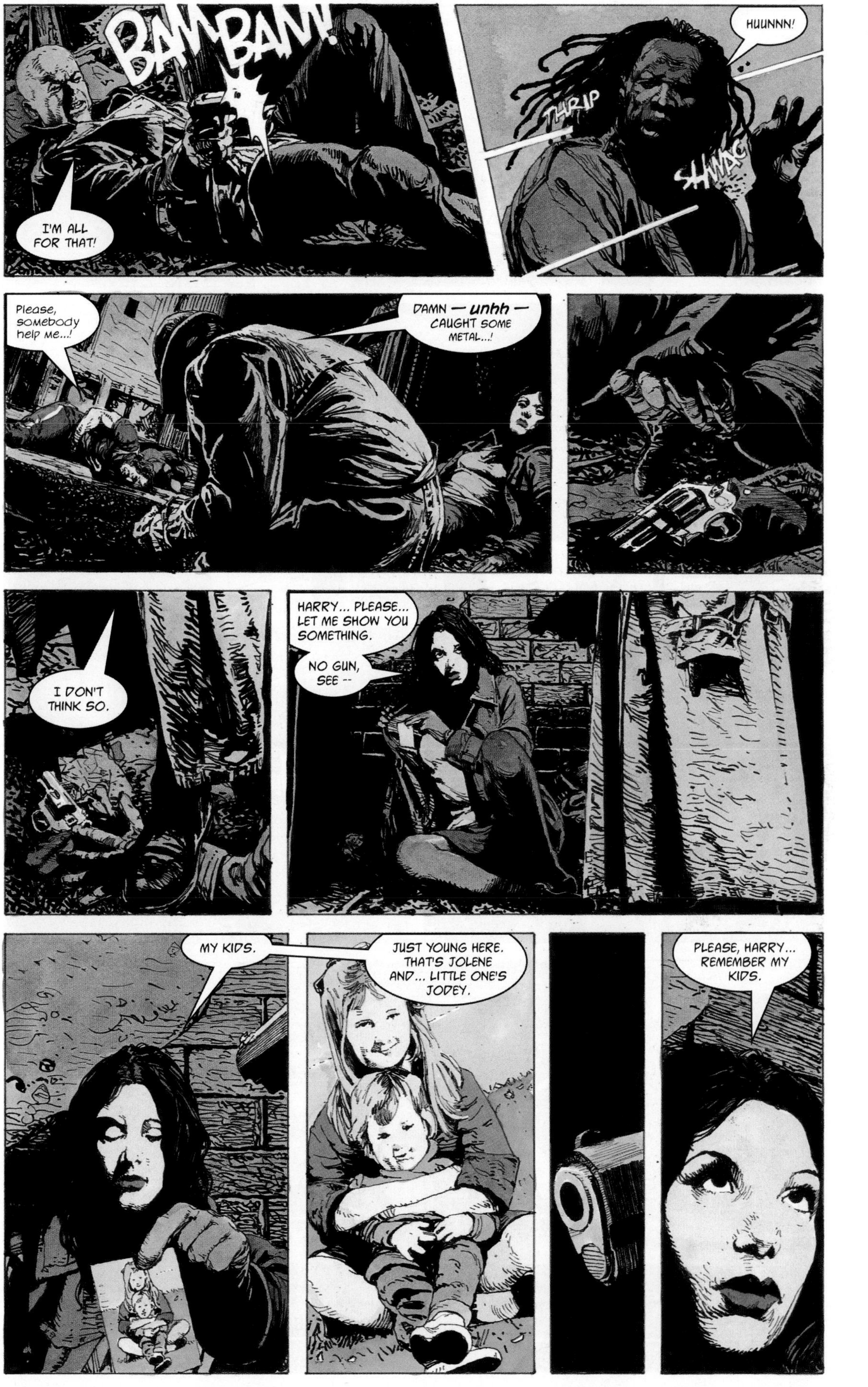

BAM BAM!
I'M ALL FOR THAT!
HUUNNN!
THRIP
SHWAC
Please, somebody help me...!
DAMN — unhh — CAUGHT SOME METAL...!
I DON'T THINK SO.
HARRY... PLEASE... LET ME SHOW YOU SOMETHING.
NO GUN, SEE --
MY KIDS.
JUST YOUNG HERE. THAT'S JOLENE AND... LITTLE ONE'S JODEY.
PLEASE, HARRY... REMEMBER MY KIDS.

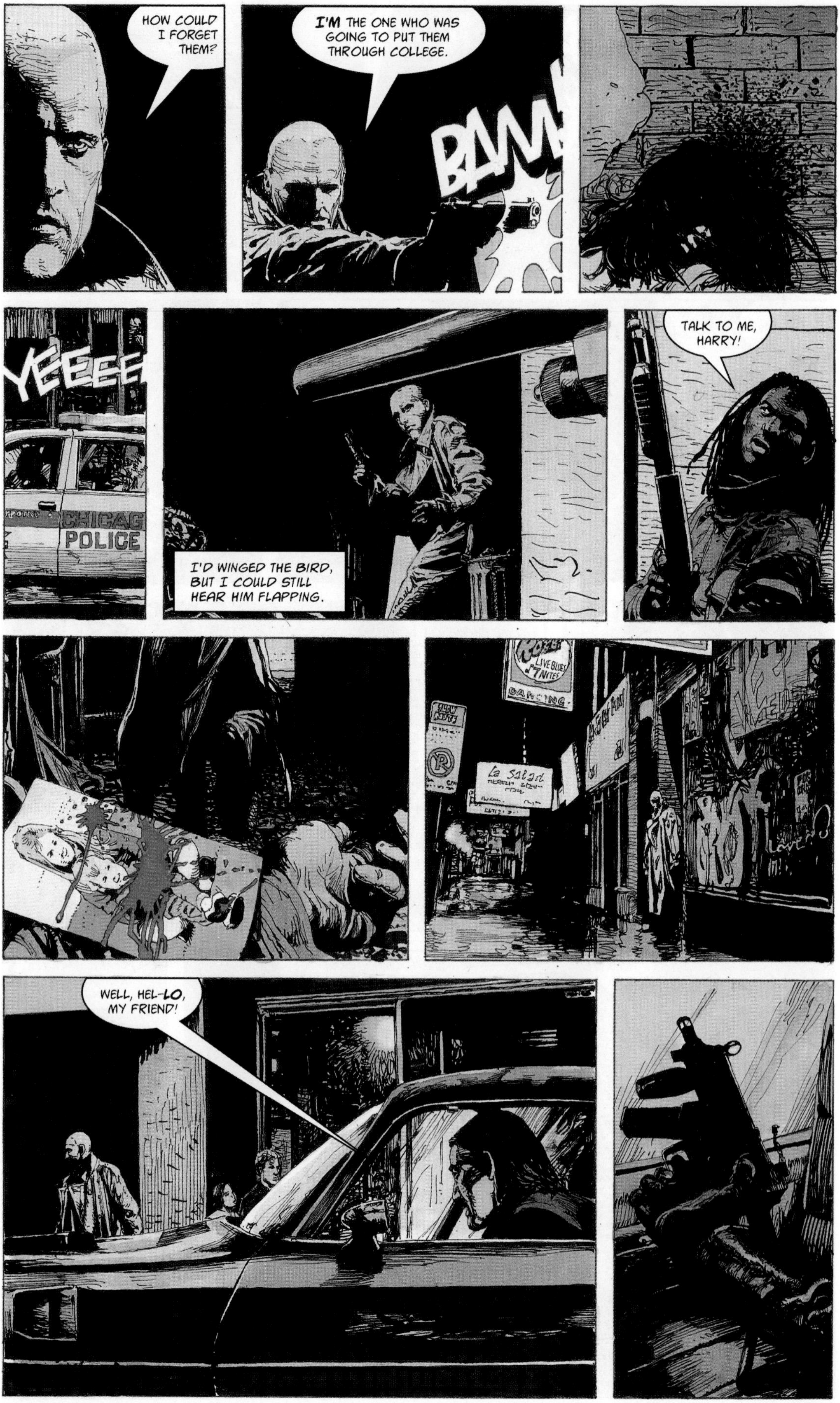
HOW COULD I FORGET THEM?
I'M THE ONE WHO WAS GOING TO PUT THEM THROUGH COLLEGE.
BAM
YEEEE
CHICAG
POLICE
I'D WINGED THE BIRD, BUT I COULD STILL HEAR HIM FLAPPING.
TALK TO ME, HARRY!
LIVE BLUES
DANCING
La Salad
WELL, HEL-LO, MY FRIEND!

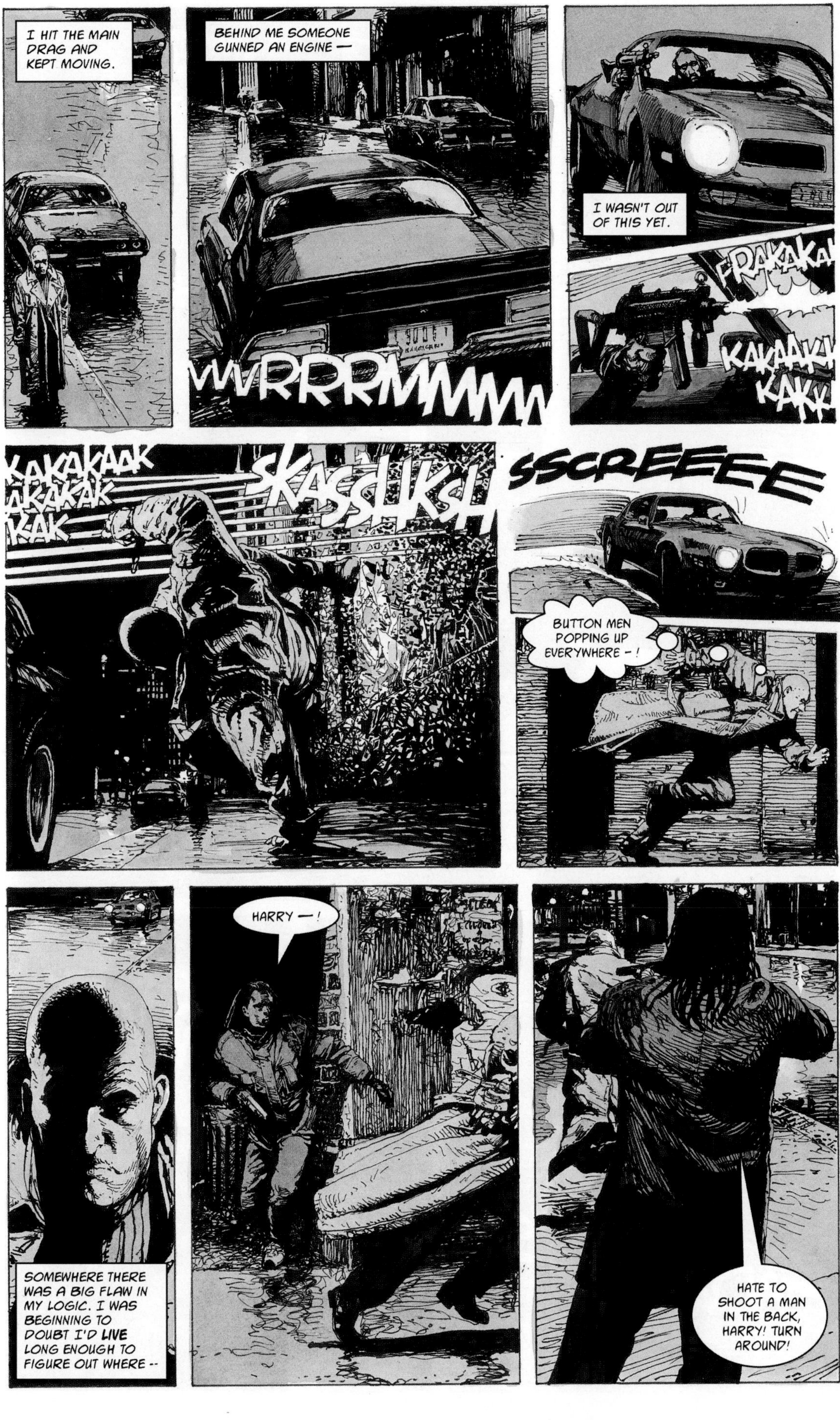

I HIT THE MAIN DRAG AND KEPT MOVING.
BEHIND ME SOMEONE GUNNED AN ENGINE —
VVVRRRRMMMMM
I WASN'T OUT OF THIS YET.
FRAKAKAK
KAKAAKK KAKK
KAKAKAAK AKAKAK KAK
SKASSLIKSH
SSCREEEEE
BUTTON MEN POPPING UP EVERYWHERE — !
SOMEWHERE THERE WAS A BIG FLAW IN MY LOGIC. I WAS BEGINNING TO DOUBT I'D **LIVE** LONG ENOUGH TO FIGURE OUT WHERE --
HARRY — !
HATE TO SHOOT A MAN IN THE BACK, HARRY! TURN AROUND!

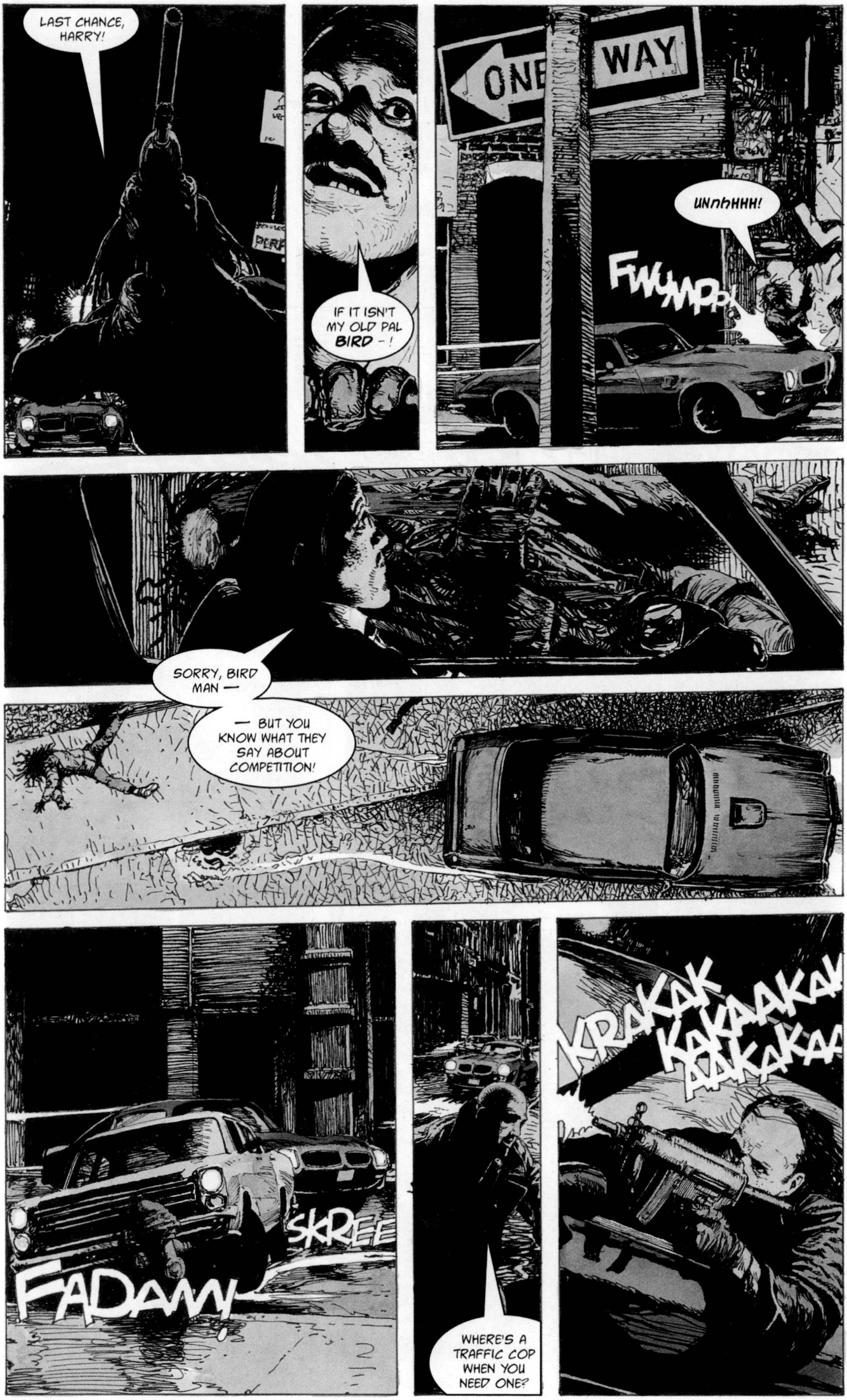
LAST CHANCE, HARRY!
IF IT ISN'T MY OLD PAL BIRD --!
ONE WAY
UNNHHHH!
FWUMPP!
SORRY, BIRD MAN --
-- BUT YOU KNOW WHAT THEY SAY ABOUT COMPETITION!
SKREEE
FADAM!
WHERE'S A TRAFFIC COP WHEN YOU NEED ONE?
KRAKAK KAKAKAKAK AKAKAKA

ZITDANGSKDANGANGADANGG

GETTING A LITTLE TOO ONE-SIDED FOR MY LIKING —!

BLAM!

BLAM! BLAM!

SKRAANG SKRAANG

SKRACH

SMG

THWUMPP!

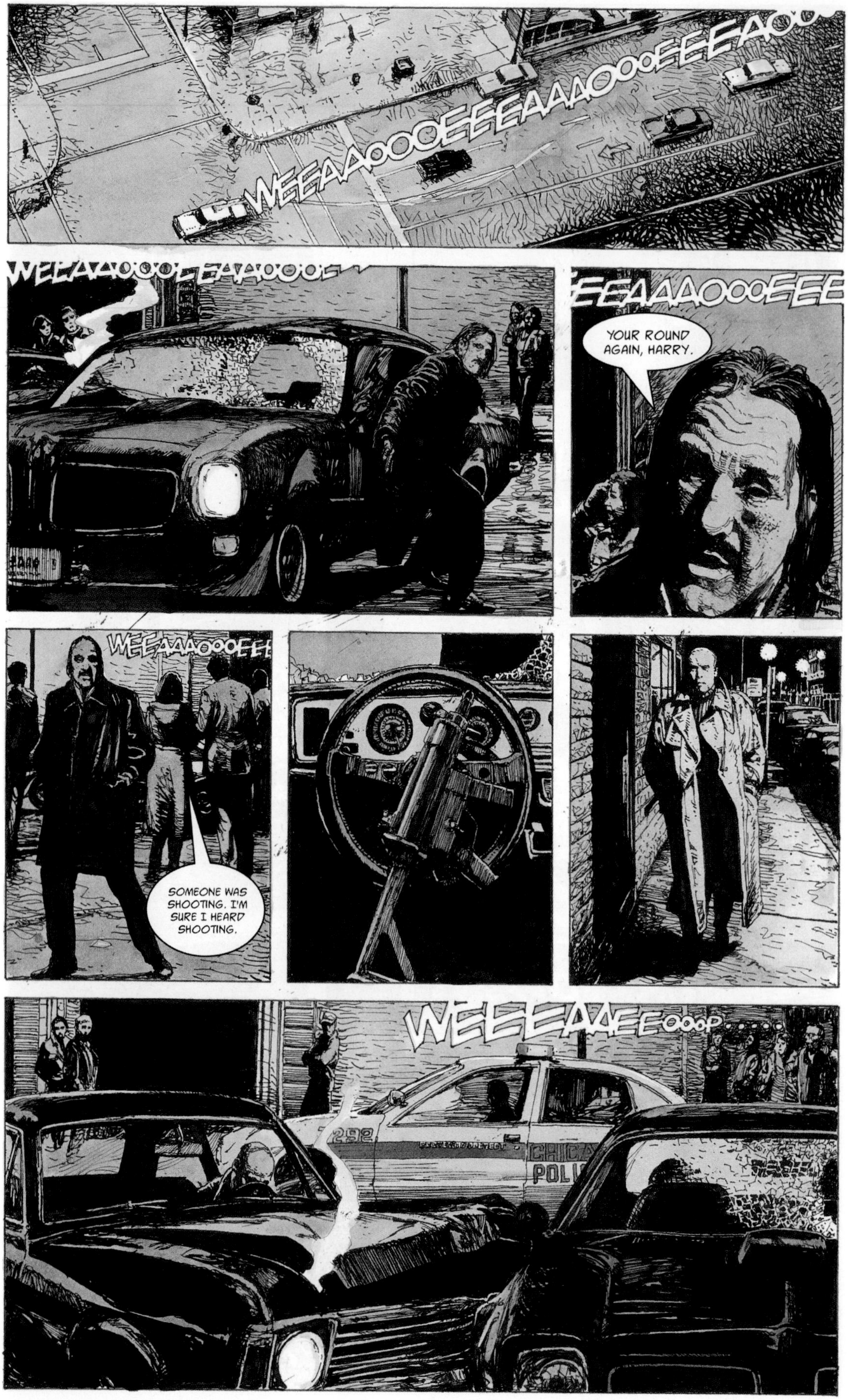
WEEAAOOOEEEEAAAOOOEEEEAOO
WEEAAOOOEEAAOOOE
EEAAAOOOEEE
YOUR ROUND AGAIN, HARRY.
WEEAAAOOOEEE
SOMEONE WAS SHOOTING. I'M SURE I HEARD SHOOTING.
WEEEAAEEOOOP...
CHICA
POLI

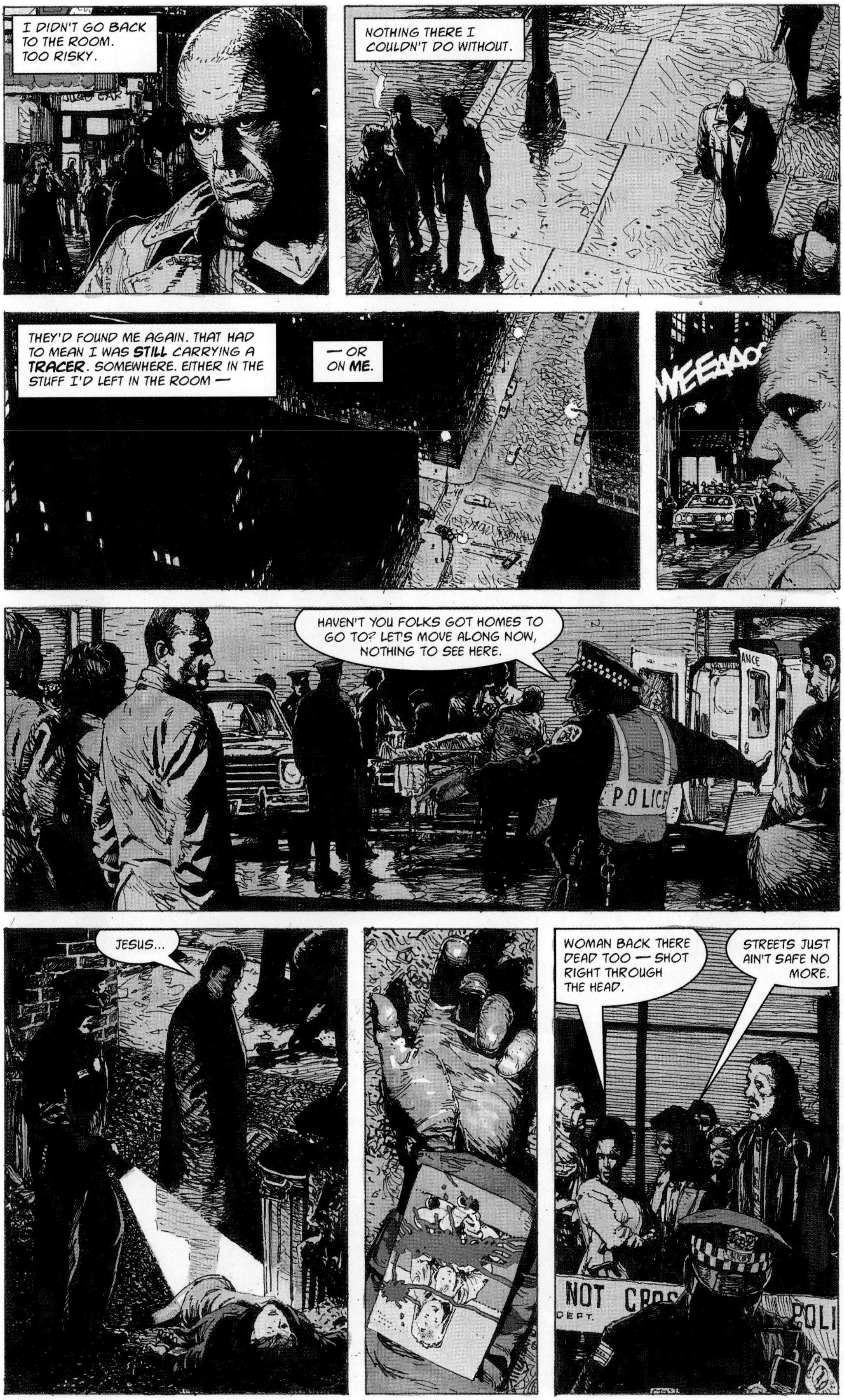
I DIDN'T GO BACK TO THE ROOM. TOO RISKY.
NOTHING THERE I COULDN'T DO WITHOUT.
THEY'D FOUND ME AGAIN. THAT HAD TO MEAN I WAS **STILL** CARRYING A **TRACER**. SOMEWHERE. EITHER IN THE STUFF I'D LEFT IN THE ROOM —
— OR ON **ME**.
HAVEN'T YOU FOLKS GOT HOMES TO GO TO? LET'S MOVE ALONG NOW, NOTHING TO SEE HERE.
POLICE
JESUS...
WOMAN BACK THERE DEAD TOO — SHOT RIGHT THROUGH THE HEAD.
STREETS JUST AIN'T SAFE NO MORE.
NOT CROS
DEPT.
POLI

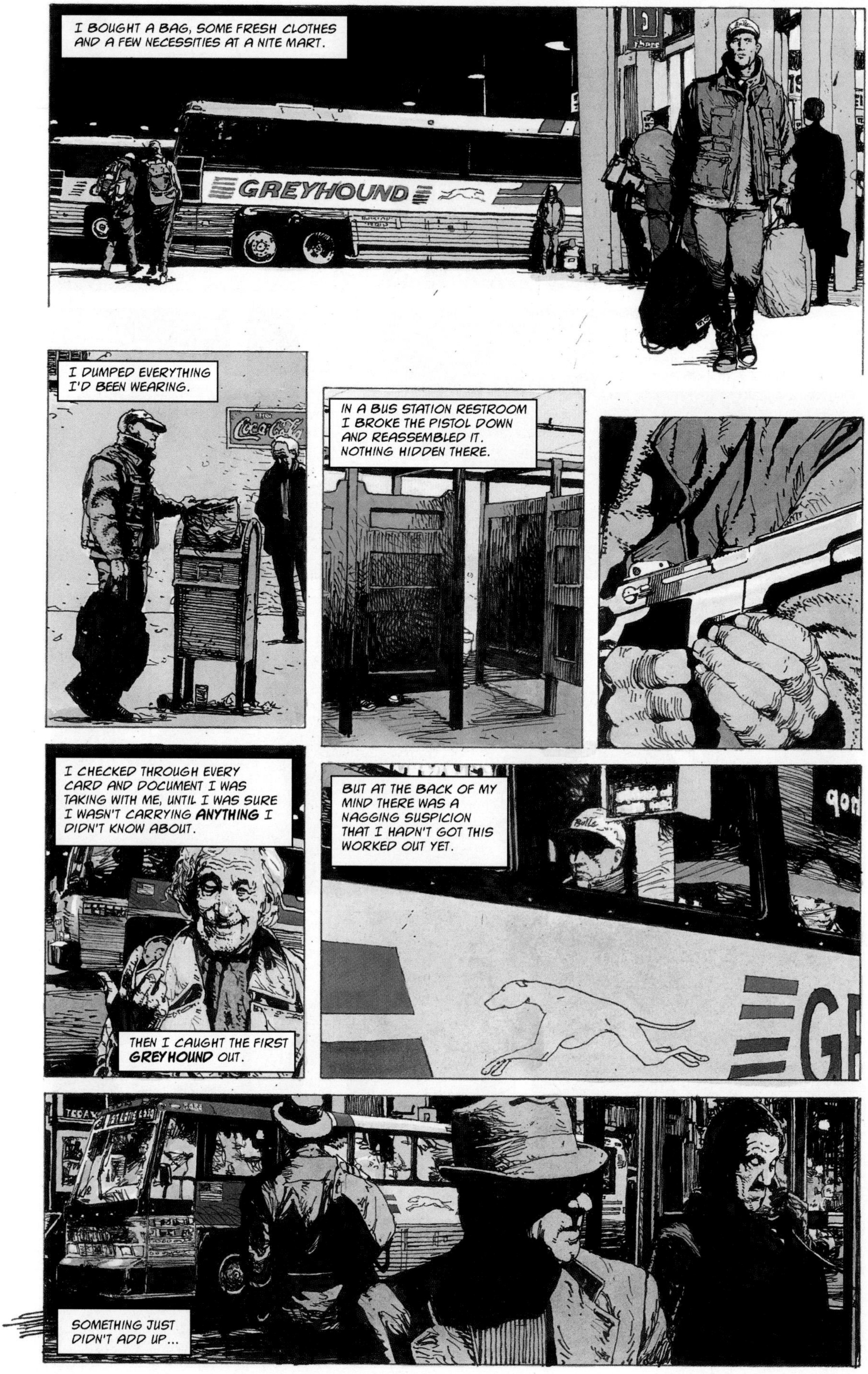
I BOUGHT A BAG, SOME FRESH CLOTHES AND A FEW NECESSITIES AT A NITE MART.
GREYHOUND
I DUMPED EVERYTHING I'D BEEN WEARING.
IN A BUS STATION RESTROOM I BROKE THE PISTOL DOWN AND REASSEMBLED IT. NOTHING HIDDEN THERE.
I CHECKED THROUGH EVERY CARD AND DOCUMENT I WAS TAKING WITH ME, UNTIL I WAS SURE I WASN'T CARRYING **ANYTHING** I DIDN'T KNOW ABOUT.
THEN I CAUGHT THE FIRST **GREYHOUND** OUT.
BUT AT THE BACK OF MY MIND THERE WAS A NAGGING SUSPICION THAT I HADN'T GOT THIS WORKED OUT YET.
SOMETHING JUST DIDN'T ADD UP...

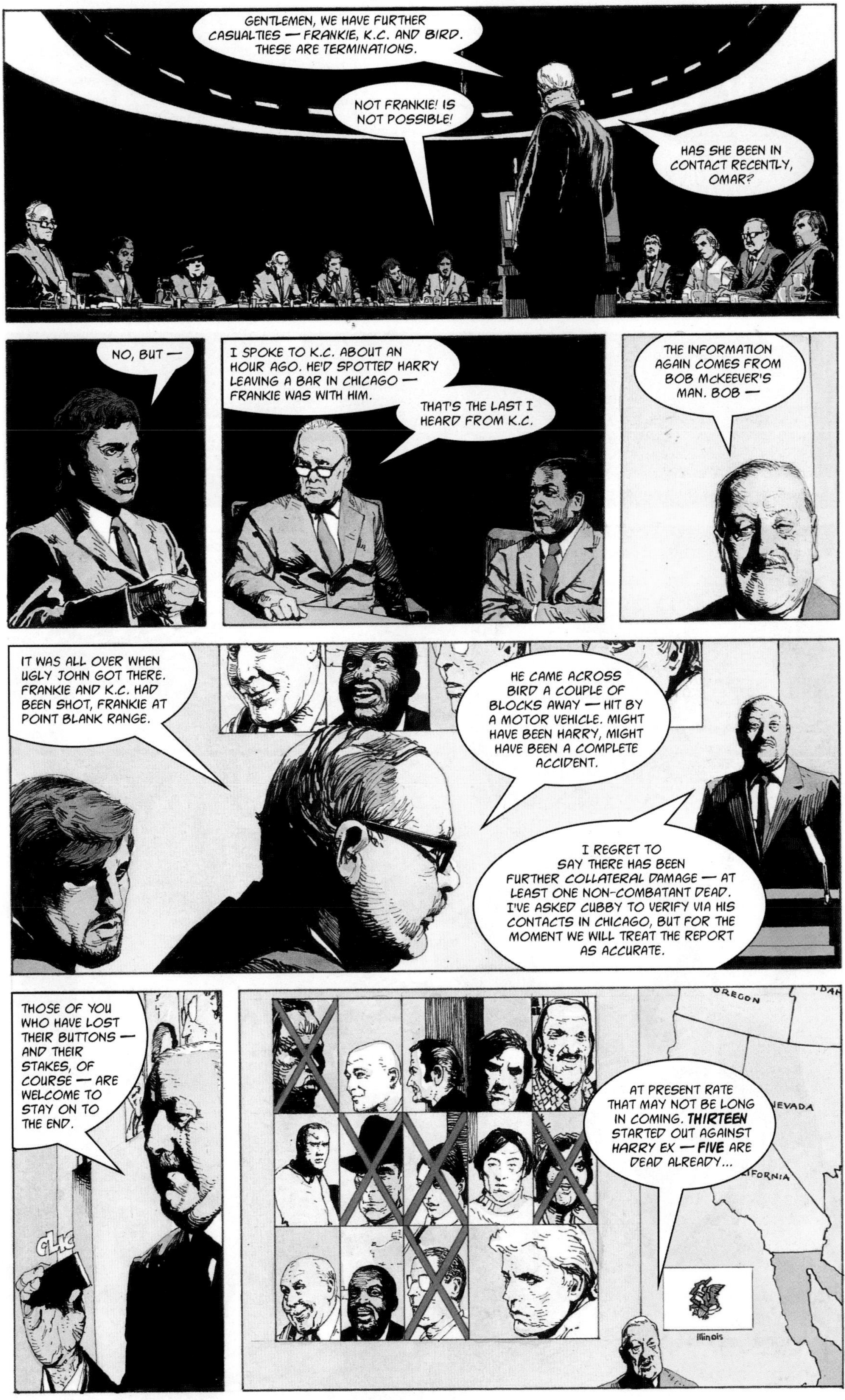
GENTLEMEN, WE HAVE FURTHER CASUALTIES — FRANKIE, K.C. AND BIRD. THESE ARE TERMINATIONS.
NOT FRANKIE! IS NOT POSSIBLE!
HAS SHE BEEN IN CONTACT RECENTLY, OMAR?
NO, BUT —
I SPOKE TO K.C. ABOUT AN HOUR AGO. HE'D SPOTTED HARRY LEAVING A BAR IN CHICAGO — FRANKIE WAS WITH HIM.
THAT'S THE LAST I HEARD FROM K.C.
THE INFORMATION AGAIN COMES FROM BOB McKEEVER'S MAN. BOB —
IT WAS ALL OVER WHEN UGLY JOHN GOT THERE. FRANKIE AND K.C. HAD BEEN SHOT, FRANKIE AT POINT BLANK RANGE.
HE CAME ACROSS BIRD A COUPLE OF BLOCKS AWAY — HIT BY A MOTOR VEHICLE. MIGHT HAVE BEEN HARRY, MIGHT HAVE BEEN A COMPLETE ACCIDENT.
I REGRET TO SAY THERE HAS BEEN FURTHER COLLATERAL DAMAGE — AT LEAST ONE NON-COMBATANT DEAD. I'VE ASKED CUBBY TO VERIFY VIA HIS CONTACTS IN CHICAGO, BUT FOR THE MOMENT WE WILL TREAT THE REPORT AS ACCURATE.
THOSE OF YOU WHO HAVE LOST THEIR BUTTONS — AND THEIR STAKES, OF COURSE — ARE WELCOME TO STAY ON TO THE END.
CLIC
OREGON
NEVADA
AT PRESENT RATE THAT MAY NOT BE LONG IN COMING. THIRTEEN STARTED OUT AGAINST HARRY EX — FIVE ARE DEAD ALREADY...
Illinois

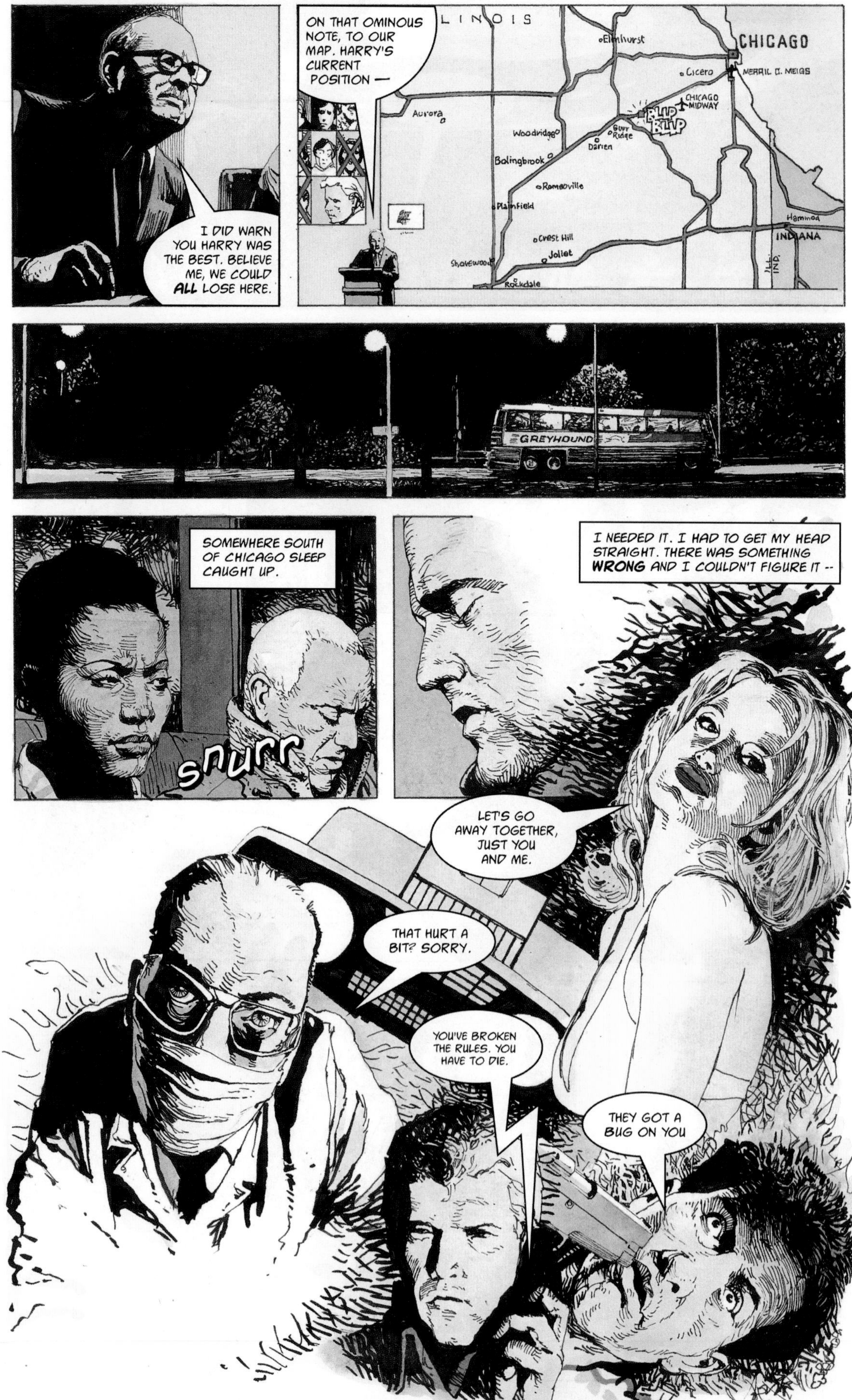
I DID WARN YOU HARRY WAS THE BEST. BELIEVE ME, WE COULD ALL LOSE HERE.
ON THAT OMINOUS NOTE, TO OUR MAP. HARRY'S CURRENT POSITION —
CHICAGO
Cicero
CHICAGO MIDWAY
BLIP BLIP
Aurora
Darien
Bolingbrook
Romeoville
Plainfield
Crest Hill
Joliet
INDIANA
SOMEWHERE SOUTH OF CHICAGO SLEEP CAUGHT UP.
GREYHOUND
snurr
I NEEDED IT. I HAD TO GET MY HEAD STRAIGHT. THERE WAS SOMETHING WRONG AND I COULDN'T FIGURE IT --
LET'S GO AWAY TOGETHER, JUST YOU AND ME.
THAT HURT A BIT? SORRY.
YOU'VE BROKEN THE RULES. YOU HAVE TO DIE.
THEY GOT A BUG ON YOU

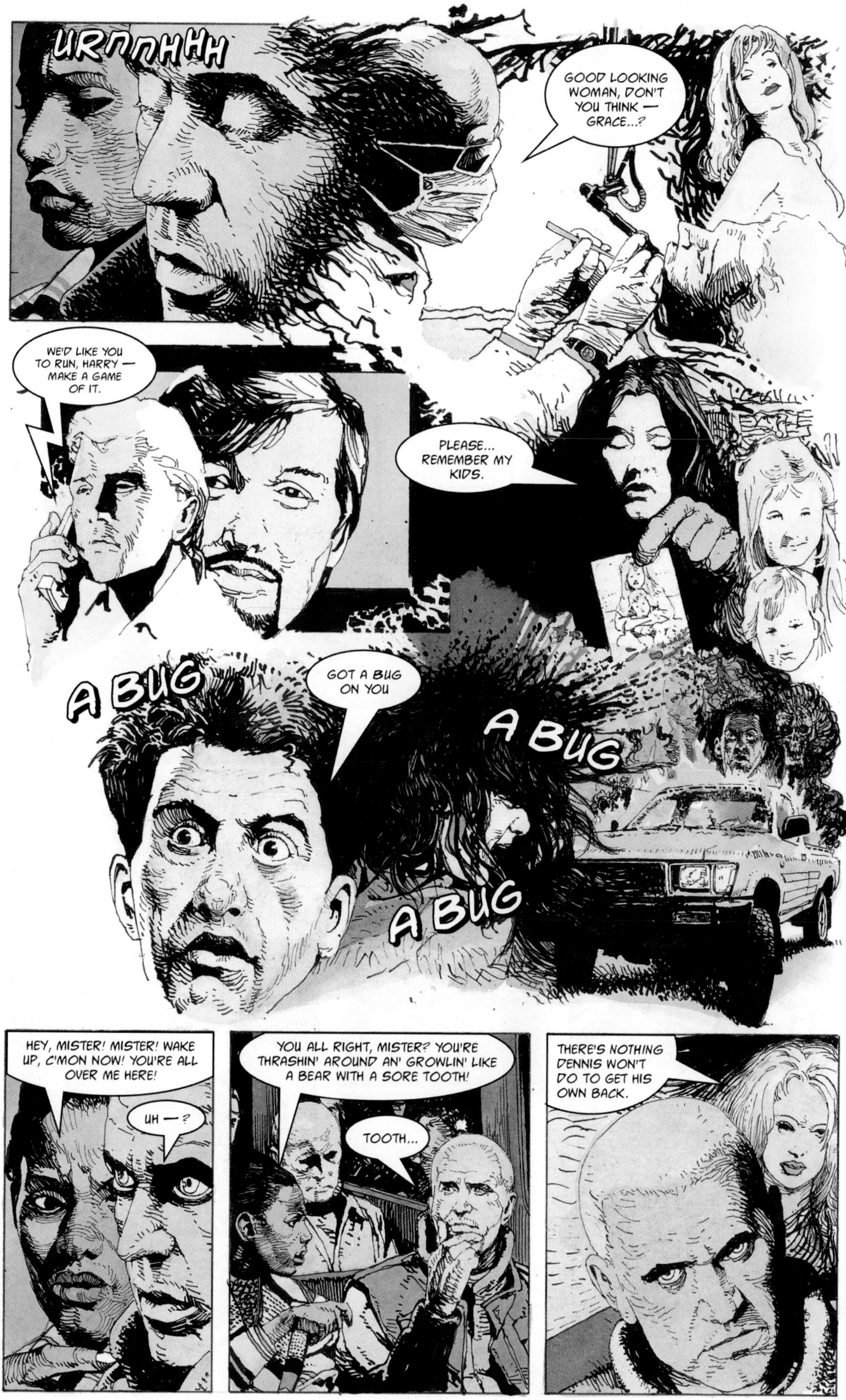
URNNHHH
GOOD LOOKING WOMAN, DON'T YOU THINK — GRACE...?
WE'D LIKE YOU TO RUN, HARRY — MAKE A GAME OF IT.
PLEASE... REMEMBER MY KIDS.
A BUG
GOT A BUG ON YOU
A BUG
A BUG
HEY, MISTER! MISTER! WAKE UP, C'MON NOW! YOU'RE ALL OVER ME HERE!
UH — ?
YOU ALL RIGHT, MISTER? YOU'RE THRASHIN' AROUND AN' GROWLIN' LIKE A BEAR WITH A SORE TOOTH!
TOOTH...
THERE'S NOTHING DENNIS WON'T DO TO GET HIS OWN BACK.

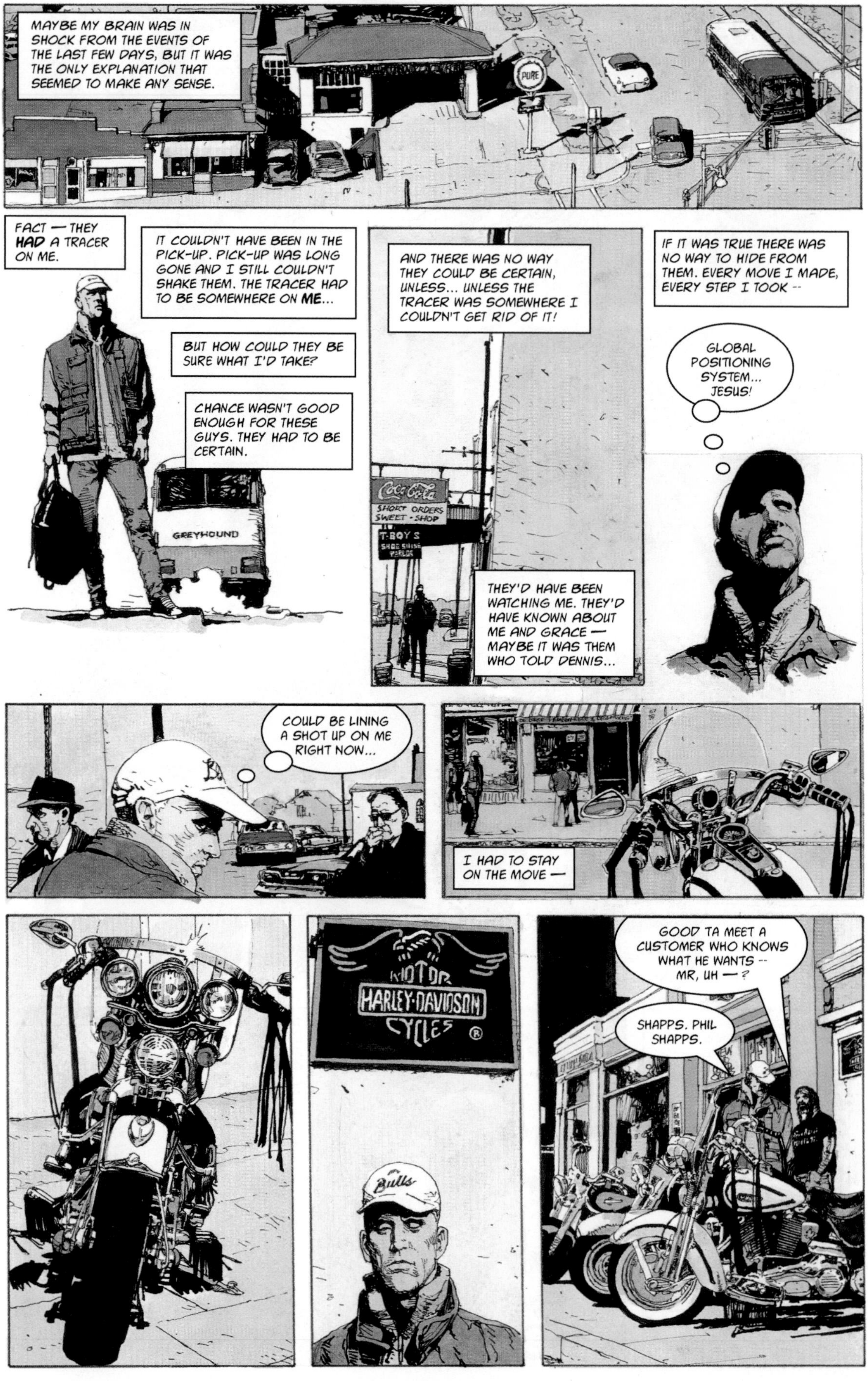
MAYBE MY BRAIN WAS IN SHOCK FROM THE EVENTS OF THE LAST FEW DAYS, BUT IT WAS THE ONLY EXPLANATION THAT SEEMED TO MAKE ANY SENSE.
PURE
FACT — THEY **HAD** A TRACER ON ME.
IT COULDN'T HAVE BEEN IN THE PICK-UP. PICK-UP WAS LONG GONE AND I STILL COULDN'T SHAKE THEM. THE TRACER HAD TO BE SOMEWHERE ON **ME**...
BUT HOW COULD THEY BE SURE WHAT I'D TAKE?
CHANCE WASN'T GOOD ENOUGH FOR THESE GUYS. THEY HAD TO BE CERTAIN.
GREYHOUND
AND THERE WAS NO WAY THEY COULD BE CERTAIN, UNLESS... UNLESS THE TRACER WAS SOMEWHERE I COULDN'T GET RID OF IT!
Coca-Cola
SHORT ORDERS SWEET - SHOP
T-BOY'S
THEY'D HAVE BEEN WATCHING ME. THEY'D HAVE KNOWN ABOUT ME AND GRACE — MAYBE IT WAS THEM WHO TOLD DENNIS...
IF IT WAS TRUE THERE WAS NO WAY TO HIDE FROM THEM. EVERY MOVE I MADE, EVERY STEP I TOOK --
GLOBAL POSITIONING SYSTEM... JESUS!
COULD BE LINING A SHOT UP ON ME RIGHT NOW...
I HAD TO STAY ON THE MOVE —
MOTOR HARLEY-DAVIDSON CYCLES ®
Bulls
GOOD TA MEET A CUSTOMER WHO KNOWS WHAT HE WANTS -- MR, UH — ?
SHAPPS. PHIL SHAPPS.

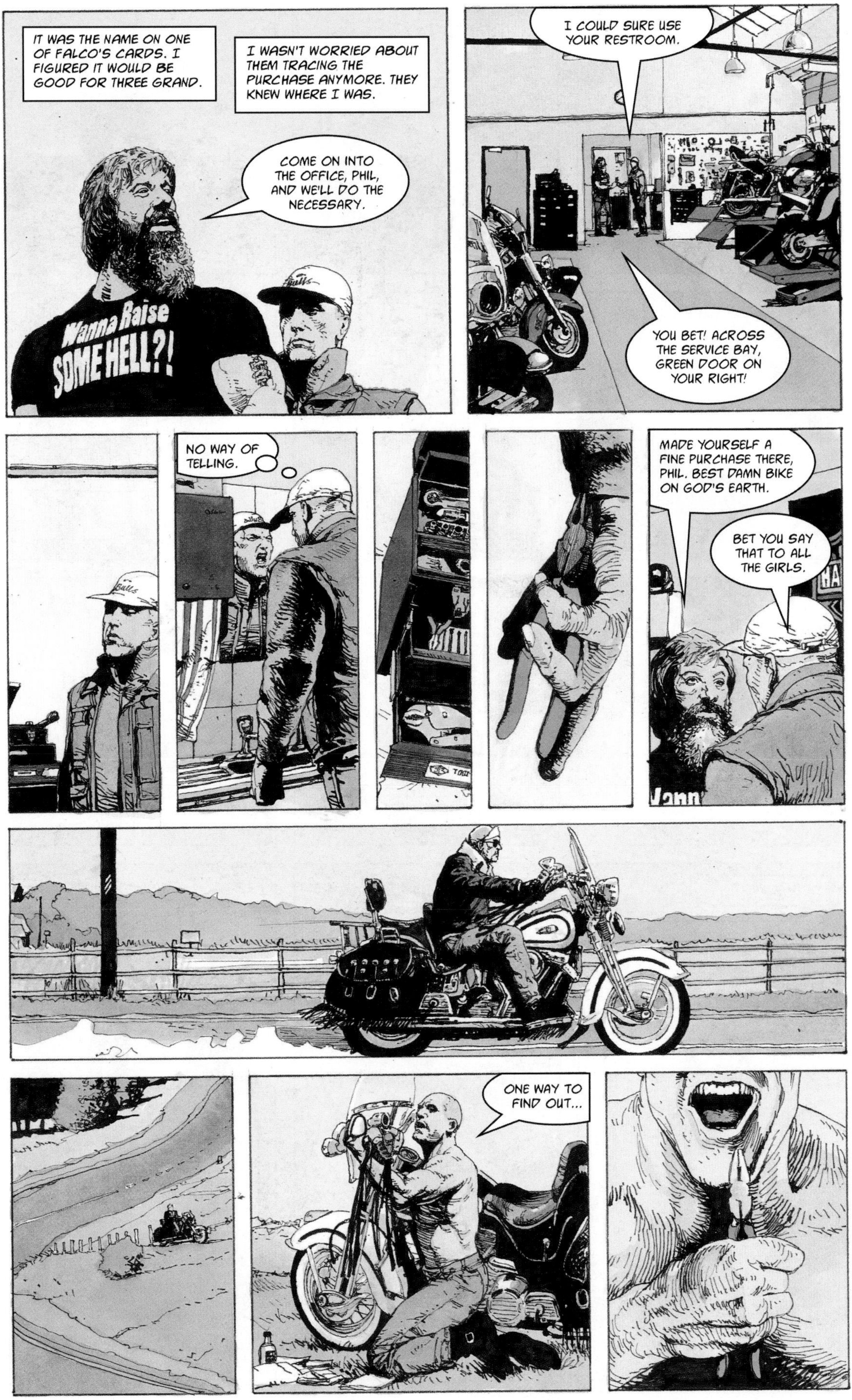
IT WAS THE NAME ON ONE OF FALCO'S CARDS. I FIGURED IT WOULD BE GOOD FOR THREE GRAND.
I WASN'T WORRIED ABOUT THEM TRACING THE PURCHASE ANYMORE. THEY KNEW WHERE I WAS.
COME ON INTO THE OFFICE, PHIL, AND WE'LL DO THE NECESSARY.
Wanna Raise SOME HELL?!
I COULD SURE USE YOUR RESTROOM.
YOU BET! ACROSS THE SERVICE BAY, GREEN DOOR ON YOUR RIGHT!
NO WAY OF TELLING.
MADE YOURSELF A FINE PURCHASE THERE, PHIL. BEST DAMN BIKE ON GOD'S EARTH.
BET YOU SAY THAT TO ALL THE GIRLS.
ONE WAY TO FIND OUT...

BETTER... GET THE RIGHT ONE...

UNNh

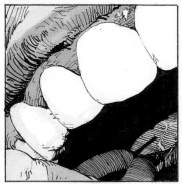

I'D PULLED A TOOTH OR TWO OUT IN THE BUSH — GLAD TO SAY, ALWAYS SOMEONE ELSE'S.

FIRST YOU GOTTA LOOSEN IT, AND THEN...

GurmonNN — !

COMIN'...!

UNNH!

NOW --

SCRCH!

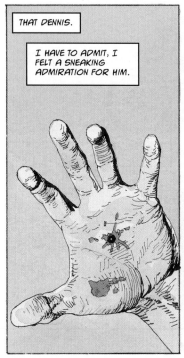

THAT DENNIS.

I HAVE TO ADMIT, I FELT A SNEAKING ADMIRATION FOR HIM.

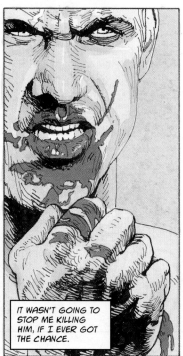

IT WASN'T GOING TO STOP ME KILLING HIM, IF I EVER GOT THE CHANCE.

I WAS GOING TO THROW IT AWAY WHEN IT CAME TO ME — EXACTLY WHAT I HAD TO DO.

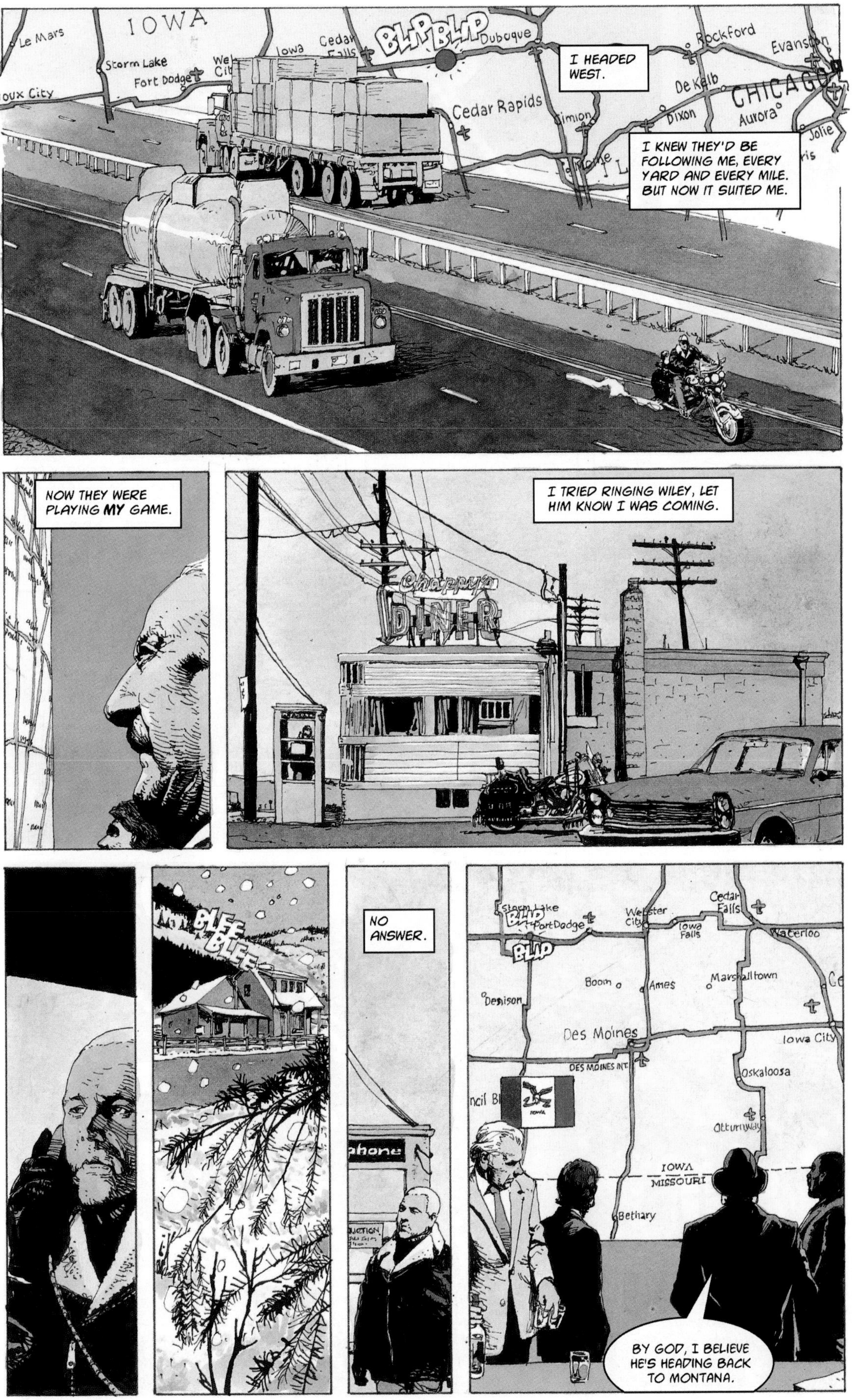
BLIP BLIP
I HEADED WEST.
I KNEW THEY'D BE FOLLOWING ME, EVERY YARD AND EVERY MILE. BUT NOW IT SUITED ME.
NOW THEY WERE PLAYING MY GAME.
I TRIED RINGING WILEY, LET HIM KNOW I WAS COMING.
Chappy's DINER
BLEE BLEE
NO ANSWER.
BLIP
BLIP
BY GOD, I BELIEVE HE'S HEADING BACK TO MONTANA.

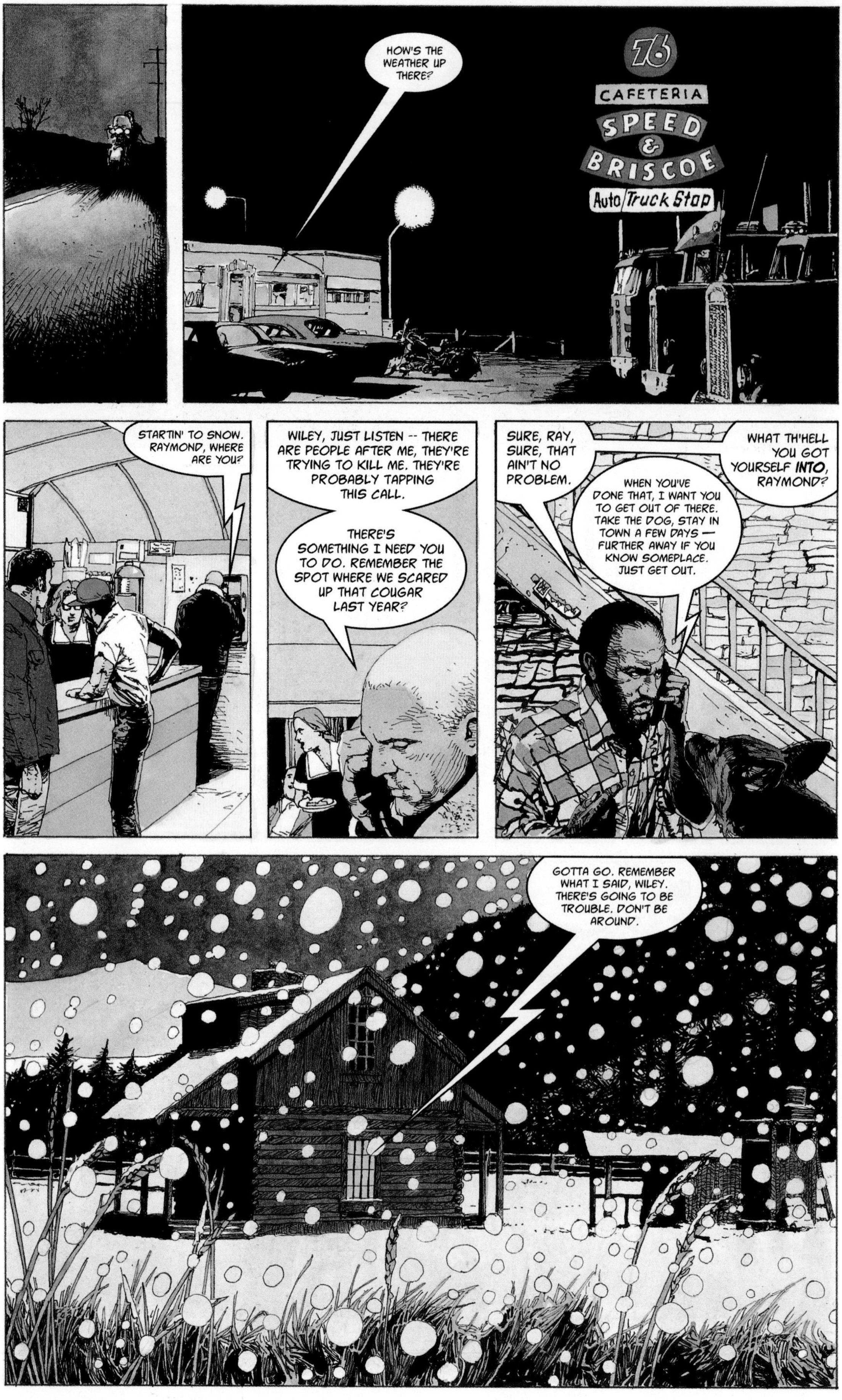

HOW'S THE WEATHER UP THERE?
76
CAFETERIA
SPEED & BRISCOE
Auto/Truck Stop
STARTIN' TO SNOW. RAYMOND, WHERE ARE YOU?
WILEY, JUST LISTEN -- THERE ARE PEOPLE AFTER ME, THEY'RE TRYING TO KILL ME. THEY'RE PROBABLY TAPPING THIS CALL.
THERE'S SOMETHING I NEED YOU TO DO. REMEMBER THE SPOT WHERE WE SCARED UP THAT COUGAR LAST YEAR?
SURE, RAY, SURE, THAT AIN'T NO PROBLEM.
WHEN YOU'VE DONE THAT, I WANT YOU TO GET OUT OF THERE. TAKE THE DOG, STAY IN TOWN A FEW DAYS — FURTHER AWAY IF YOU KNOW SOMEPLACE. JUST GET OUT.
WHAT TH'HELL YOU GOT YOURSELF INTO, RAYMOND?
GOTTA GO. REMEMBER WHAT I SAID, WILEY. THERE'S GOING TO BE TROUBLE. DON'T BE AROUND.

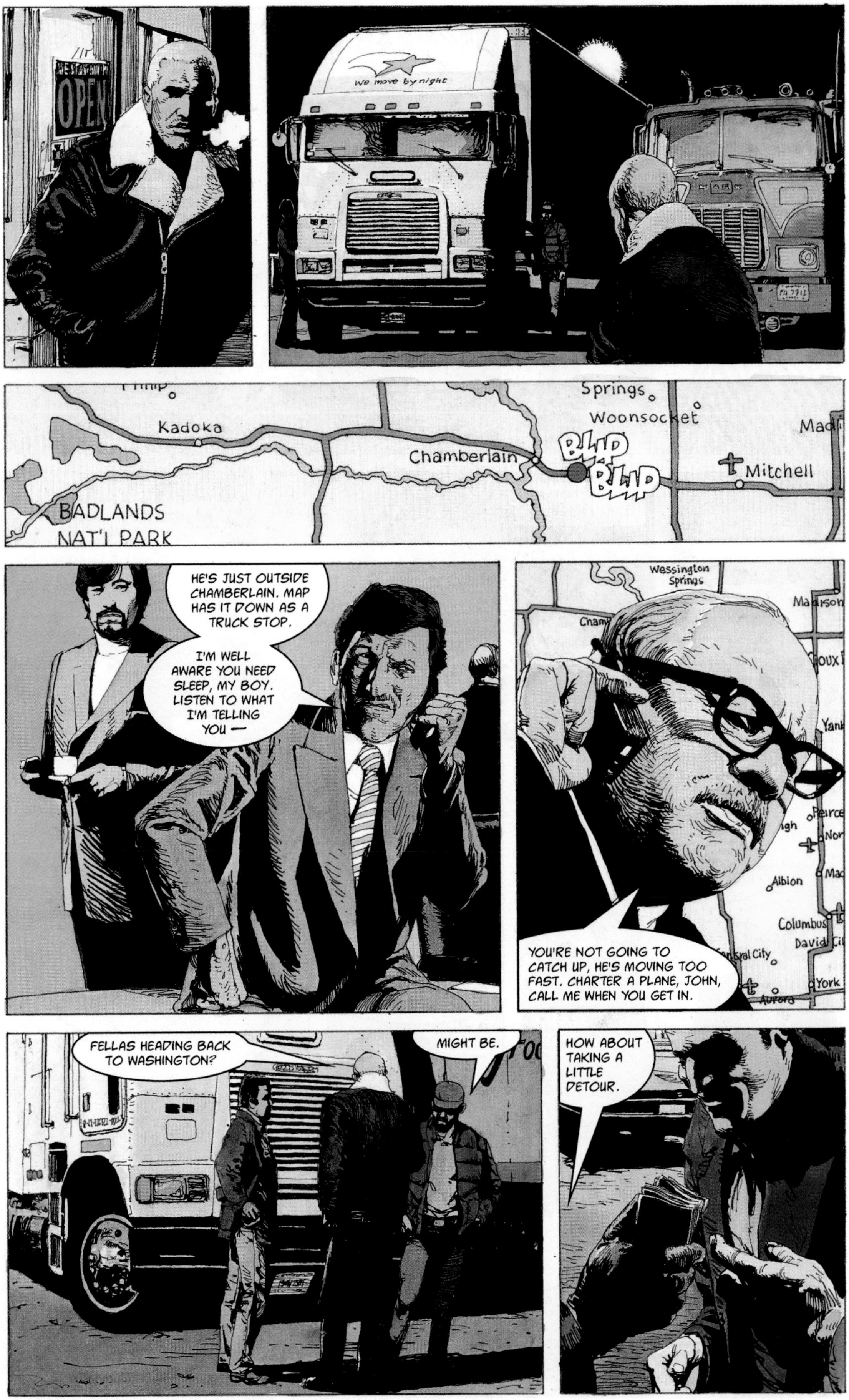
OPEN
We move by night
Springs
Woonsocket
Kadoka
Chamberlain
BLIP
BLIP
Mitchell
BADLANDS
NAT'L PARK
HE'S JUST OUTSIDE CHAMBERLAIN. MAP HAS IT DOWN AS A TRUCK STOP.
I'M WELL AWARE YOU NEED SLEEP, MY BOY. LISTEN TO WHAT I'M TELLING YOU —
Wessington Springs
Madison
Albion
Columbus
YOU'RE NOT GOING TO CATCH UP, HE'S MOVING TOO FAST. CHARTER A PLANE, JOHN, CALL ME WHEN YOU GET IN.
FELLAS HEADING BACK TO WASHINGTON?
MIGHT BE.
HOW ABOUT TAKING A LITTLE DETOUR.

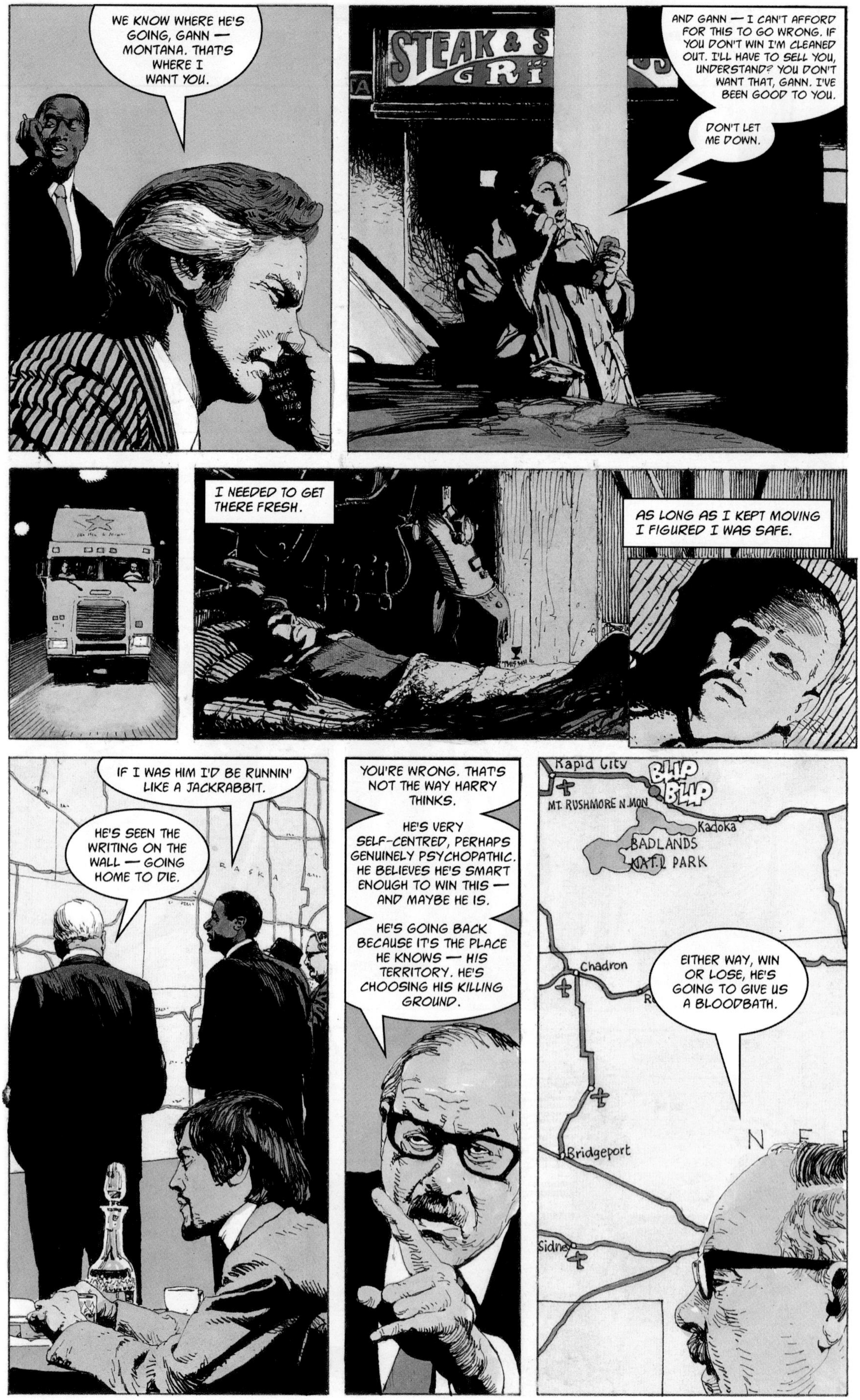
WE KNOW WHERE HE'S GOING, GANN — MONTANA. THAT'S WHERE I WANT YOU.
AND GANN — I CAN'T AFFORD FOR THIS TO GO WRONG. IF YOU DON'T WIN I'M CLEANED OUT. I'LL HAVE TO SELL YOU, UNDERSTAND? YOU DON'T WANT THAT, GANN. I'VE BEEN GOOD TO YOU.
DON'T LET ME DOWN.
I NEEDED TO GET THERE FRESH.
AS LONG AS I KEPT MOVING I FIGURED I WAS SAFE.
IF I WAS HIM I'D BE RUNNIN' LIKE A JACKRABBIT.
HE'S SEEN THE WRITING ON THE WALL — GOING HOME TO DIE.
YOU'RE WRONG. THAT'S NOT THE WAY HARRY THINKS.
HE'S VERY SELF-CENTRED, PERHAPS GENUINELY PSYCHOPATHIC. HE BELIEVES HE'S SMART ENOUGH TO WIN THIS — AND MAYBE HE IS.
HE'S GOING BACK BECAUSE IT'S THE PLACE HE KNOWS — HIS TERRITORY. HE'S CHOOSING HIS KILLING GROUND.
Rapid City
BLIP BLIP
MT. RUSHMORE N.MON
Kadoka
BADLANDS NAT.L PARK
Chadron
Bridgeport
Sidney
EITHER WAY, WIN OR LOSE, HE'S GOING TO GIVE US A BLOODBATH.

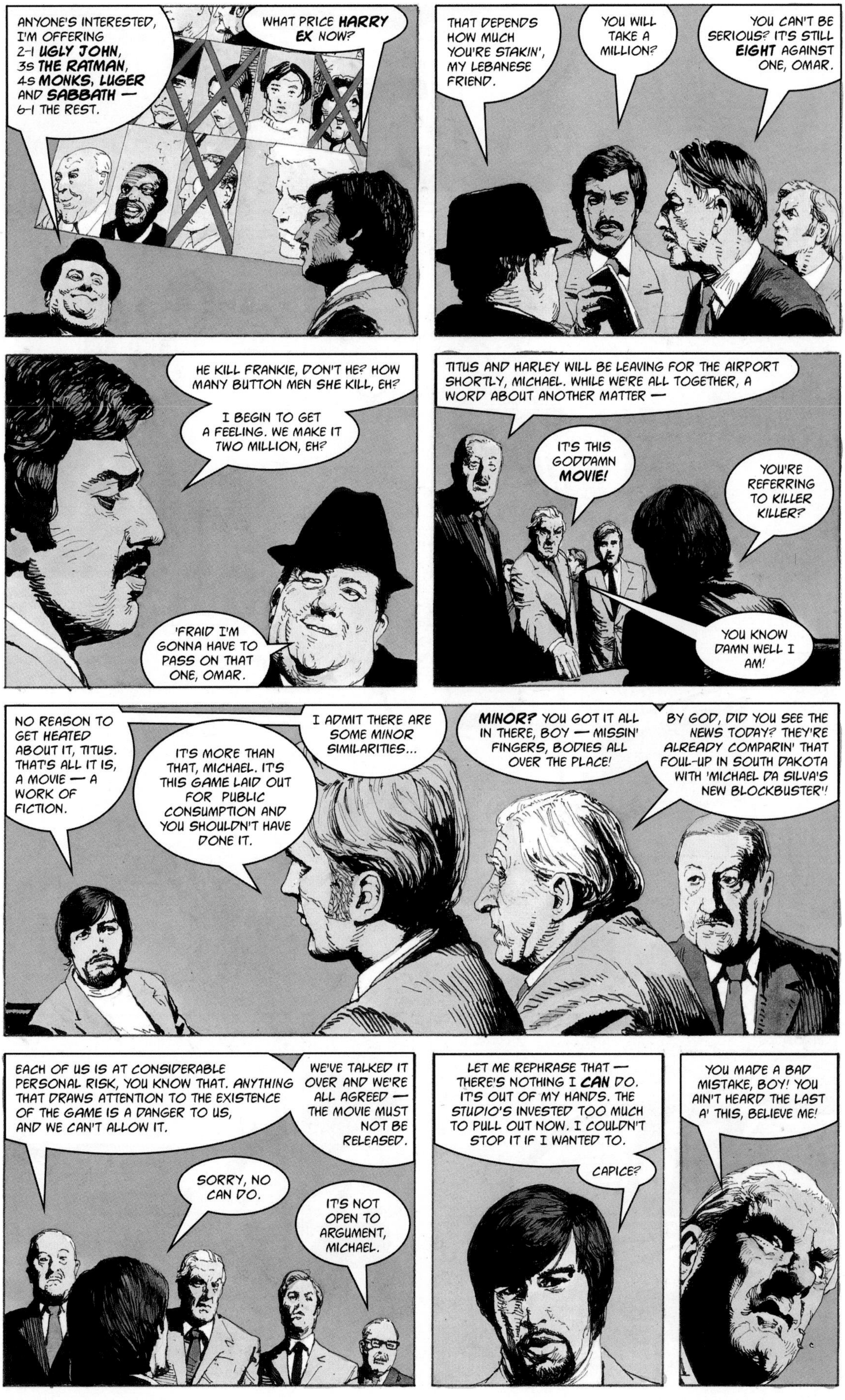
ANYONE'S INTERESTED, I'M OFFERING 2-1 UGLY JOHN, 3s THE RATMAN, 4s MONKS, LUGER AND SABBATH — 6-1 THE REST.
WHAT PRICE HARRY EX NOW?
THAT DEPENDS HOW MUCH YOU'RE STAKIN', MY LEBANESE FRIEND.
YOU WILL TAKE A MILLION?
YOU CAN'T BE SERIOUS? IT'S STILL EIGHT AGAINST ONE, OMAR.
HE KILL FRANKIE, DON'T HE? HOW MANY BUTTON MEN SHE KILL, EH?
I BEGIN TO GET A FEELING. WE MAKE IT TWO MILLION, EH?
'FRAID I'M GONNA HAVE TO PASS ON THAT ONE, OMAR.
TITUS AND HARLEY WILL BE LEAVING FOR THE AIRPORT SHORTLY, MICHAEL. WHILE WE'RE ALL TOGETHER, A WORD ABOUT ANOTHER MATTER —
IT'S THIS GODDAMN MOVIE!
YOU'RE REFERRING TO KILLER KILLER?
YOU KNOW DAMN WELL I AM!
NO REASON TO GET HEATED ABOUT IT, TITUS. THAT'S ALL IT IS, A MOVIE — A WORK OF FICTION.
I ADMIT THERE ARE SOME MINOR SIMILARITIES...
IT'S MORE THAN THAT, MICHAEL. IT'S THIS GAME LAID OUT FOR PUBLIC CONSUMPTION AND YOU SHOULDN'T HAVE DONE IT.
MINOR? YOU GOT IT ALL IN THERE, BOY — MISSIN' FINGERS, BODIES ALL OVER THE PLACE!
BY GOD, DID YOU SEE THE NEWS TODAY? THEY'RE ALREADY COMPARIN' THAT FOUL-UP IN SOUTH DAKOTA WITH 'MICHAEL DA SILVA'S NEW BLOCKBUSTER'!
EACH OF US IS AT CONSIDERABLE PERSONAL RISK, YOU KNOW THAT. ANYTHING THAT DRAWS ATTENTION TO THE EXISTENCE OF THE GAME IS A DANGER TO US, AND WE CAN'T ALLOW IT.
WE'VE TALKED IT OVER AND WE'RE ALL AGREED — THE MOVIE MUST NOT BE RELEASED.
SORRY, NO CAN DO.
IT'S NOT OPEN TO ARGUMENT, MICHAEL.
LET ME REPHRASE THAT — THERE'S NOTHING I CAN DO. IT'S OUT OF MY HANDS. THE STUDIO'S INVESTED TOO MUCH TO PULL OUT NOW. I COULDN'T STOP IT IF I WANTED TO.
CAPICE?
YOU MADE A BAD MISTAKE, BOY! YOU AIN'T HEARD THE LAST A' THIS, BELIEVE ME!

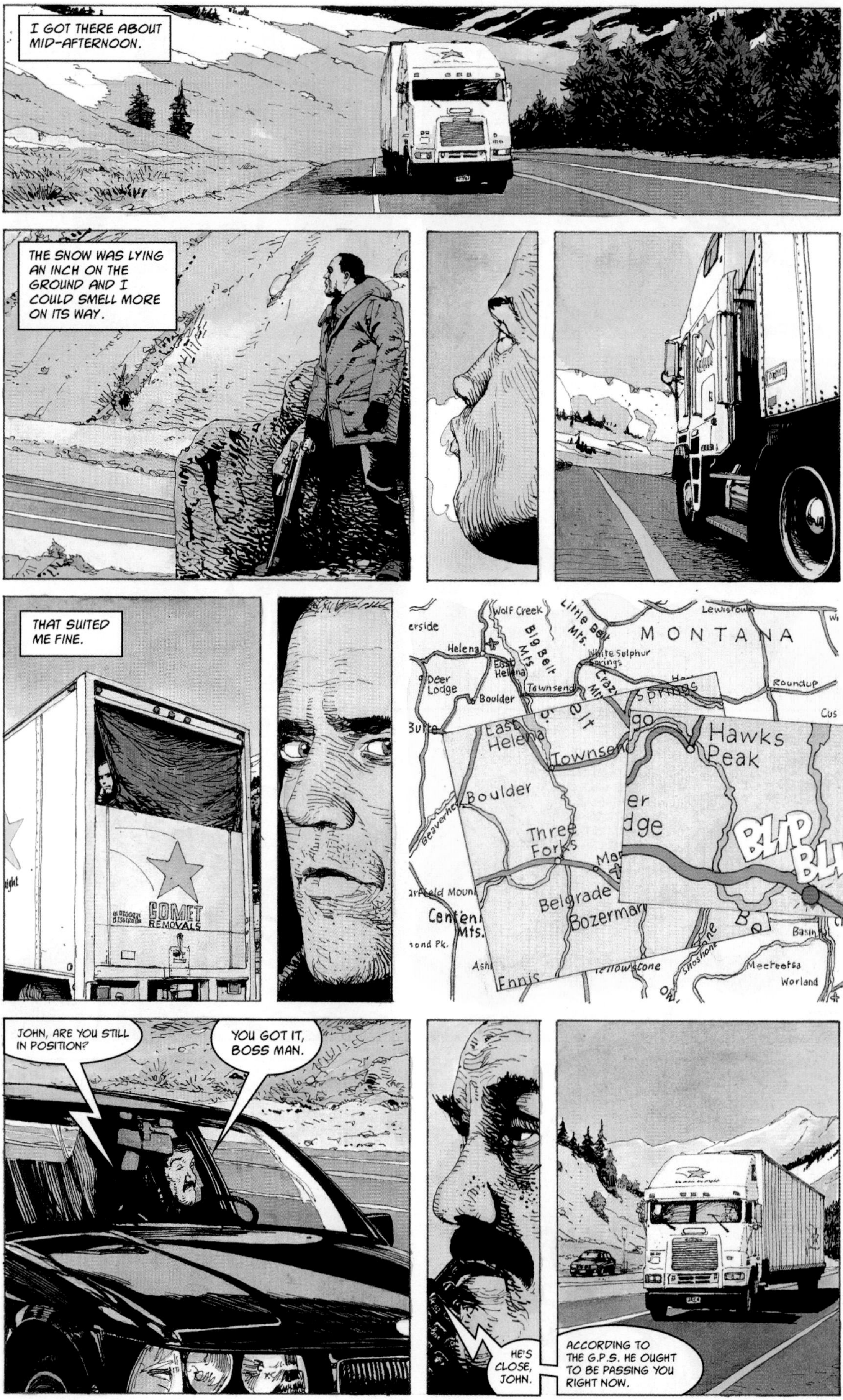
I GOT THERE ABOUT MID-AFTERNOON.
THE SNOW WAS LYING AN INCH ON THE GROUND AND I COULD SMELL MORE ON ITS WAY.
THAT SUITED ME FINE.
COMET REMOVALS
MONTANA
Helena
Boulder
Townsend
Hawks Peak
Three Forks
Belgrade
Bozerman
BLIP
BLIP
JOHN, ARE YOU STILL IN POSITION?
YOU GOT IT, BOSS MAN.
HE'S CLOSE, JOHN.
ACCORDING TO THE G.P.S. HE OUGHT TO BE PASSING YOU RIGHT NOW.

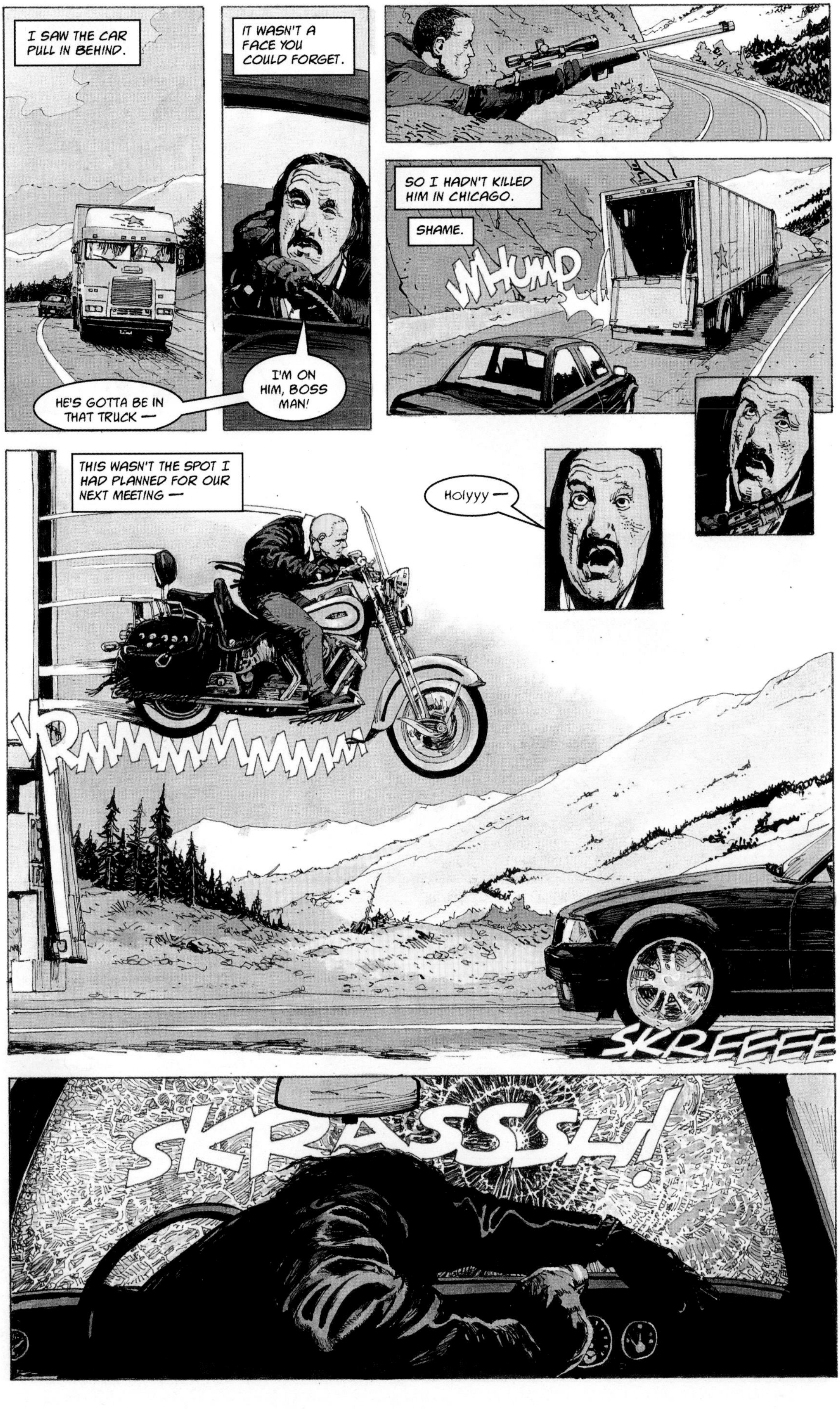
I SAW THE CAR PULL IN BEHIND.
IT WASN'T A FACE YOU COULD FORGET.
HE'S GOTTA BE IN THAT TRUCK —
I'M ON HIM, BOSS MAN!
SO I HADN'T KILLED HIM IN CHICAGO.
SHAME.
WHUMP
THIS WASN'T THE SPOT I HAD PLANNED FOR OUR NEXT MEETING —
Holyyy —
VRMMMMMMMM
SKREEEEE
SKRASSSH!

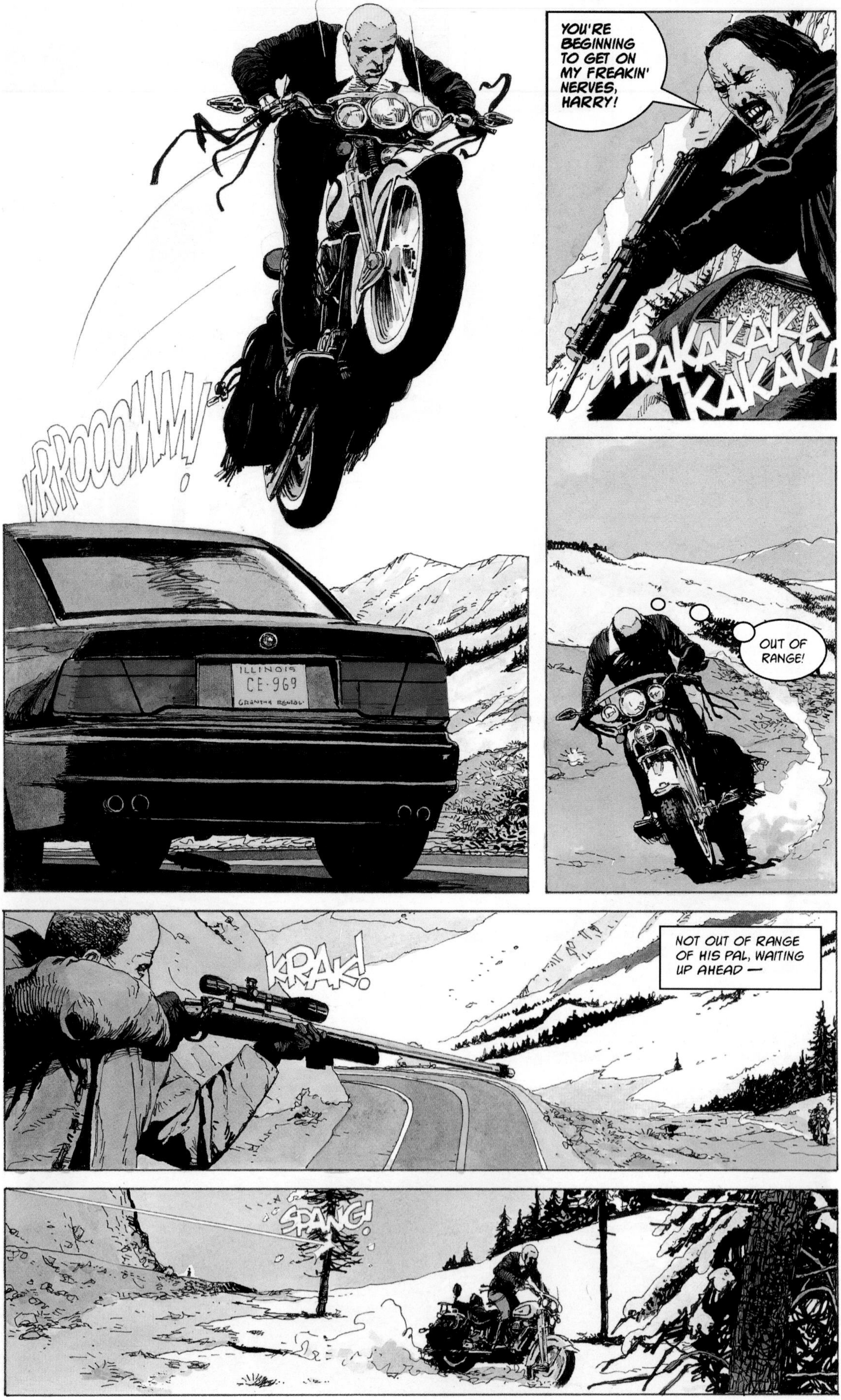

VRROOOMMM!
YOU'RE BEGINNING TO GET ON MY FREAKIN' NERVES, HARRY!
FRAKAKAKA KAKAKA
ILLINOIS CE-969
OUT OF RANGE!
KRAK!
NOT OUT OF RANGE OF HIS PAL, WAITING UP AHEAD —
SPANG!

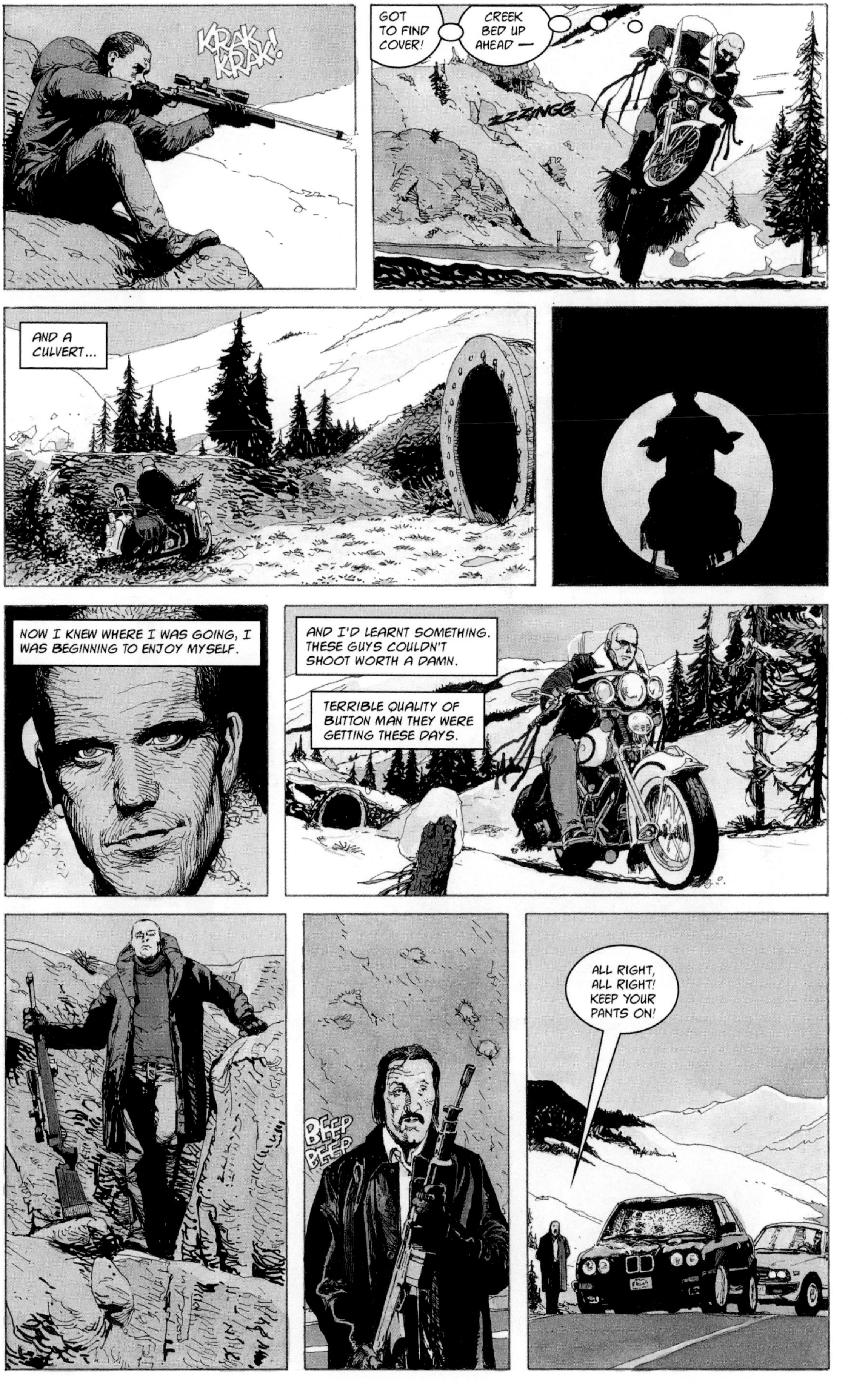
KRAK KRAK!
GOT TO FIND COVER!
CREEK BED UP AHEAD —
ZZZINGG
AND A CULVERT...
NOW I KNEW WHERE I WAS GOING, I WAS BEGINNING TO ENJOY MYSELF.
AND I'D LEARNT SOMETHING. THESE GUYS COULDN'T SHOOT WORTH A DAMN.
TERRIBLE QUALITY OF BUTTON MAN THEY WERE GETTING THESE DAYS.
BEEP BEEP
ALL RIGHT, ALL RIGHT! KEEP YOUR PANTS ON!

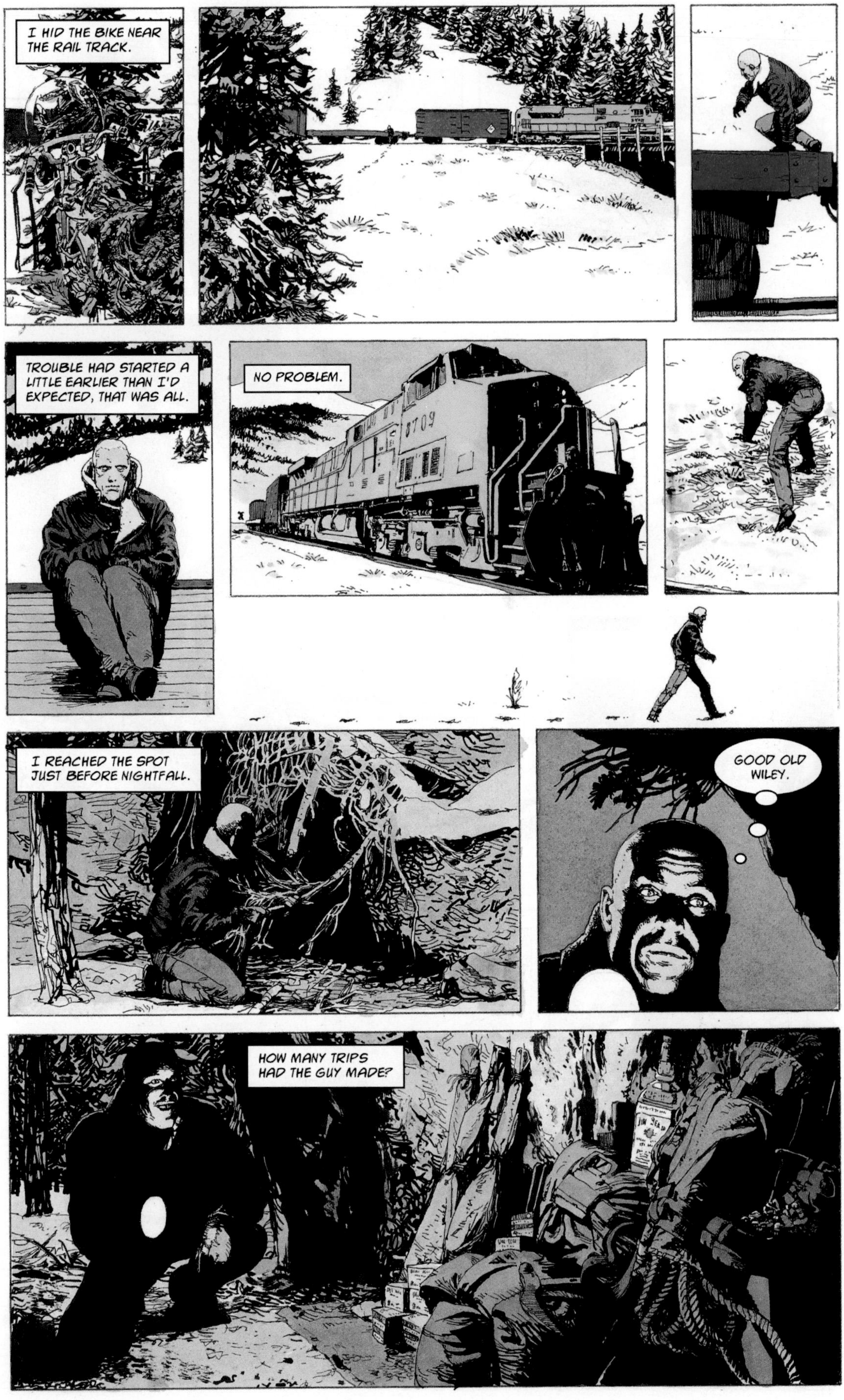
I HID THE BIKE NEAR THE RAIL TRACK.
TROUBLE HAD STARTED A LITTLE EARLIER THAN I'D EXPECTED, THAT WAS ALL.
NO PROBLEM.
I REACHED THE SPOT JUST BEFORE NIGHTFALL.
GOOD OLD WILEY.
HOW MANY TRIPS HAD THE GUY MADE?

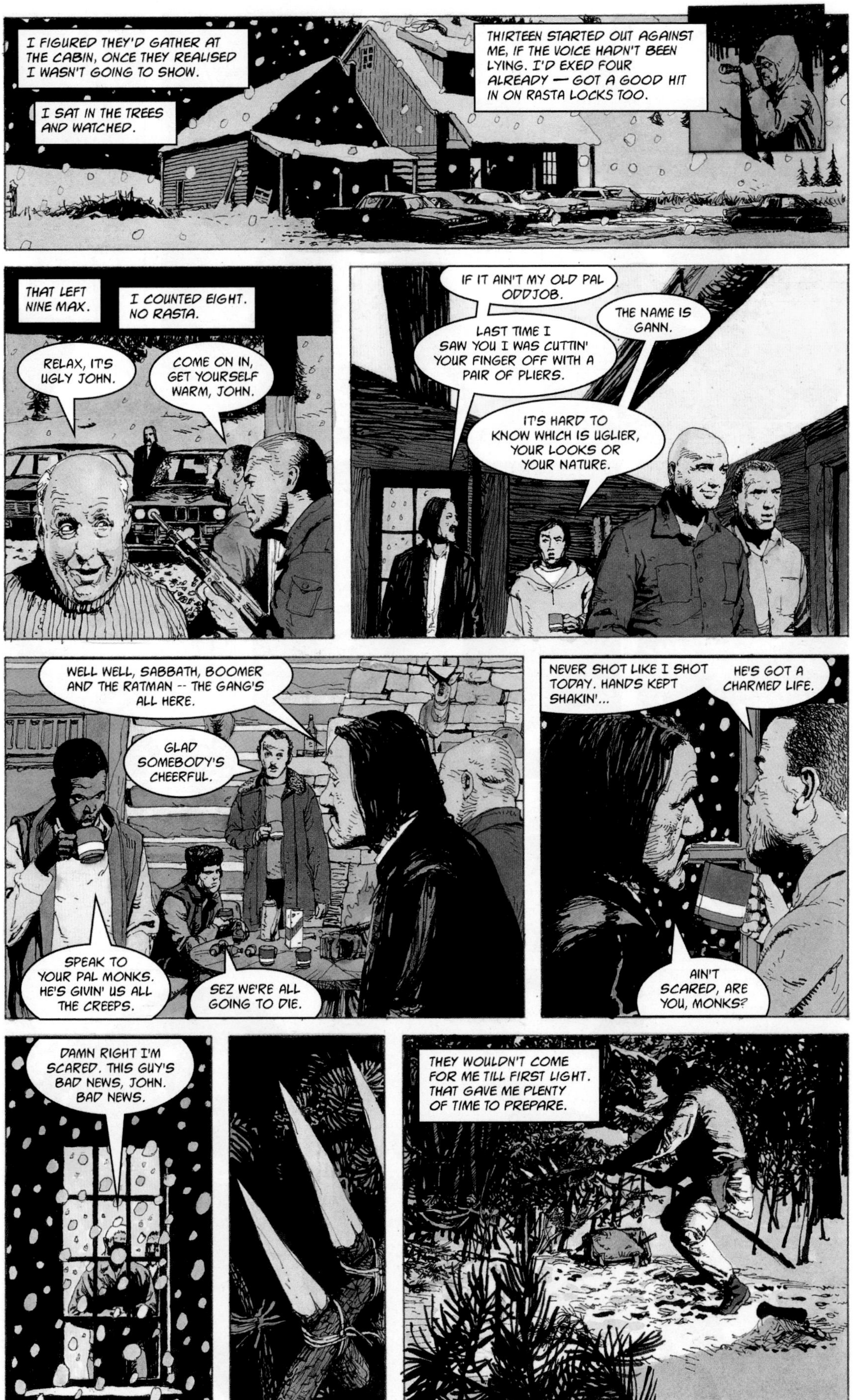
I FIGURED THEY'D GATHER AT THE CABIN, ONCE THEY REALISED I WASN'T GOING TO SHOW.
I SAT IN THE TREES AND WATCHED.
THIRTEEN STARTED OUT AGAINST ME, IF THE VOICE HADN'T BEEN LYING. I'D EXED FOUR ALREADY — GOT A GOOD HIT IN ON RASTA LOCKS TOO.
THAT LEFT NINE MAX.
I COUNTED EIGHT. NO RASTA.
RELAX, IT'S UGLY JOHN.
COME ON IN, GET YOURSELF WARM, JOHN.
IF IT AIN'T MY OLD PAL ODDJOB.
LAST TIME I SAW YOU I WAS CUTTIN' YOUR FINGER OFF WITH A PAIR OF PLIERS.
THE NAME IS GANN.
IT'S HARD TO KNOW WHICH IS UGLIER, YOUR LOOKS OR YOUR NATURE.
WELL WELL, SABBATH, BOOMER AND THE RATMAN -- THE GANG'S ALL HERE.
GLAD SOMEBODY'S CHEERFUL.
SPEAK TO YOUR PAL MONKS. HE'S GIVIN' US ALL THE CREEPS.
SEZ WE'RE ALL GOING TO DIE.
NEVER SHOT LIKE I SHOT TODAY. HANDS KEPT SHAKIN'...
HE'S GOT A CHARMED LIFE.
AIN'T SCARED, ARE YOU, MONKS?
DAMN RIGHT I'M SCARED. THIS GUY'S BAD NEWS, JOHN. BAD NEWS.
THEY WOULDN'T COME FOR ME TILL FIRST LIGHT. THAT GAVE ME PLENTY OF TIME TO PREPARE.

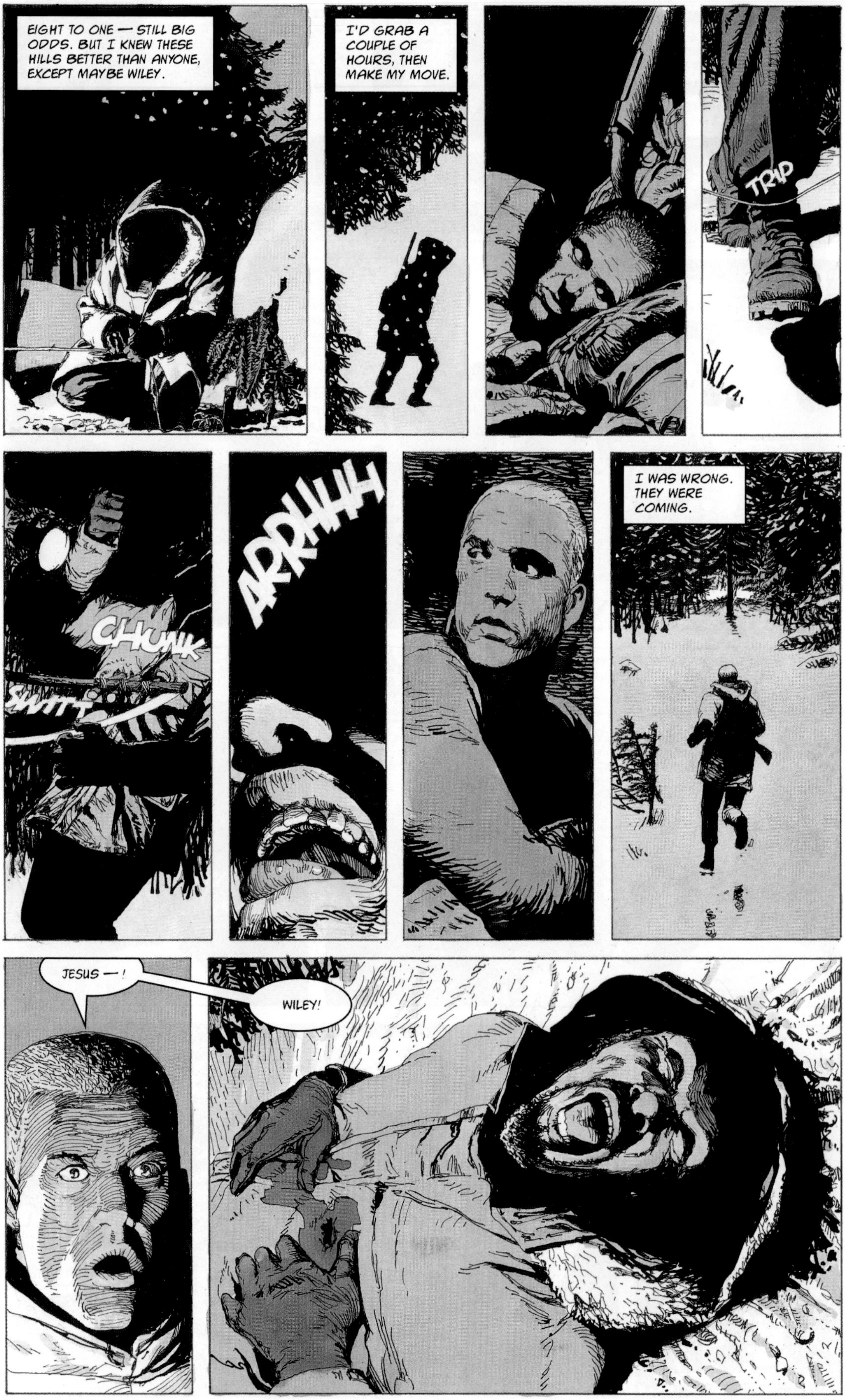
EIGHT TO ONE — STILL BIG ODDS. BUT I KNEW THESE HILLS BETTER THAN ANYONE, EXCEPT MAYBE WILEY.
I'D GRAB A COUPLE OF HOURS, THEN MAKE MY MOVE.
TRIP
CHUNK
SWITT
ARRHHH
I WAS WRONG. THEY WERE COMING.
JESUS —!
WILEY!

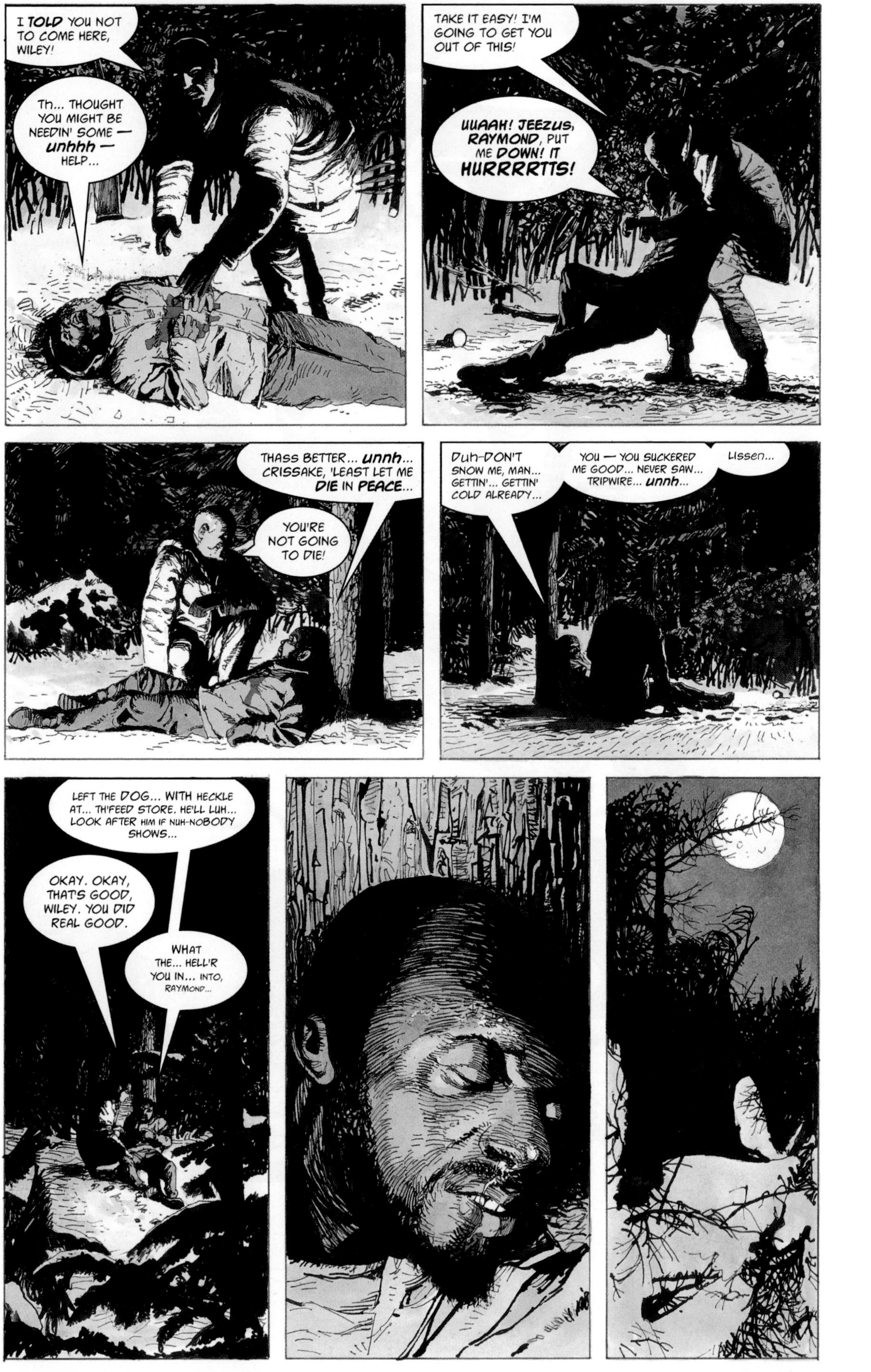
I TOLD YOU NOT TO COME HERE, WILEY!
Th... THOUGHT YOU MIGHT BE NEEDIN' SOME — unhhh — HELP...
TAKE IT EASY! I'M GOING TO GET YOU OUT OF THIS!
UUAAH! JEEZUS, RAYMOND, PUT ME DOWN! IT HURRRRTTS!
THASS BETTER... unnh... CRISSAKE, 'LEAST LET ME DIE IN PEACE...
YOU'RE NOT GOING TO DIE!
Duh-DON'T SNOW ME, MAN... GETTIN'... GETTIN' COLD ALREADY...
YOU — YOU SUCKERED ME GOOD... NEVER SAW... TRIPWIRE... unnh...
Lissen...
LEFT THE DOG... WITH HECKLE AT... TH'FEED STORE. HE'LL LUH... LOOK AFTER HIM IF NUH-NOBODY SHOWS...
OKAY. OKAY, THAT'S GOOD, WILEY. YOU DID REAL GOOD.
WHAT THE... HELL'R YOU IN... INTO, RAYMOND...

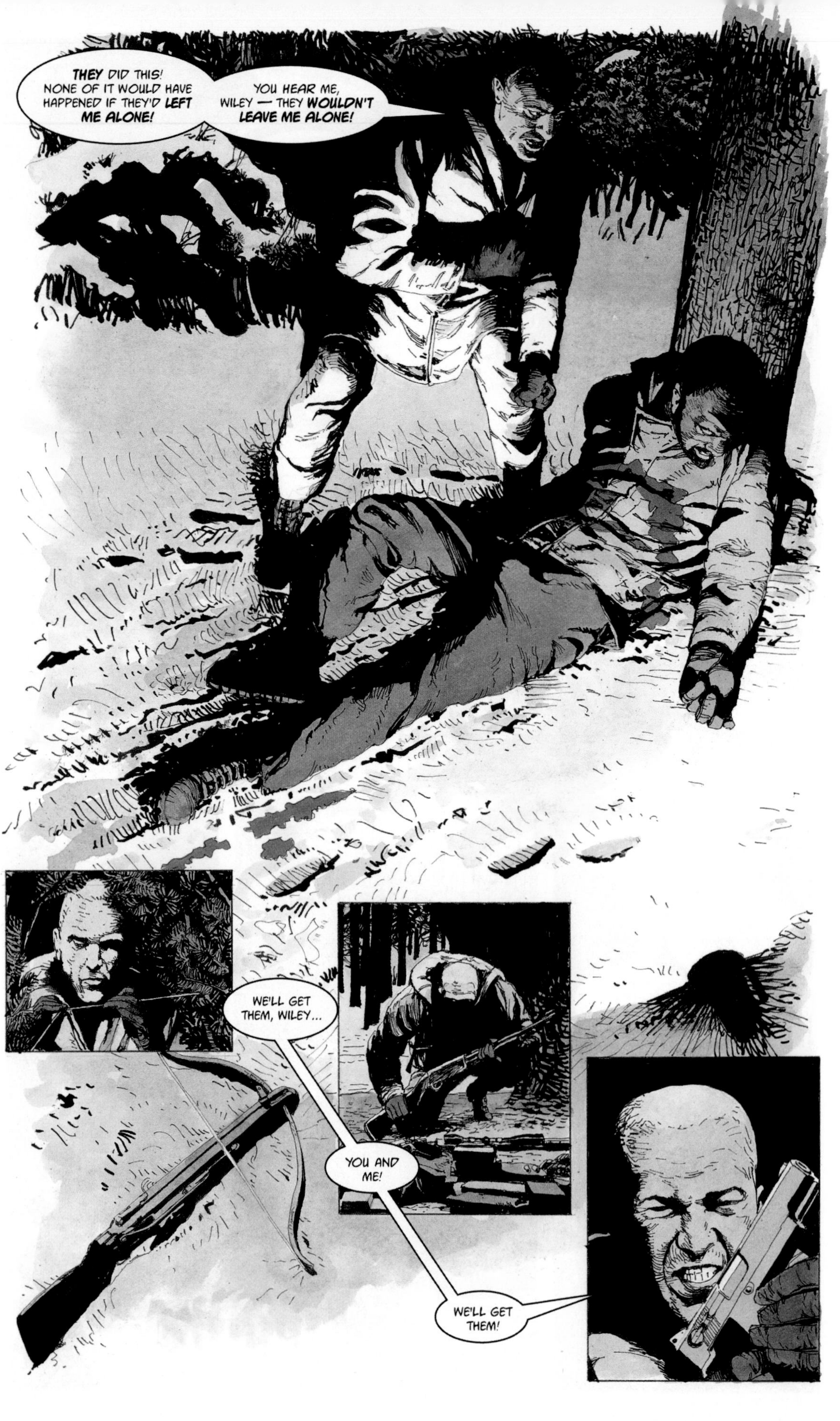
THEY DID THIS! NONE OF IT WOULD HAVE HAPPENED IF THEY'D LEFT ME ALONE!
YOU HEAR ME, WILEY — THEY WOULDN'T LEAVE ME ALONE!
WE'LL GET THEM, WILEY...
YOU AND ME!
WE'LL GET THEM!

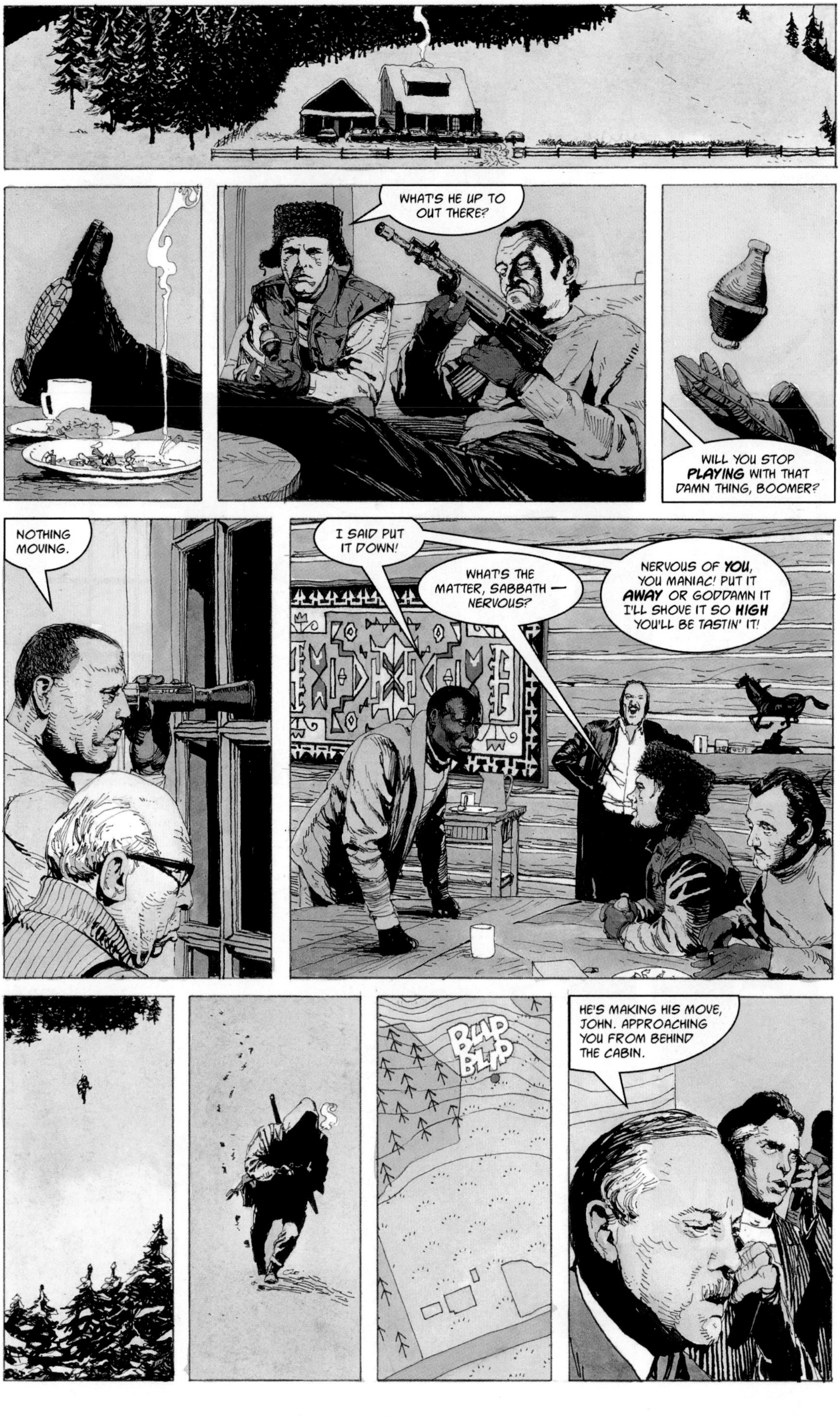
WHAT'S HE UP TO OUT THERE?
WILL YOU STOP PLAYING WITH THAT DAMN THING, BOOMER?
NOTHING MOVING.
I SAID PUT IT DOWN!
WHAT'S THE MATTER, SABBATH — NERVOUS?
NERVOUS OF YOU, YOU MANIAC! PUT IT AWAY OR GODDAMN IT I'LL SHOVE IT SO HIGH YOU'LL BE TASTIN' IT!
BLIP BLIP
HE'S MAKING HIS MOVE, JOHN. APPROACHING YOU FROM BEHIND THE CABIN.

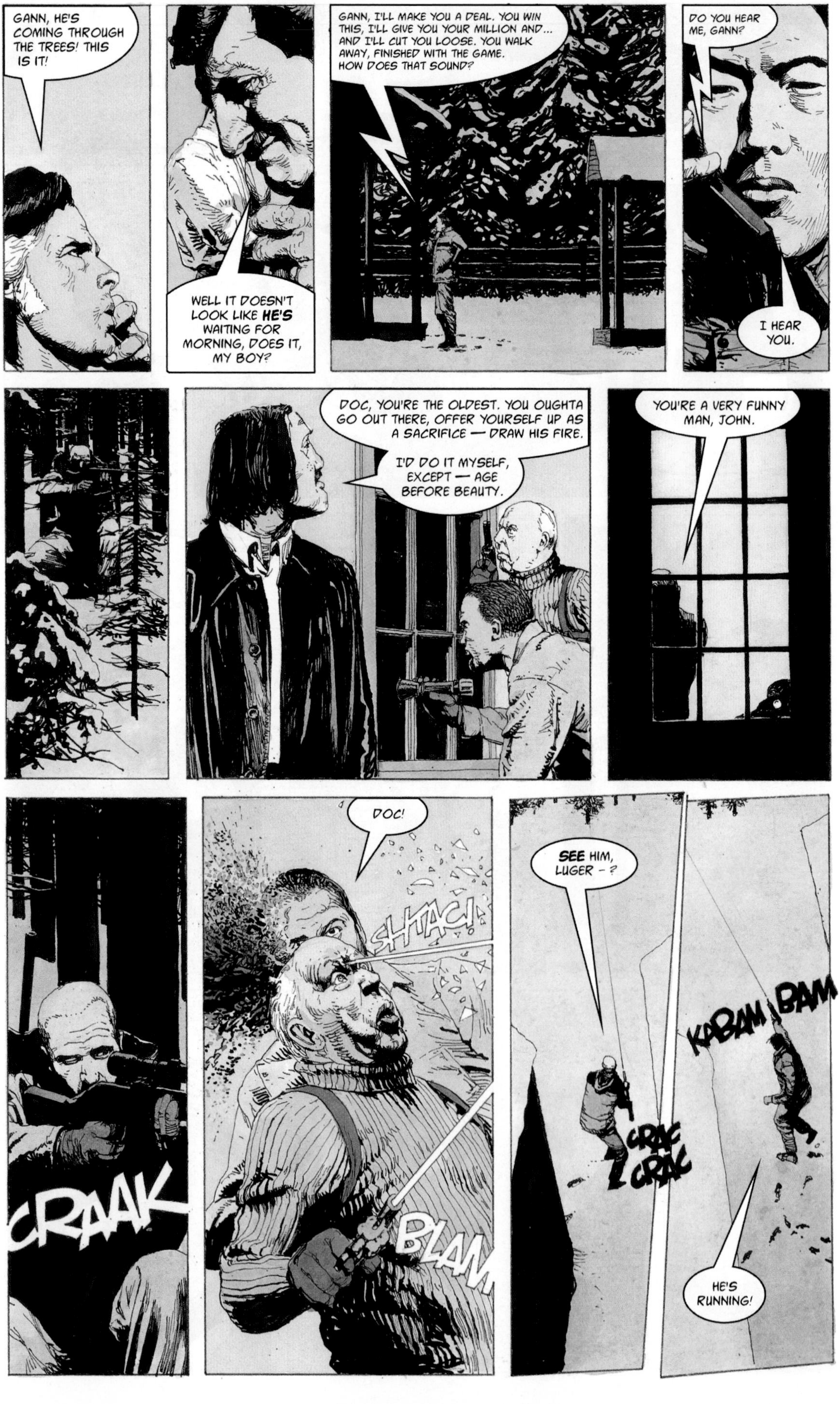
GANN, HE'S COMING THROUGH THE TREES! THIS IS IT!
WELL IT DOESN'T LOOK LIKE **HE'S** WAITING FOR MORNING, DOES IT, MY BOY?
GANN, I'LL MAKE YOU A DEAL. YOU WIN THIS, I'LL GIVE YOU YOUR MILLION AND... AND I'LL CUT YOU LOOSE. YOU WALK AWAY, FINISHED WITH THE GAME. HOW DOES THAT SOUND?
DO YOU HEAR ME, GANN?
I HEAR YOU.
DOC, YOU'RE THE OLDEST. YOU OUGHTA GO OUT THERE, OFFER YOURSELF UP AS A SACRIFICE — DRAW HIS FIRE.
I'D DO IT MYSELF, EXCEPT — AGE BEFORE BEAUTY.
YOU'RE A VERY FUNNY MAN, JOHN.
CRAAK
DOC!
SHTAC!
BLAM
SEE HIM, LUGER – ?
CRAC CRAC
KABAM BAM
HE'S RUNNING!

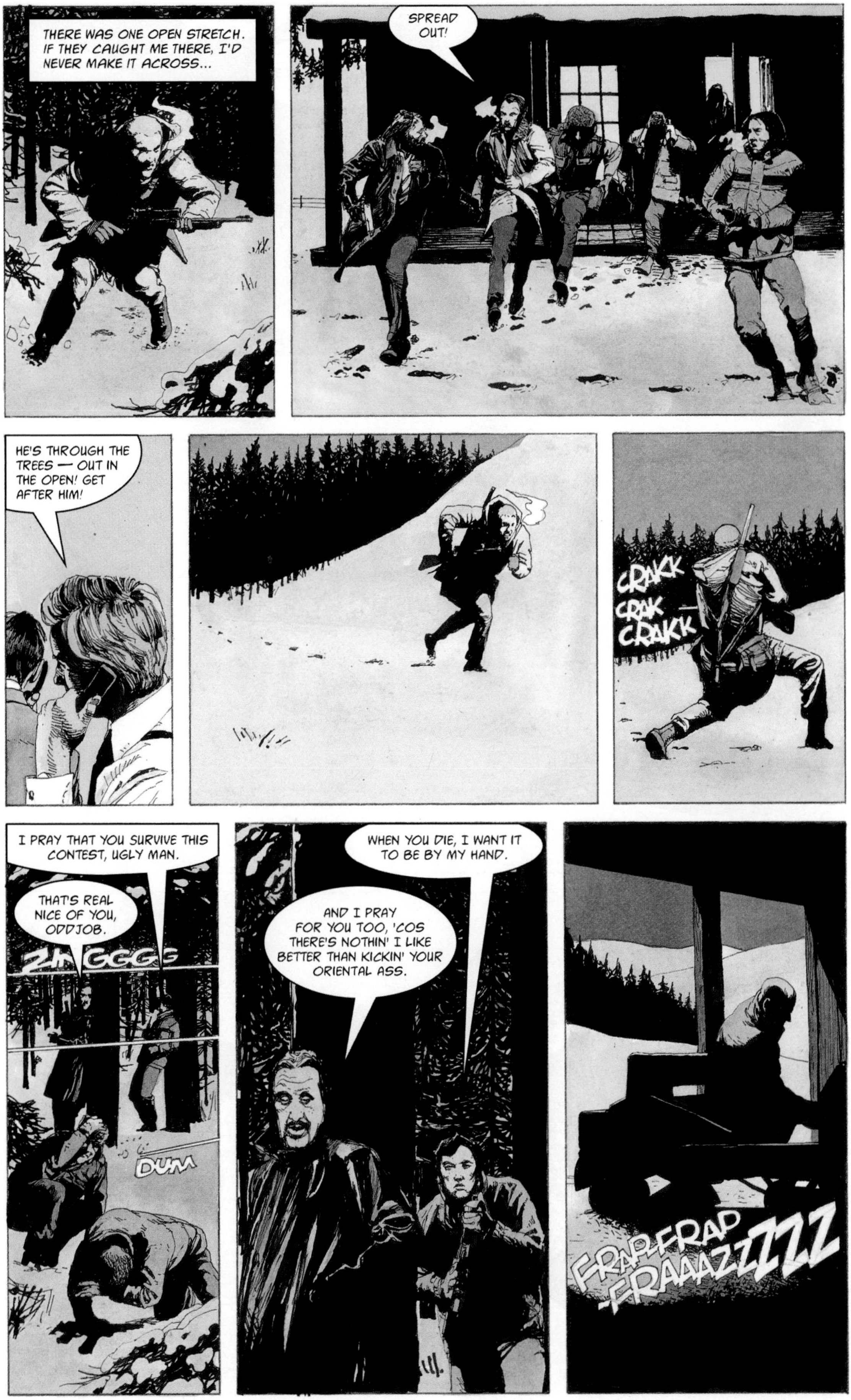
THERE WAS ONE OPEN STRETCH. IF THEY CAUGHT ME THERE, I'D NEVER MAKE IT ACROSS...
SPREAD OUT!
HE'S THROUGH THE TREES — OUT IN THE OPEN! GET AFTER HIM!
CRAKK
CRAK
CRAKK
I PRAY THAT YOU SURVIVE THIS CONTEST, UGLY MAN.
THAT'S REAL NICE OF YOU, ODDJOB.
ZINGGGG
DUM
WHEN YOU DIE, I WANT IT TO BE BY MY HAND.
AND I PRAY FOR YOU TOO, 'COS THERE'S NOTHIN' I LIKE BETTER THAN KICKIN' YOUR ORIENTAL ASS.
FRAPFRAP
-FRAAAZZZZZ

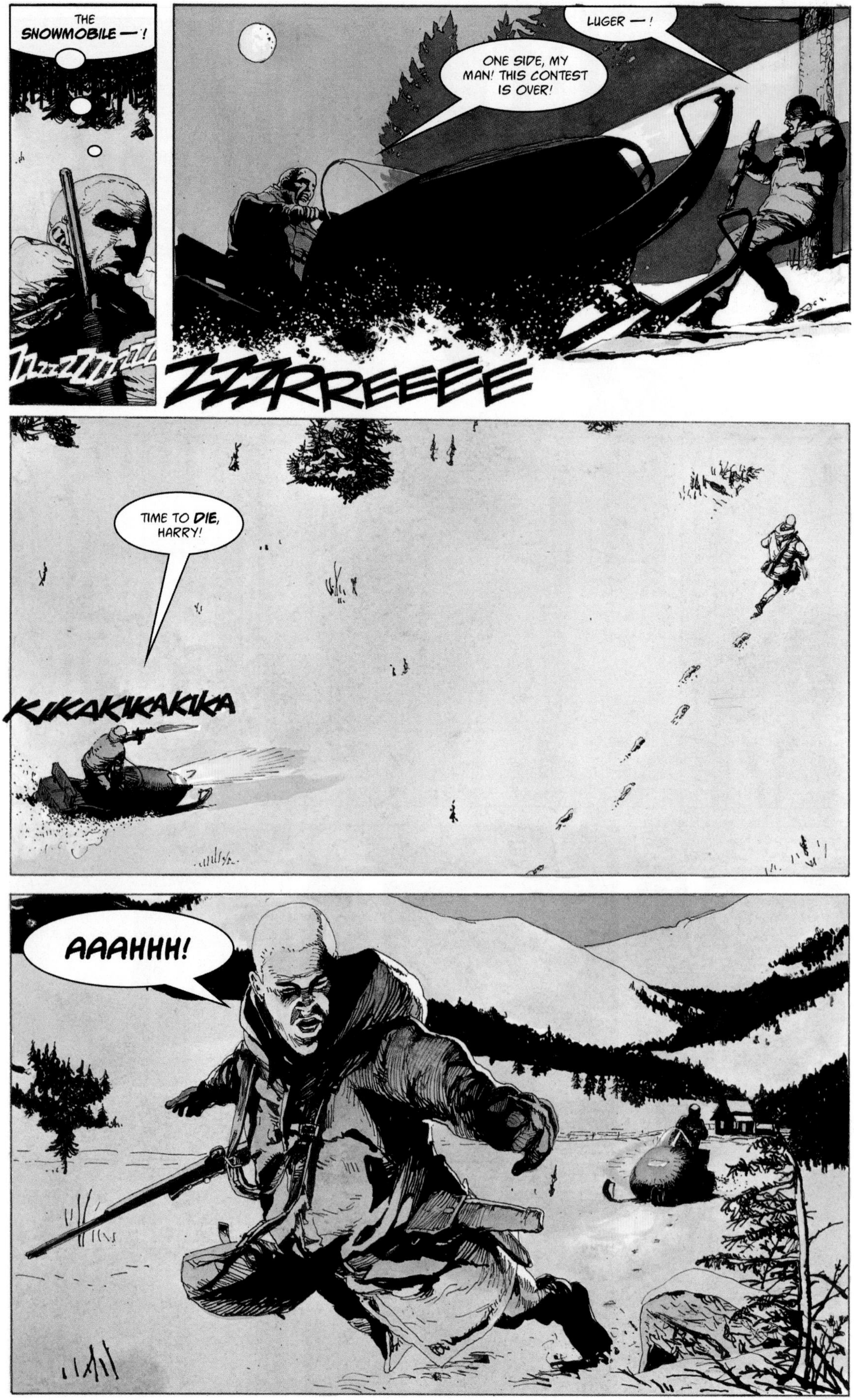

THE **SNOWMOBILE**—!
LUGER—!
ONE SIDE, MY MAN! THIS CONTEST IS OVER!
ZZZRREEEEE
TIME TO **DIE**, HARRY!
KIKAKIKAKIKA
AAAHHH!

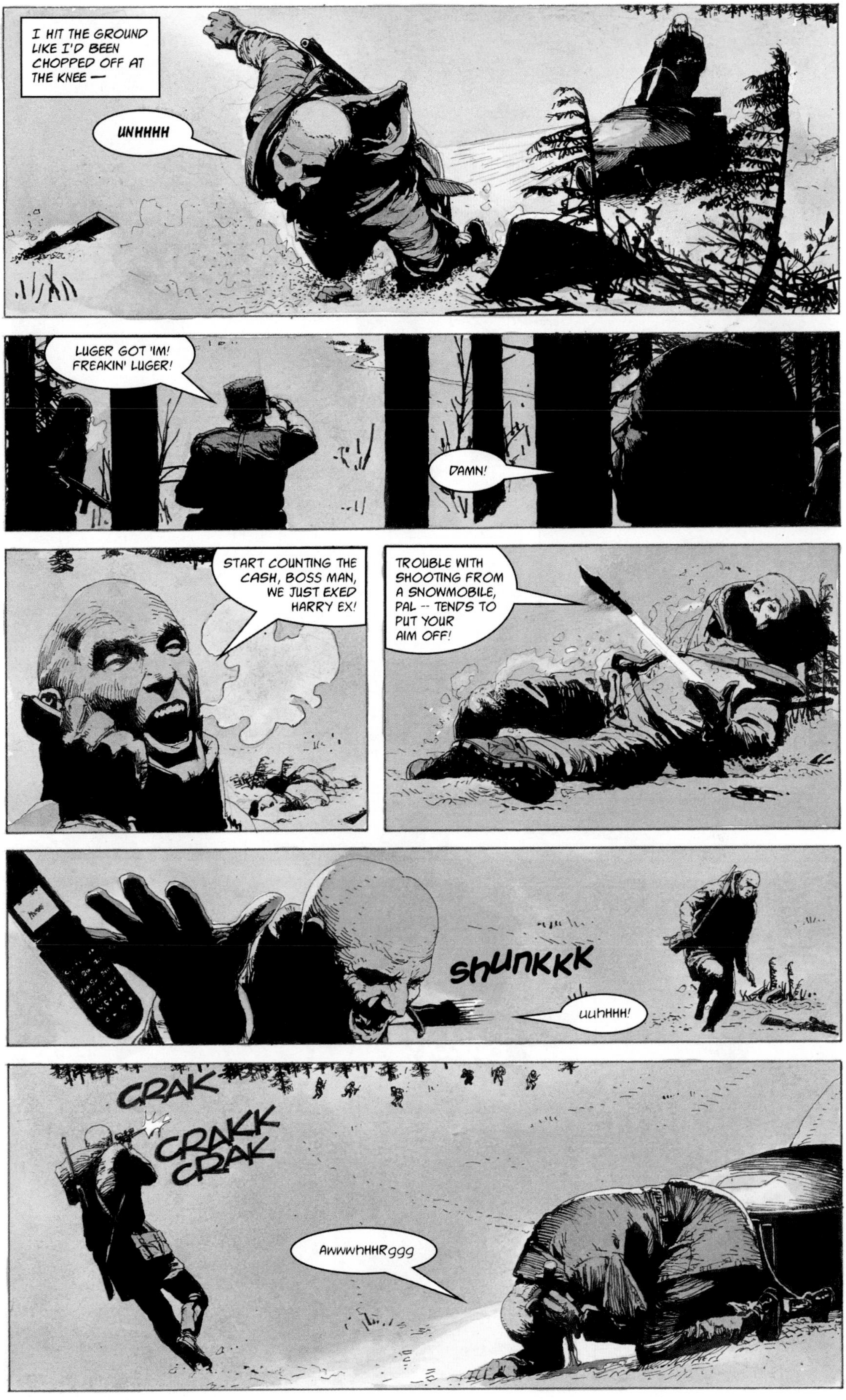
I HIT THE GROUND LIKE I'D BEEN CHOPPED OFF AT THE KNEE —
UNHHHH
LUGER GOT 'IM! FREAKIN' LUGER!
DAMN!
START COUNTING THE CASH, BOSS MAN, WE JUST EXED HARRY EX!
TROUBLE WITH SHOOTING FROM A SNOWMOBILE, PAL -- TENDS TO PUT YOUR AIM OFF!
SHUNKKK
UUHHHH!
CRAK
CRAKK
CRAK
AWWWHHHRGGG

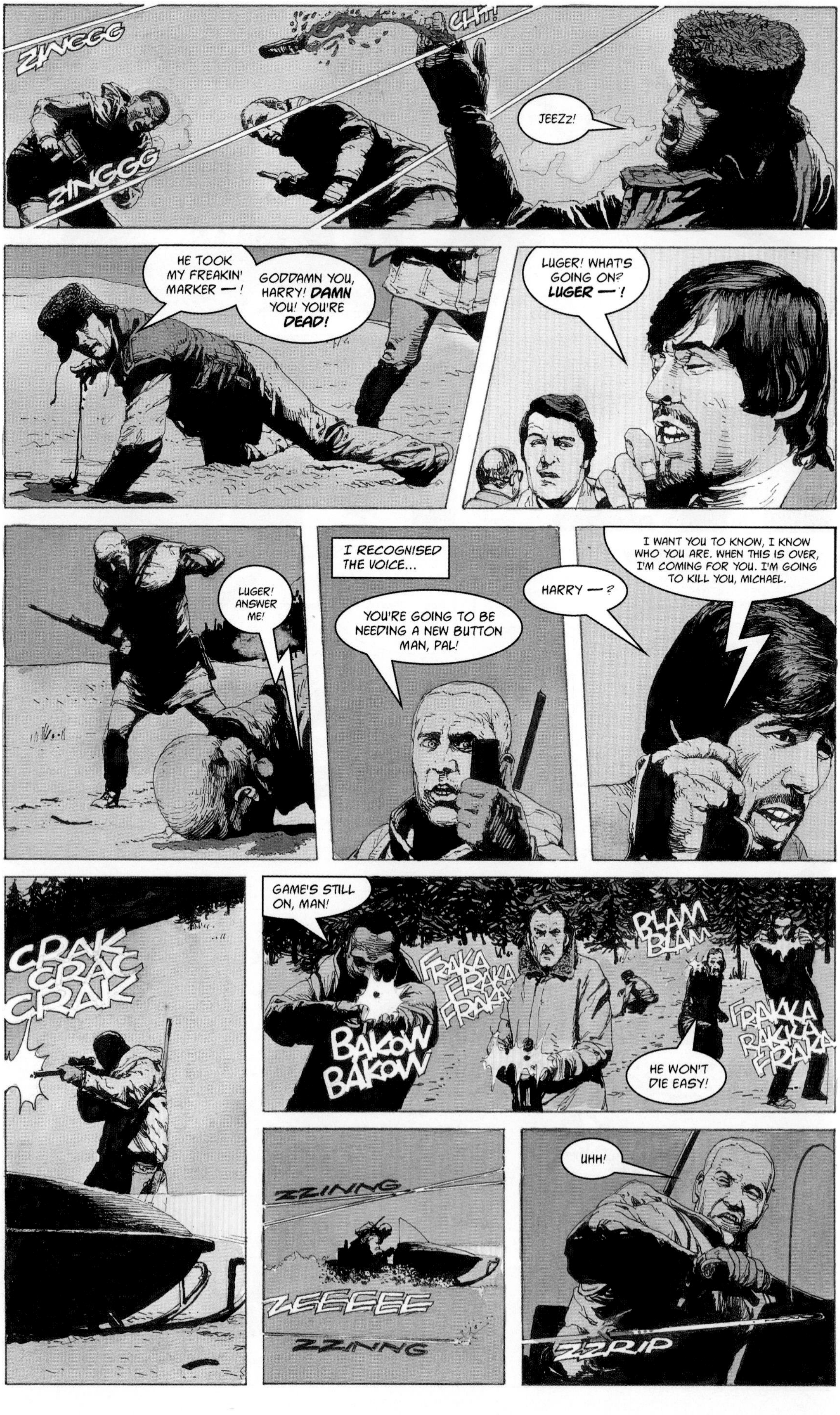
ZINGGG
CHT!
ZINGGG
JEEZz!
HE TOOK MY FREAKIN' MARKER —!
GODDAMN YOU, HARRY! DAMN YOU! YOU'RE DEAD!
LUGER! WHAT'S GOING ON? LUGER —!
LUGER! ANSWER ME!
I RECOGNISED THE VOICE...
YOU'RE GOING TO BE NEEDING A NEW BUTTON MAN, PAL!
HARRY —?
I WANT YOU TO KNOW, I KNOW WHO YOU ARE. WHEN THIS IS OVER, I'M COMING FOR YOU. I'M GOING TO KILL YOU, MICHAEL.
CRAK CRAC CRAK
GAME'S STILL ON, MAN!
FRAKA FRAKA FRAKA
BLAM BLAM
BAKOW BAKOW
FRAKKA RAKKA FRAKA
HE WON'T DIE EASY!
ZZINNG
ZEEEEEE
ZZINNG
UHH!
ZZRIP

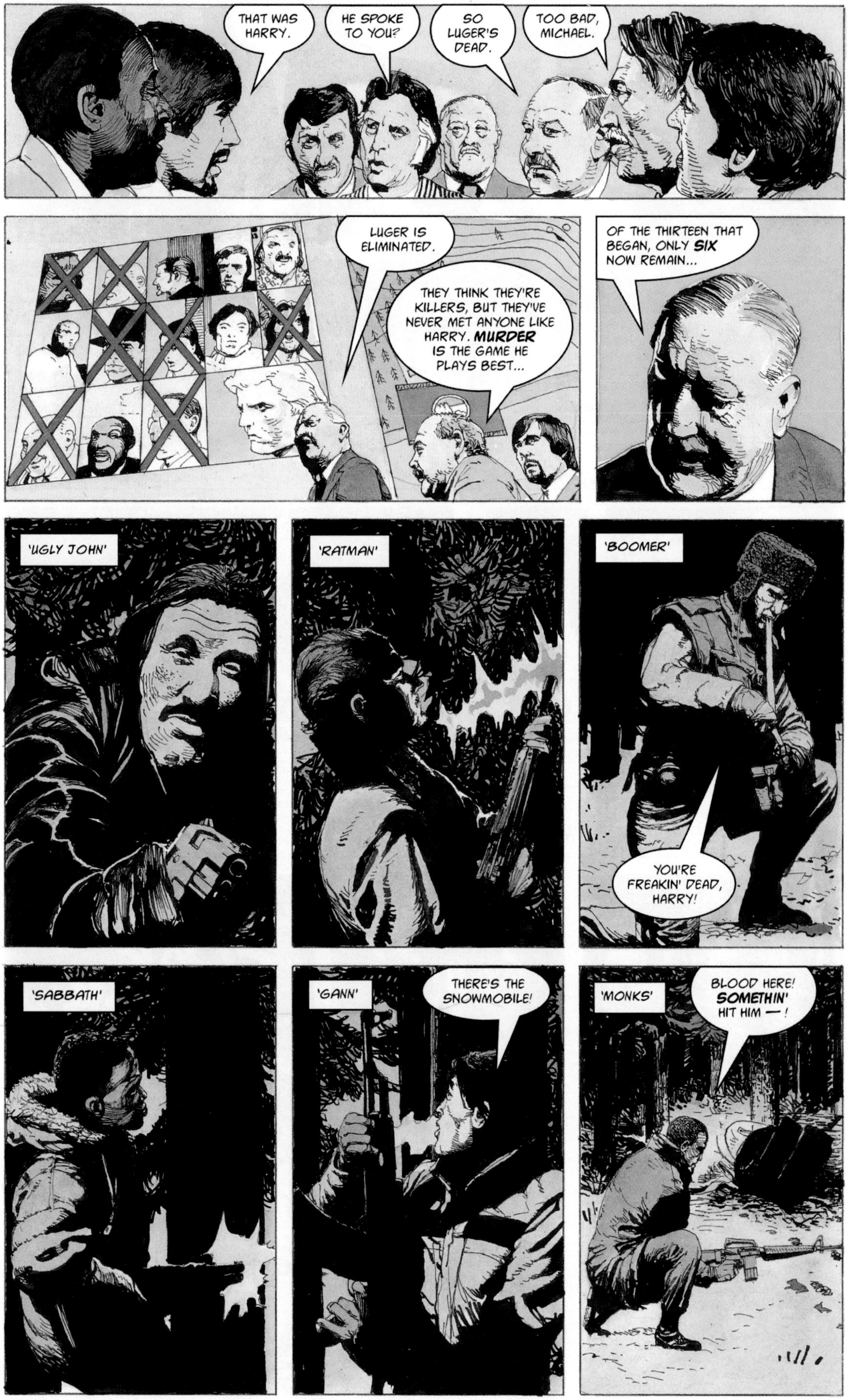
THAT WAS HARRY.
HE SPOKE TO YOU?
SO LUGER'S DEAD.
TOO BAD, MICHAEL.
LUGER IS ELIMINATED.
THEY THINK THEY'RE KILLERS, BUT THEY'VE NEVER MET ANYONE LIKE HARRY. MURDER IS THE GAME HE PLAYS BEST...
OF THE THIRTEEN THAT BEGAN, ONLY SIX NOW REMAIN...
'UGLY JOHN'
'RATMAN'
'BOOMER'
YOU'RE FREAKIN' DEAD, HARRY!
'SABBATH'
'GANN'
THERE'S THE SNOWMOBILE!
'MONKS'
BLOOD HERE! SOMETHIN' HIT HIM — !

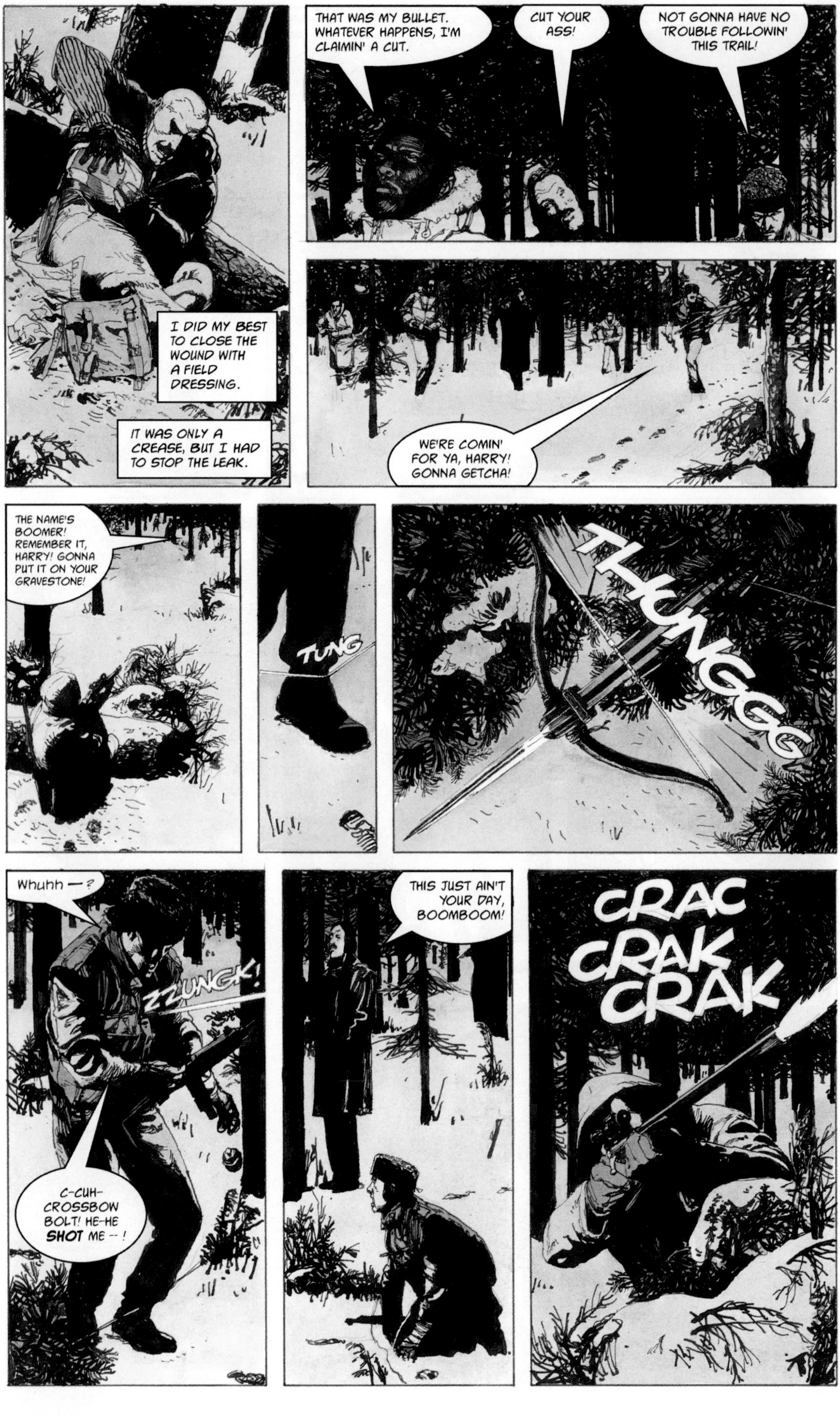
I DID MY BEST TO CLOSE THE WOUND WITH A FIELD DRESSING.
IT WAS ONLY A CREASE, BUT I HAD TO STOP THE LEAK.
THAT WAS MY BULLET. WHATEVER HAPPENS, I'M CLAIMIN' A CUT.
CUT YOUR ASS!
NOT GONNA HAVE NO TROUBLE FOLLOWIN' THIS TRAIL!
WE'RE COMIN' FOR YA, HARRY! GONNA GETCHA!
THE NAME'S BOOMER! REMEMBER IT, HARRY! GONNA PUT IT ON YOUR GRAVESTONE!
TUNG
THUNGGG
Whuhh — ?
ZZUNGK!
C-CUH-CROSSBOW BOLT! HE-HE **SHOT** ME -- !
THIS JUST AIN'T YOUR DAY, BOOMBOOM!
CRAC
CRAK
CRAK

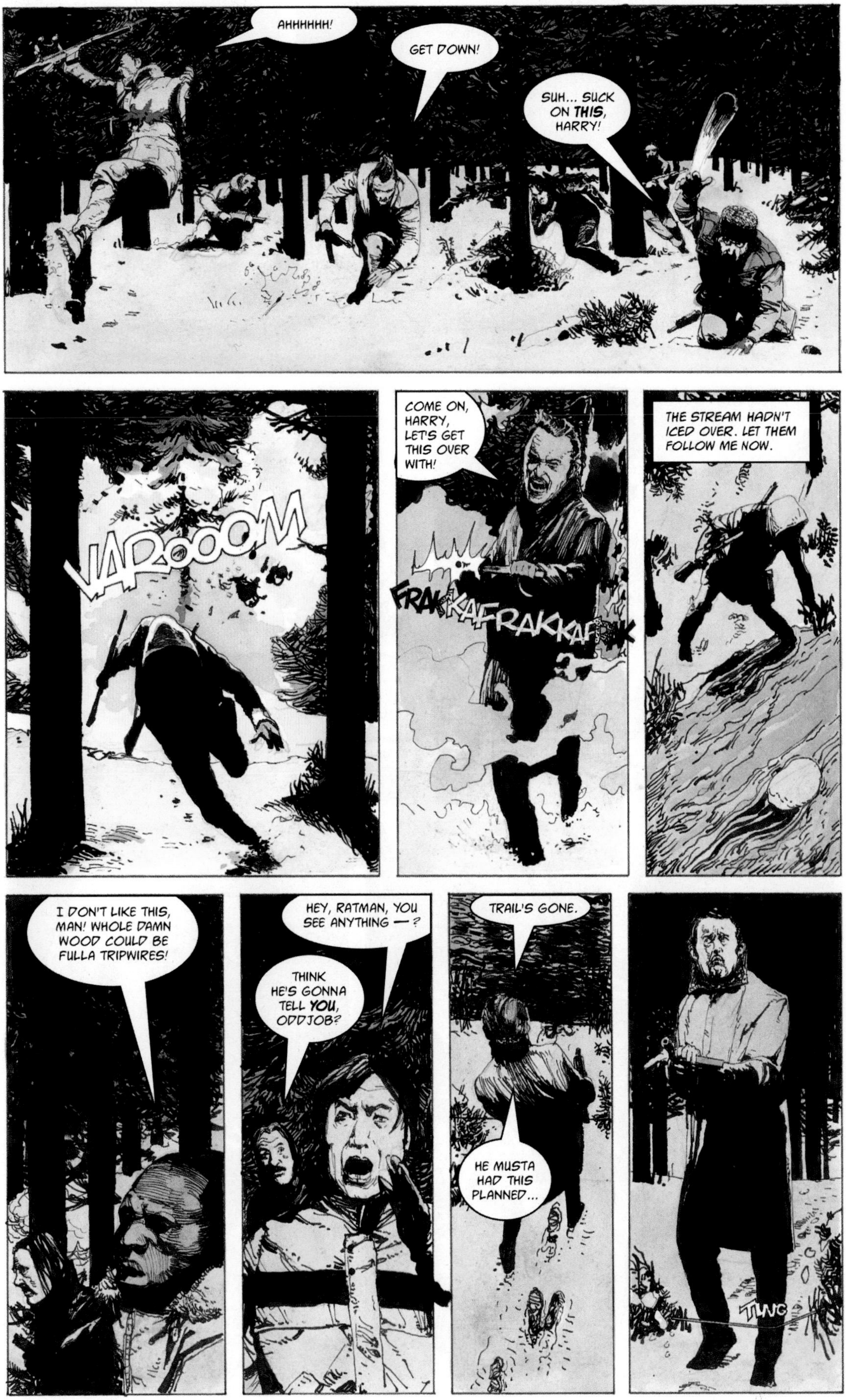
AHHHHHH!
GET DOWN!
SUH... SUCK ON **THIS**, HARRY!
VAROOOM
COME ON, HARRY, LET'S GET THIS OVER WITH!
FRAKKAFRAKKAFRAK
THE STREAM HADN'T ICED OVER. LET THEM FOLLOW ME NOW.
I DON'T LIKE THIS, MAN! WHOLE DAMN WOOD COULD BE FULLA TRIPWIRES!
HEY, RATMAN, YOU SEE ANYTHING — ?
THINK HE'S GONNA TELL **YOU**, ODDJOB?
TRAIL'S GONE.
HE MUSTA HAD THIS PLANNED...
TWNG

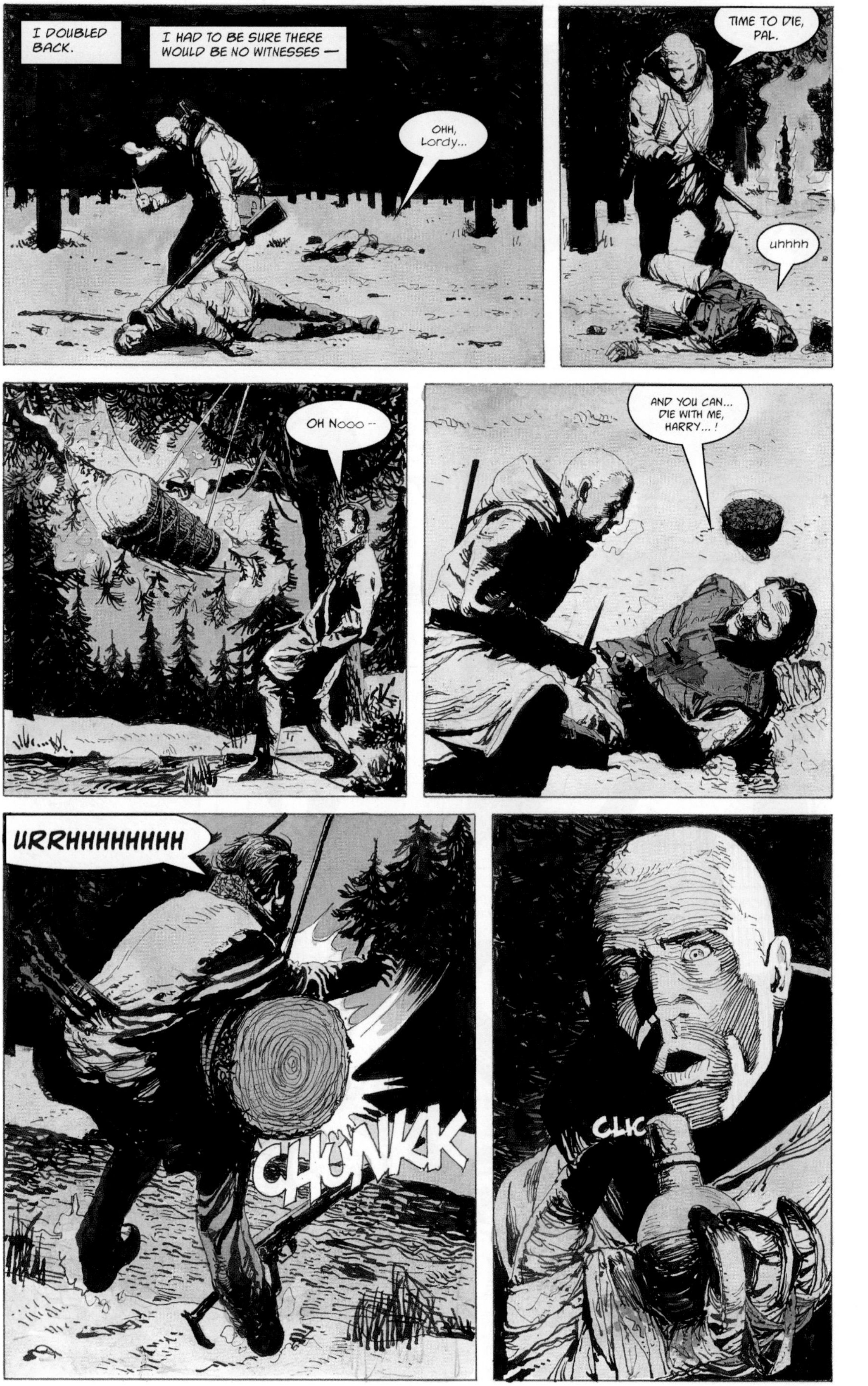
I DOUBLED BACK.
I HAD TO BE SURE THERE WOULD BE NO WITNESSES —
OHH, Lordy...
TIME TO DIE, PAL.
uhhhh
OH Nooo --
AND YOU CAN... DIE WITH ME, HARRY... !
URRHHHHHHHH
CHUNKK
CLIC

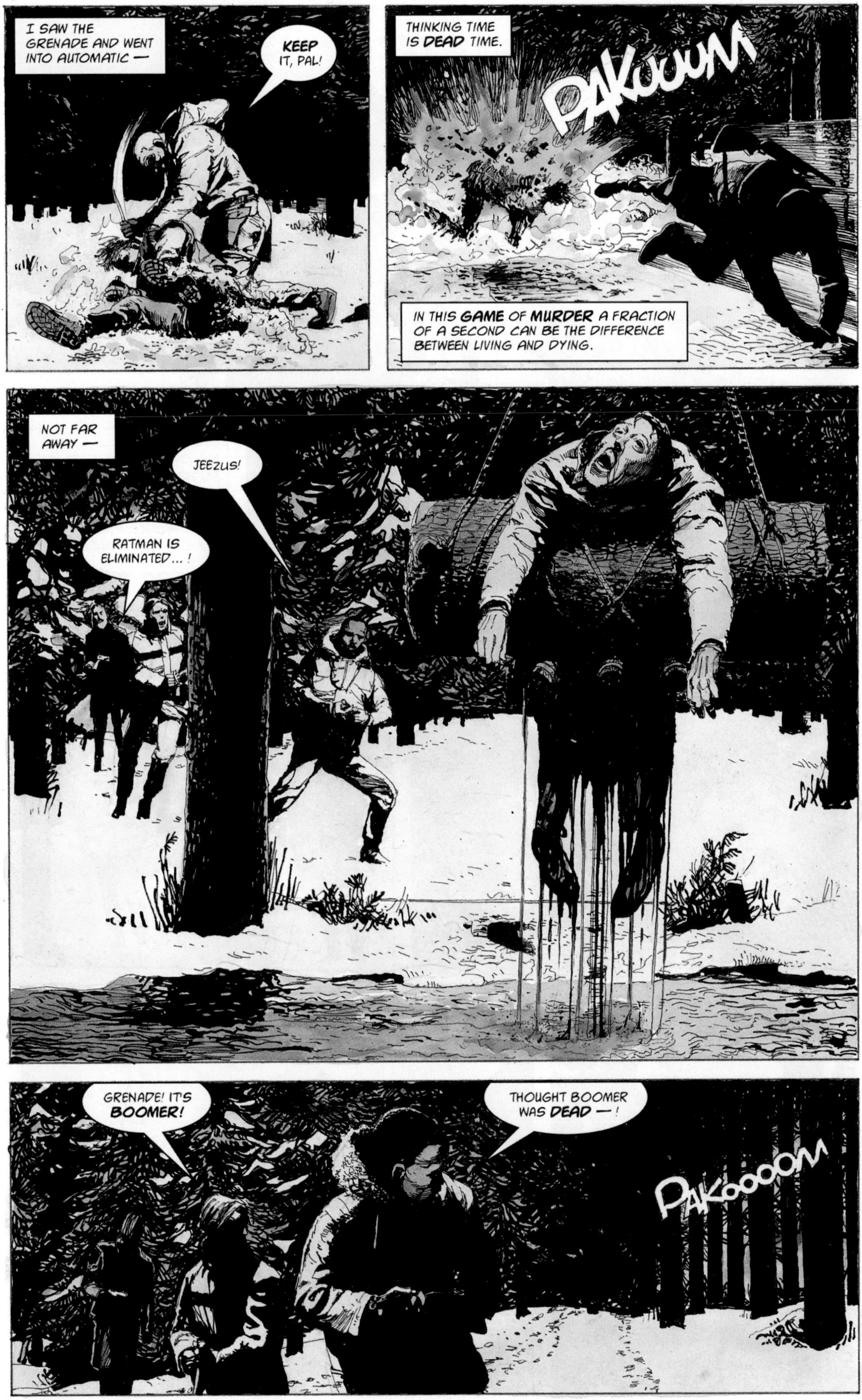

I SAW THE GRENADE AND WENT INTO AUTOMATIC —
KEEP IT, PAL!
THINKING TIME IS DEAD TIME.
PAKUUUM
IN THIS GAME OF MURDER A FRACTION OF A SECOND CAN BE THE DIFFERENCE BETWEEN LIVING AND DYING.
NOT FAR AWAY —
JEEZUS!
RATMAN IS ELIMINATED... !
GRENADE! IT'S BOOMER!
THOUGHT BOOMER WAS DEAD — !
PAKOOOOM

NICE TRY, PAL.

THIS AIN'T WORKIN', MAN! THIS IS HIS GROUND! HE'S GONNA *EX* US ALL!

I HAVE HAD A BAD FEELING ABOUT THIS ONE FROM THE BEGINNING. WE ALL KNEW HIS REPUTATION...

DUNNO 'BOUT YOU GUYS BUT I'M OUTA HERE.

HE IS *BEHIND* US NOW... CUTTING US OFF.

LET'S TALK, HARRY!

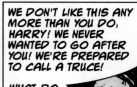

WE DON'T LIKE THIS ANY MORE THAN YOU DO, HARRY! WE NEVER WANTED TO GO AFTER YOU! WE'RE PREPARED TO CALL A TRUCE!

WHAT DO YOU SAY, HARRY?

HUH?

BREE BREE

THAT YOURS OR MINE?

KEEP MEANIN' TO GET ONE OF THEM FANCY RINGS --

BREE BREE

NOT ME.

FREAKIN' GETTIN' MY ASS SHOT OFF —!

WHAT'S THE SITUATION? I'M REAL GLAD YOU CALLED TO ASK ME THAT, BOSS MAN, 'COS SPEAKIN' TO YOU IS JUST WHAT I NEED RIGHT NOW!

WELL, I CAN TELL YOU, THE SITUATION IS NOT TOO DAMN GOOD.

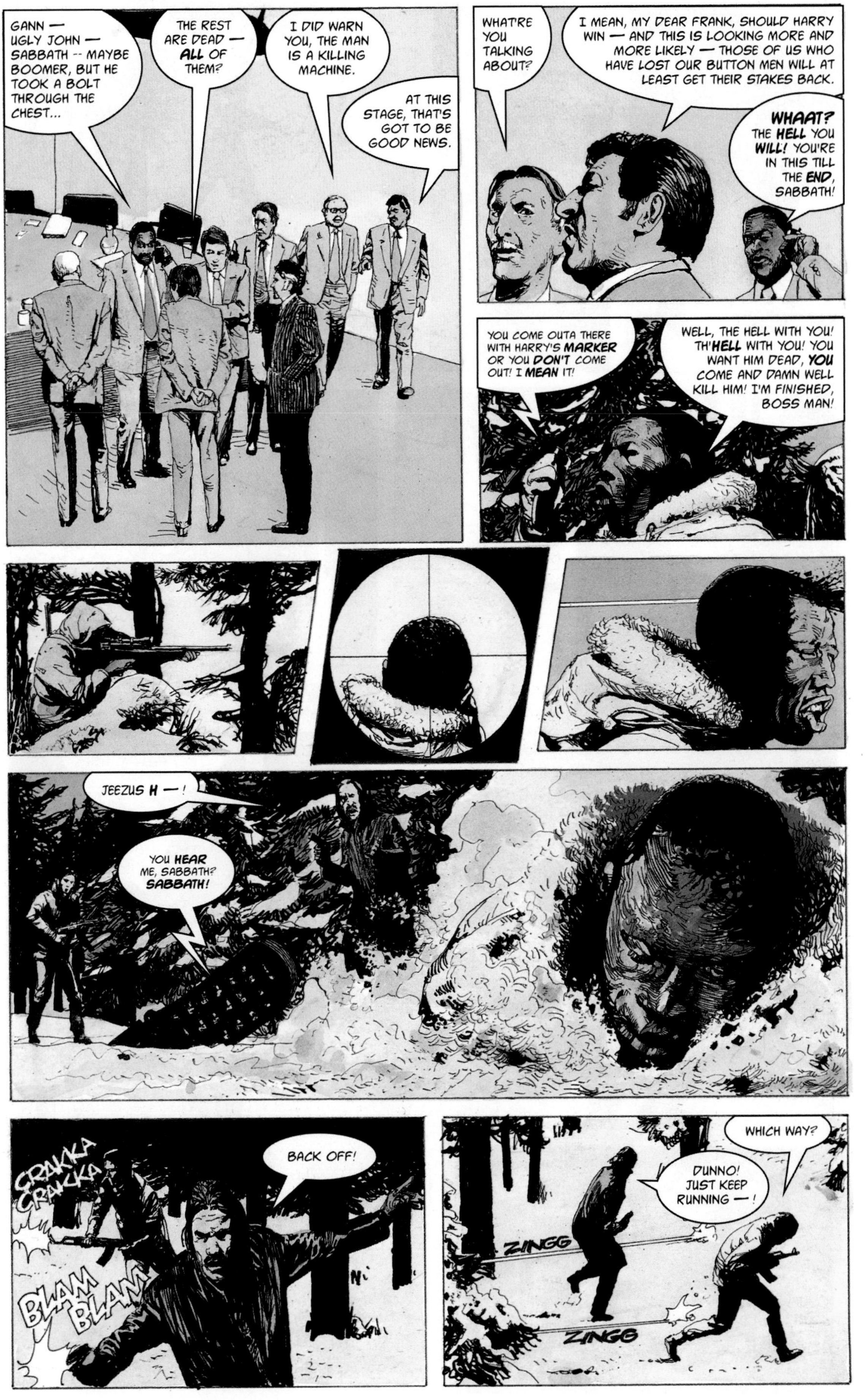
GANN — UGLY JOHN — SABBATH -- MAYBE BOOMER, BUT HE TOOK A BOLT THROUGH THE CHEST...
THE REST ARE DEAD — ALL OF THEM?
I DID WARN YOU, THE MAN IS A KILLING MACHINE.
AT THIS STAGE, THAT'S GOT TO BE GOOD NEWS.
WHAT'RE YOU TALKING ABOUT?
I MEAN, MY DEAR FRANK, SHOULD HARRY WIN — AND THIS IS LOOKING MORE AND MORE LIKELY — THOSE OF US WHO HAVE LOST OUR BUTTON MEN WILL AT LEAST GET THEIR STAKES BACK.
WHAAT? THE HELL YOU WILL! YOU'RE IN THIS TILL THE END, SABBATH!
YOU COME OUTA THERE WITH HARRY'S MARKER OR YOU DON'T COME OUT! I MEAN IT!
WELL, THE HELL WITH YOU! TH'HELL WITH YOU! YOU WANT HIM DEAD, YOU COME AND DAMN WELL KILL HIM! I'M FINISHED, BOSS MAN!
JEEZUS H — !
YOU HEAR ME, SABBATH? SABBATH!
CRACKA CRACKA
BLAM BLAM
BACK OFF!
WHICH WAY?
DUNNO! JUST KEEP RUNNING — !
ZINGG
ZINGG

UNHHH!

CRASH!

FREAKIN' SPIKES! JEEZUSSS!

GIMME A HAND, ODDJOB!

I TOLD YOU BEFORE, THE NAME IS *GANN*.

I'LL **REMEMBER** THIS, ODDJOB!

YOU AN' ME AIN'T FRIENDS NO MORE!

UNNNH!

DON'T SHOOT, UGLY MAN.

TRIPWIRE. LOOK OVER THERE.

WHO THE HELL IS *HE*?

I DON'T KNOW. THE ONE WHO WAS LOOKING AFTER HARRY'S CABIN, PERHAPS.

DON'T EVEN PAY TO BE **FRIENDS** WITH THE GUY!

MUCH AS IT GRIEVES ME TO SAY IT, WE GOT TO STICK TOGETHER, ODDJOB —

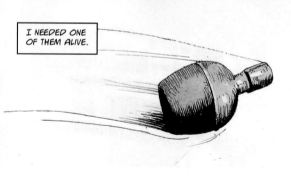

I NEEDED ONE OF THEM ALIVE.

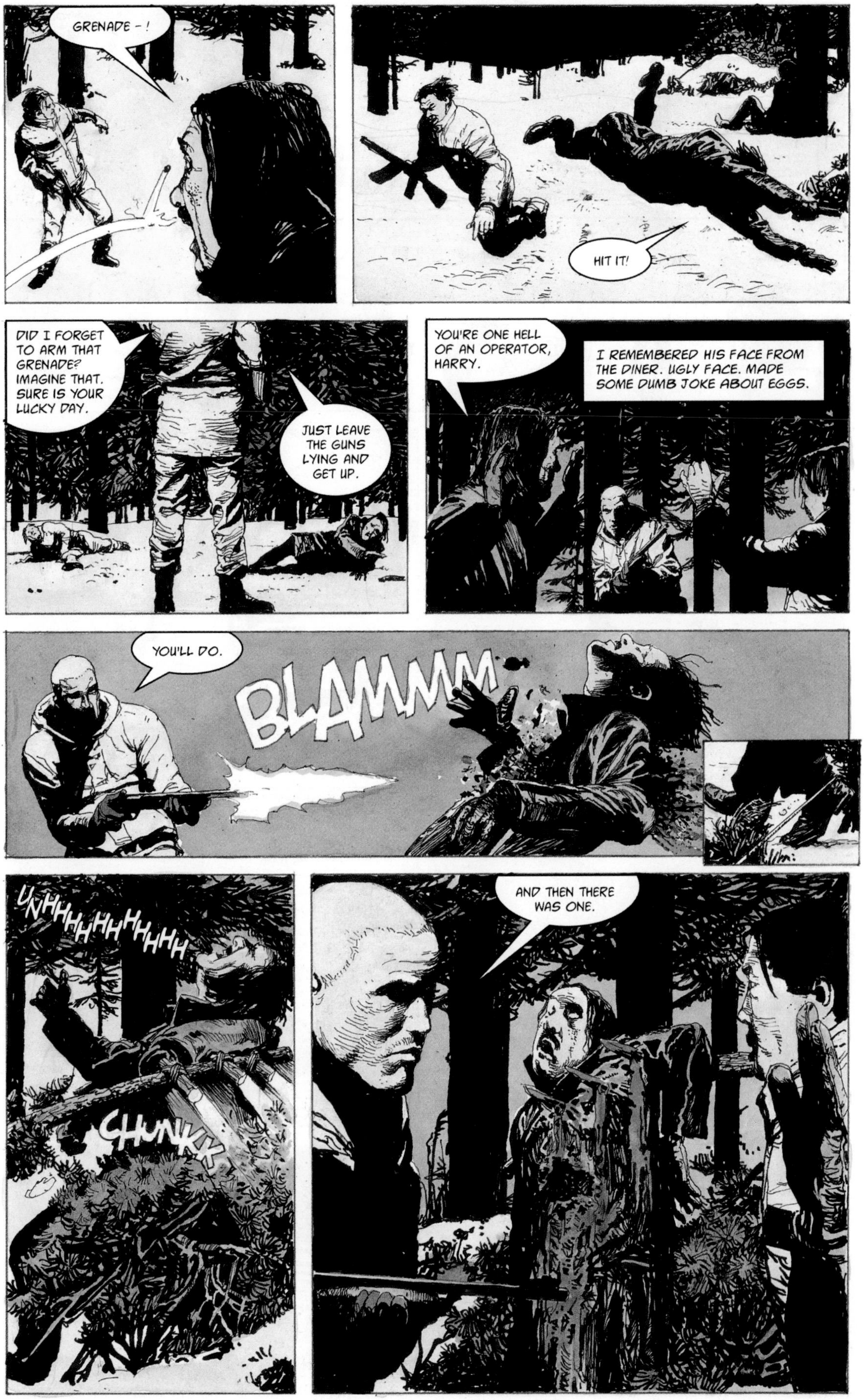
GRENADE -!
HIT IT!
DID I FORGET TO ARM THAT GRENADE? IMAGINE THAT. SURE IS YOUR LUCKY DAY.
JUST LEAVE THE GUNS LYING AND GET UP.
YOU'RE ONE HELL OF AN OPERATOR, HARRY.
I REMEMBERED HIS FACE FROM THE DINER. UGLY FACE. MADE SOME DUMB JOKE ABOUT EGGS.
YOU'LL DO.
BLAMMM
UNHHHHHHHHHHHH
CHUNKK
AND THEN THERE WAS ONE.

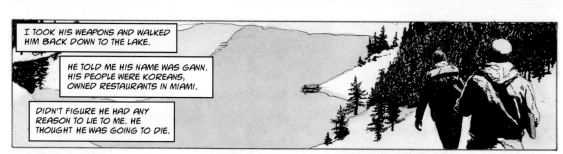

I TOOK HIS WEAPONS AND WALKED HIM BACK DOWN TO THE LAKE.

HE TOLD ME HIS NAME WAS GANN. HIS PEOPLE WERE KOREANS, OWNED RESTAURANTS IN MIAMI.

DIDN'T FIGURE HE HAD ANY REASON TO LIE TO ME. HE THOUGHT HE WAS GOING TO DIE.

HE'S MOVING OUT ONTO THE LAKE... ?

THERE IS A BOAT — A DINGHY.

ANSWER ME, GANN!

I CAN'T RAISE UGLY JOHN EITHER.

WHAT'S HE UP TO?

BLIP

YOU WILL FIND THIS IRONIC... MY VOICE PROMISED HE WOULD PERMIT ME TO QUIT -- IF I WON. IF I KILLED YOU.

AND YOU BELIEVED HIM?

PROBABLY NOT. IT WOULD HAVE BEEN INTERESTING TO... FIND OUT.

YOUR VOICE IS GETTING ANXIOUS.

HE'S A WORRIER.

BREE BREE

WHY ARE YOU DOING THIS, HARRY? IF YOU ARE GOING TO KILL ME, WHY LIKE THIS — ?

MAYBE YOU DON'T HAVE TO DIE, GANN. MAYBE YOU AND I CAN DO A DEAL.

I SHOWED HIM THE TRACER I'D TAKEN FROM MY TOOTH, AND I LAID THE WHOLE SCAM OUT FOR HIM.

SEE, GANN, I'M THE ONE WHO'S GOT TO DIE...

PLIP

AND IT WAS HIS TURN TO SEE THE FUNNY SIDE —

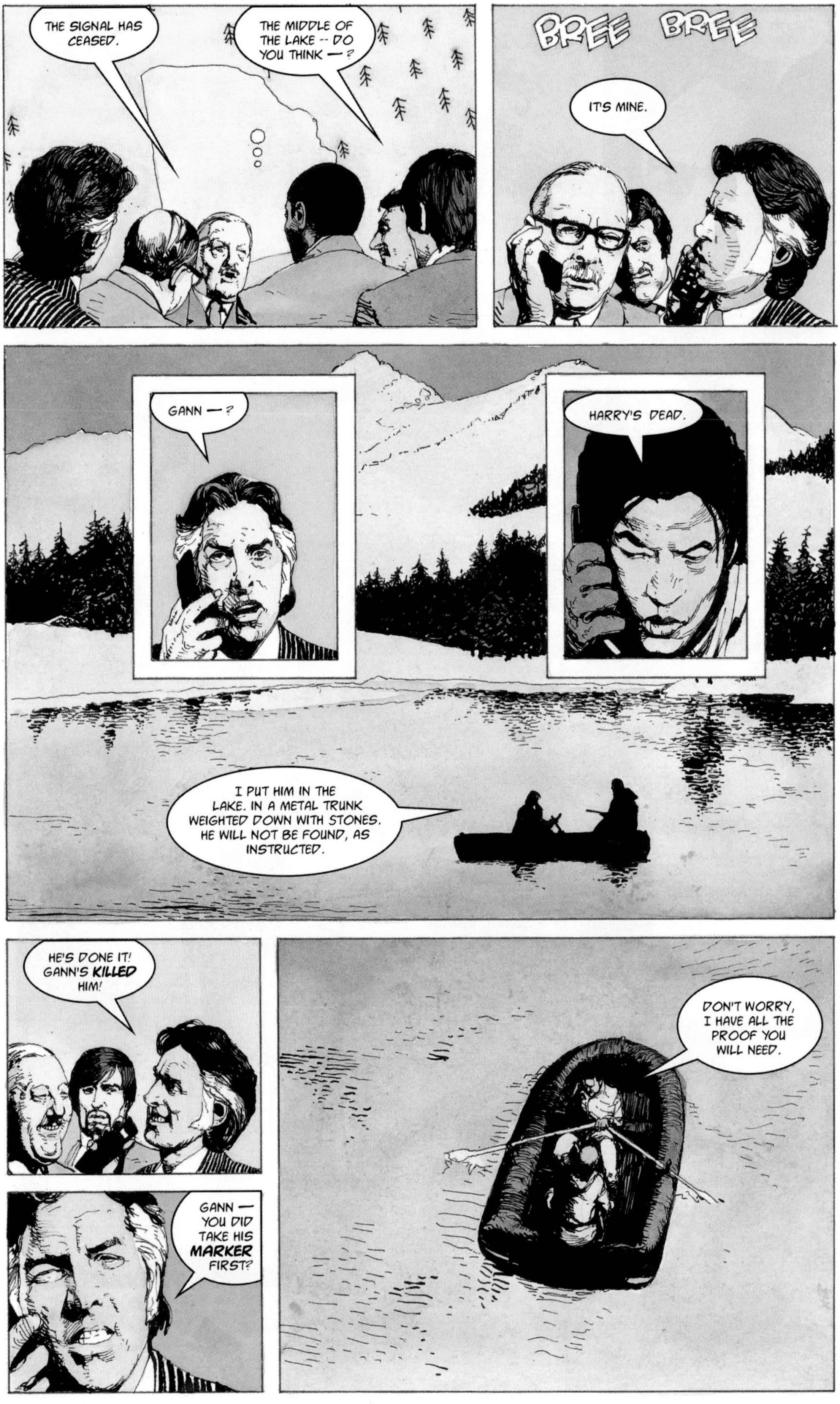
THE SIGNAL HAS CEASED.
THE MIDDLE OF THE LAKE -- DO YOU THINK —?
BREE BREE
IT'S MINE.
GANN —?
HARRY'S DEAD.
I PUT HIM IN THE LAKE. IN A METAL TRUNK WEIGHTED DOWN WITH STONES. HE WILL NOT BE FOUND, AS INSTRUCTED.
HE'S DONE IT! GANN'S KILLED HIM!
GANN — YOU DID TAKE HIS MARKER FIRST?
DON'T WORRY, I HAVE ALL THE PROOF YOU WILL NEED.

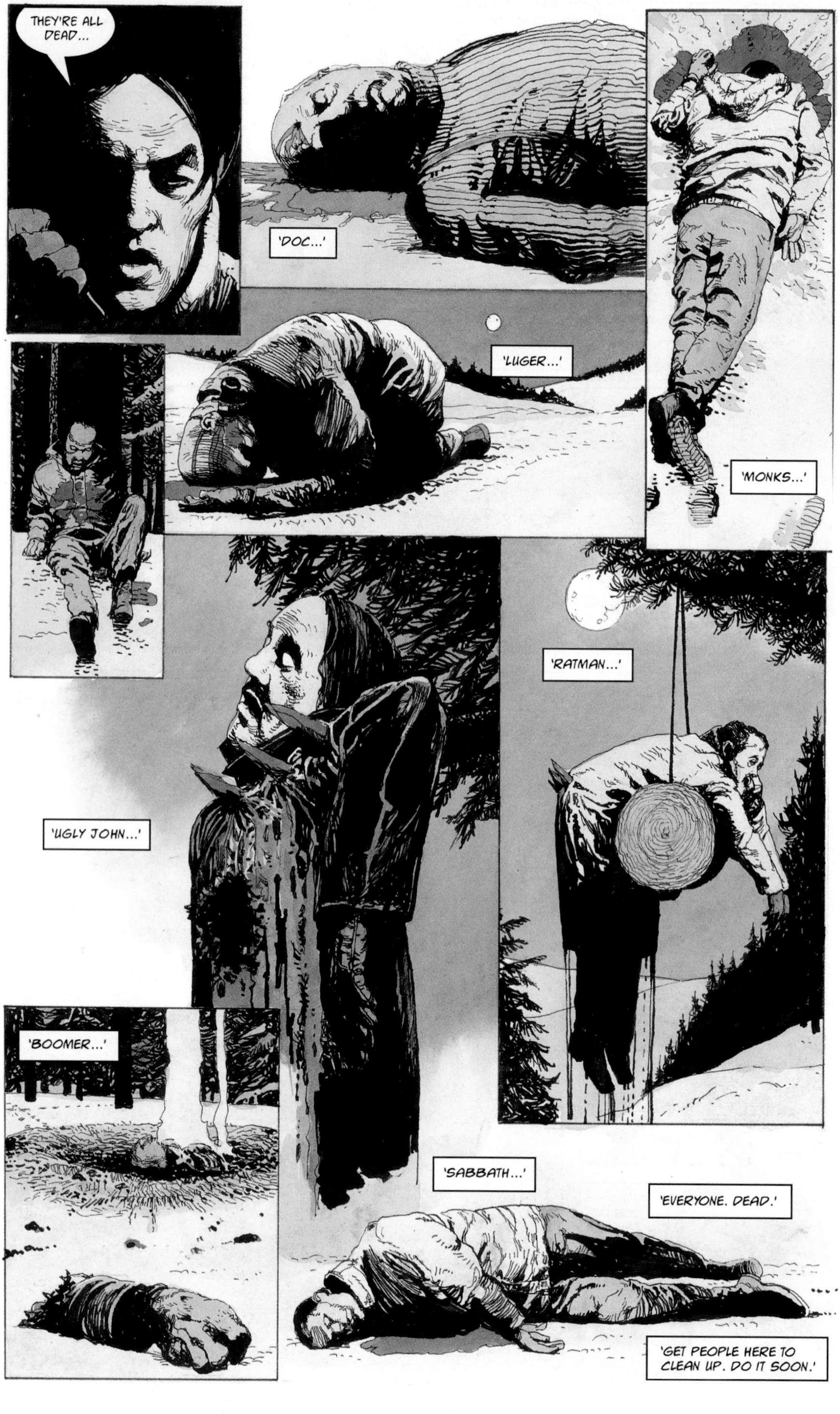
THEY'RE ALL DEAD...
'DOC...'
'LUGER...'
'MONKS...'
'RATMAN...'
'UGLY JOHN...'
'BOOMER...'
'SABBATH...'
'EVERYONE. DEAD.'
'GET PEOPLE HERE TO CLEAN UP. DO IT SOON.'

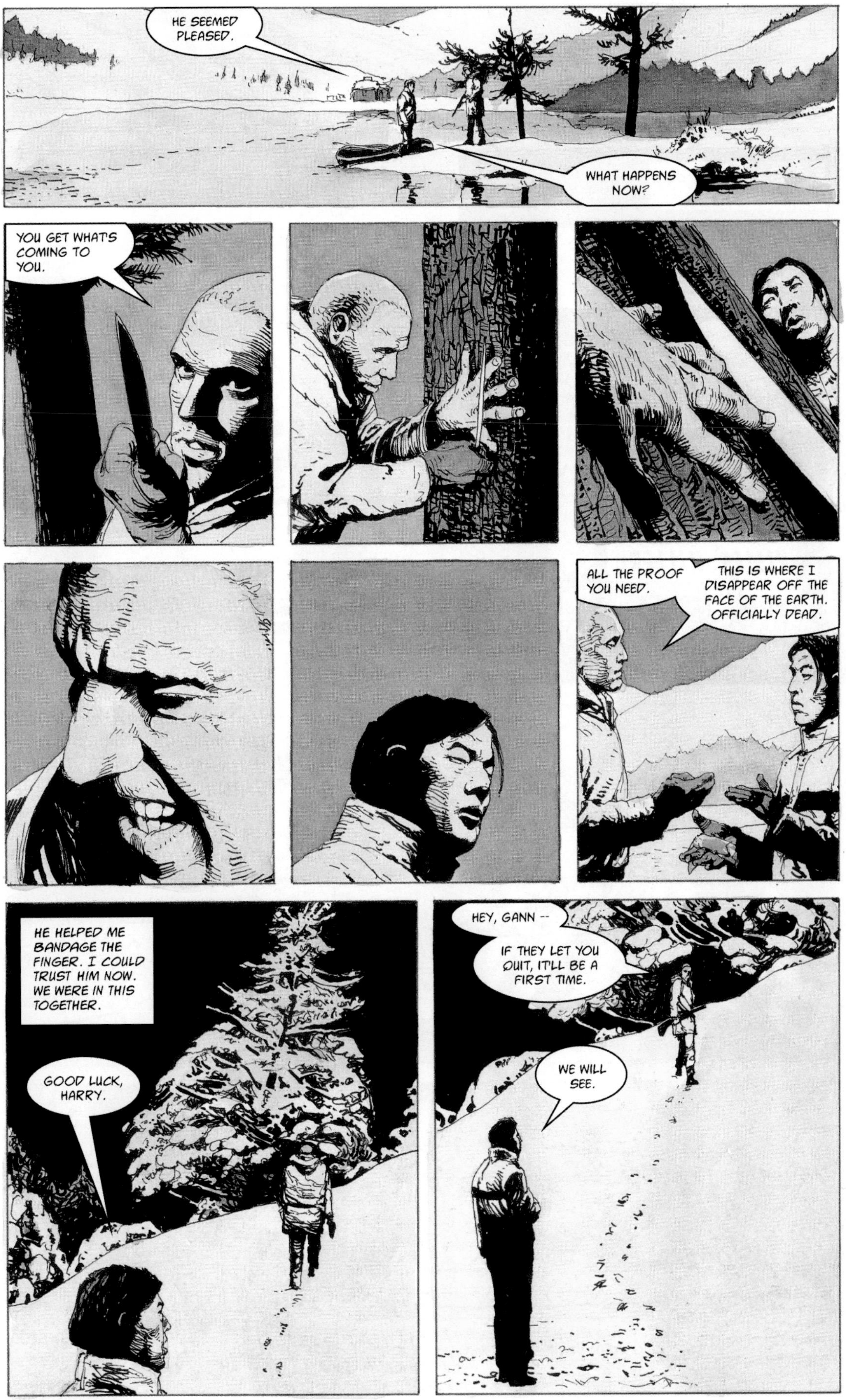
HE SEEMED PLEASED.
WHAT HAPPENS NOW?
YOU GET WHAT'S COMING TO YOU.
ALL THE PROOF YOU NEED.
THIS IS WHERE I DISAPPEAR OFF THE FACE OF THE EARTH. OFFICIALLY DEAD.
HE HELPED ME BANDAGE THE FINGER. I COULD TRUST HIM NOW. WE WERE IN THIS TOGETHER.
GOOD LUCK, HARRY.
HEY, GANN --
IF THEY LET YOU QUIT, IT'LL BE A FIRST TIME.
WE WILL SEE.

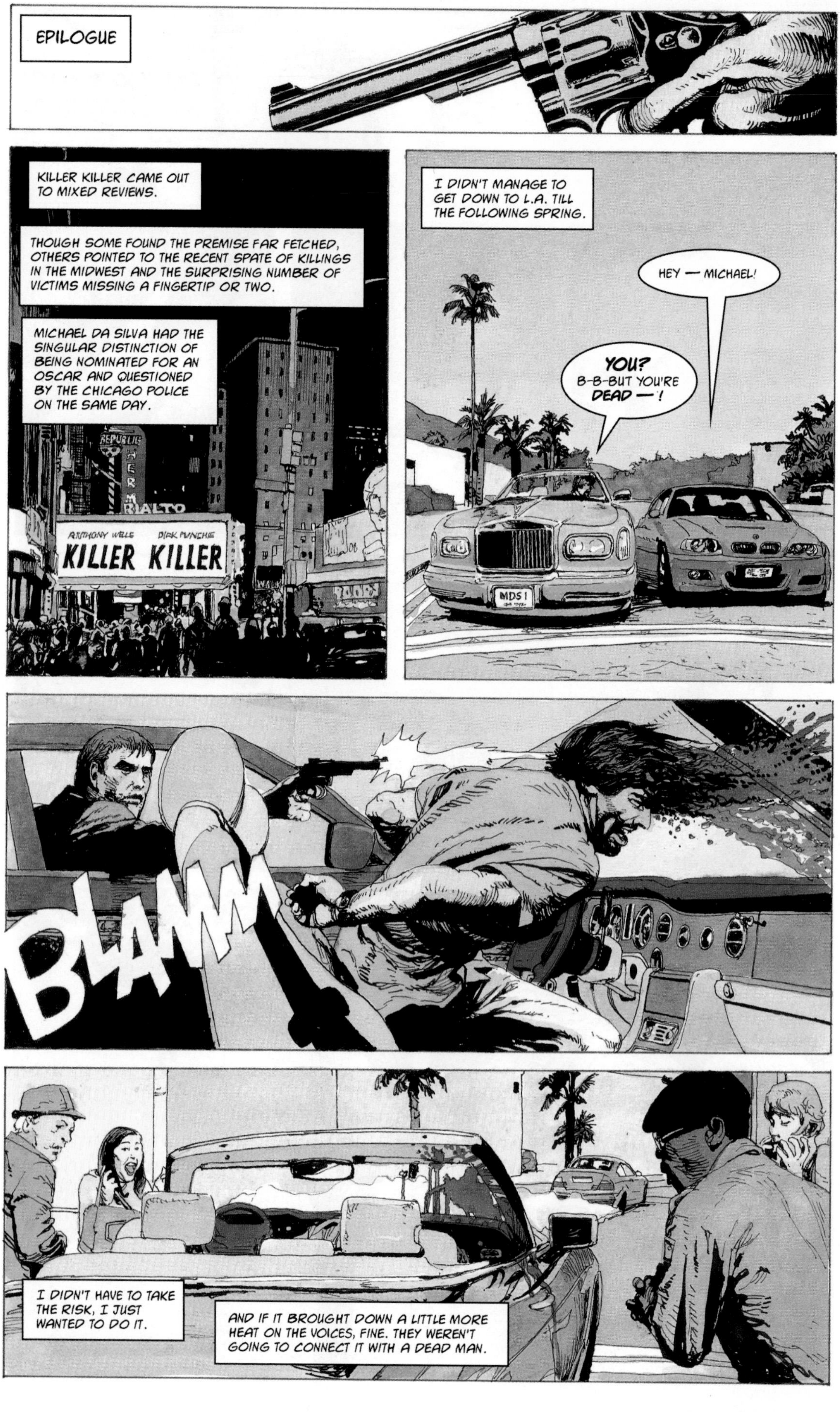
EPILOGUE
KILLER KILLER CAME OUT TO MIXED REVIEWS.
THOUGH SOME FOUND THE PREMISE FAR FETCHED, OTHERS POINTED TO THE RECENT SPATE OF KILLINGS IN THE MIDWEST AND THE SURPRISING NUMBER OF VICTIMS MISSING A FINGERTIP OR TWO.
MICHAEL DA SILVA HAD THE SINGULAR DISTINCTION OF BEING NOMINATED FOR AN OSCAR AND QUESTIONED BY THE CHICAGO POLICE ON THE SAME DAY.
RIALTO
KILLER KILLER
I DIDN'T MANAGE TO GET DOWN TO L.A. TILL THE FOLLOWING SPRING.
HEY — MICHAEL!
YOU? B-B-BUT YOU'RE DEAD —!
MDS 1
BLAMM
I DIDN'T HAVE TO TAKE THE RISK, I JUST WANTED TO DO IT.
AND IF IT BROUGHT DOWN A LITTLE MORE HEAT ON THE VOICES, FINE. THEY WEREN'T GOING TO CONNECT IT WITH A DEAD MAN.

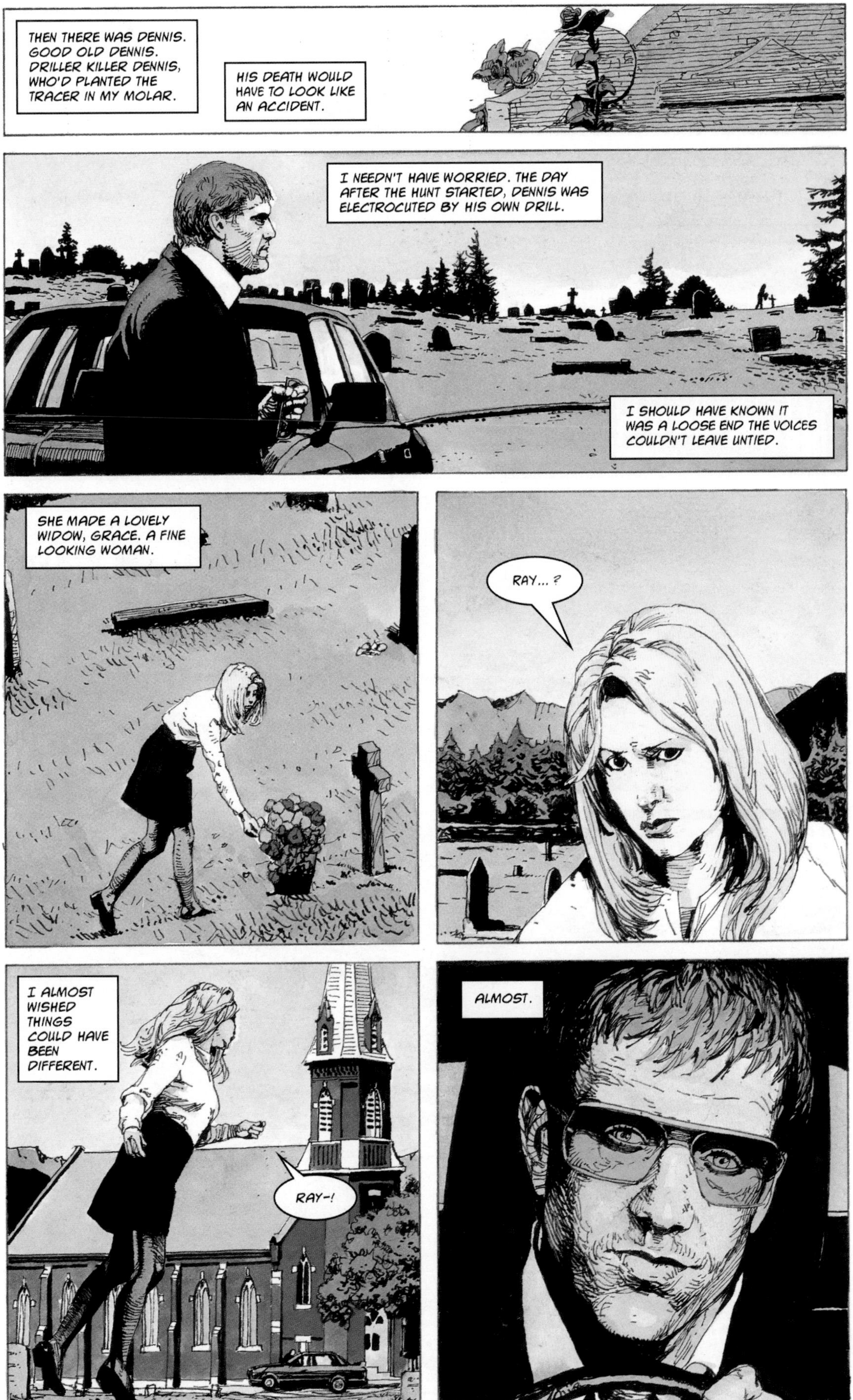
THEN THERE WAS DENNIS. GOOD OLD DENNIS. DRILLER KILLER DENNIS, WHO'D PLANTED THE TRACER IN MY MOLAR.
HIS DEATH WOULD HAVE TO LOOK LIKE AN ACCIDENT.
I NEEDN'T HAVE WORRIED. THE DAY AFTER THE HUNT STARTED, DENNIS WAS ELECTROCUTED BY HIS OWN DRILL.
I SHOULD HAVE KNOWN IT WAS A LOOSE END THE VOICES COULDN'T LEAVE UNTIED.
SHE MADE A LOVELY WIDOW, GRACE. A FINE LOOKING WOMAN.
RAY... ?
I ALMOST WISHED THINGS COULD HAVE BEEN DIFFERENT.
RAY-!
ALMOST.

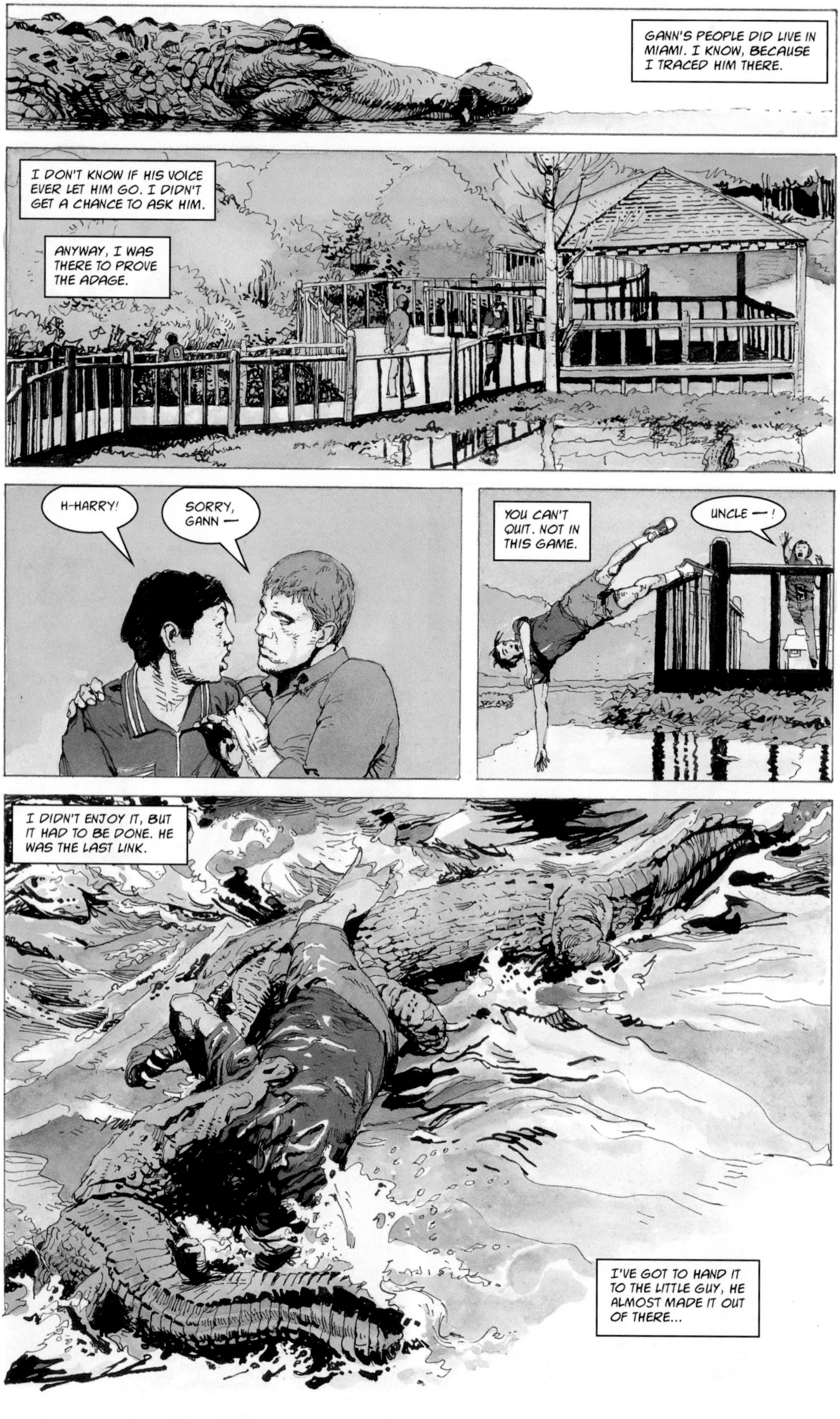
GANN'S PEOPLE DID LIVE IN MIAMI. I KNOW, BECAUSE I TRACED HIM THERE.
I DON'T KNOW IF HIS VOICE EVER LET HIM GO. I DIDN'T GET A CHANCE TO ASK HIM.
ANYWAY, I WAS THERE TO PROVE THE ADAGE.
H-HARRY!
SORRY, GANN —
YOU CAN'T QUIT. NOT IN THIS GAME.
UNCLE — !
I DIDN'T ENJOY IT, BUT IT HAD TO BE DONE. HE WAS THE LAST LINK.
I'VE GOT TO HAND IT TO THE LITTLE GUY, HE ALMOST MADE IT OUT OF THERE...

THE END

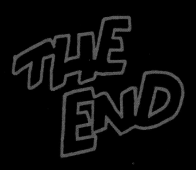

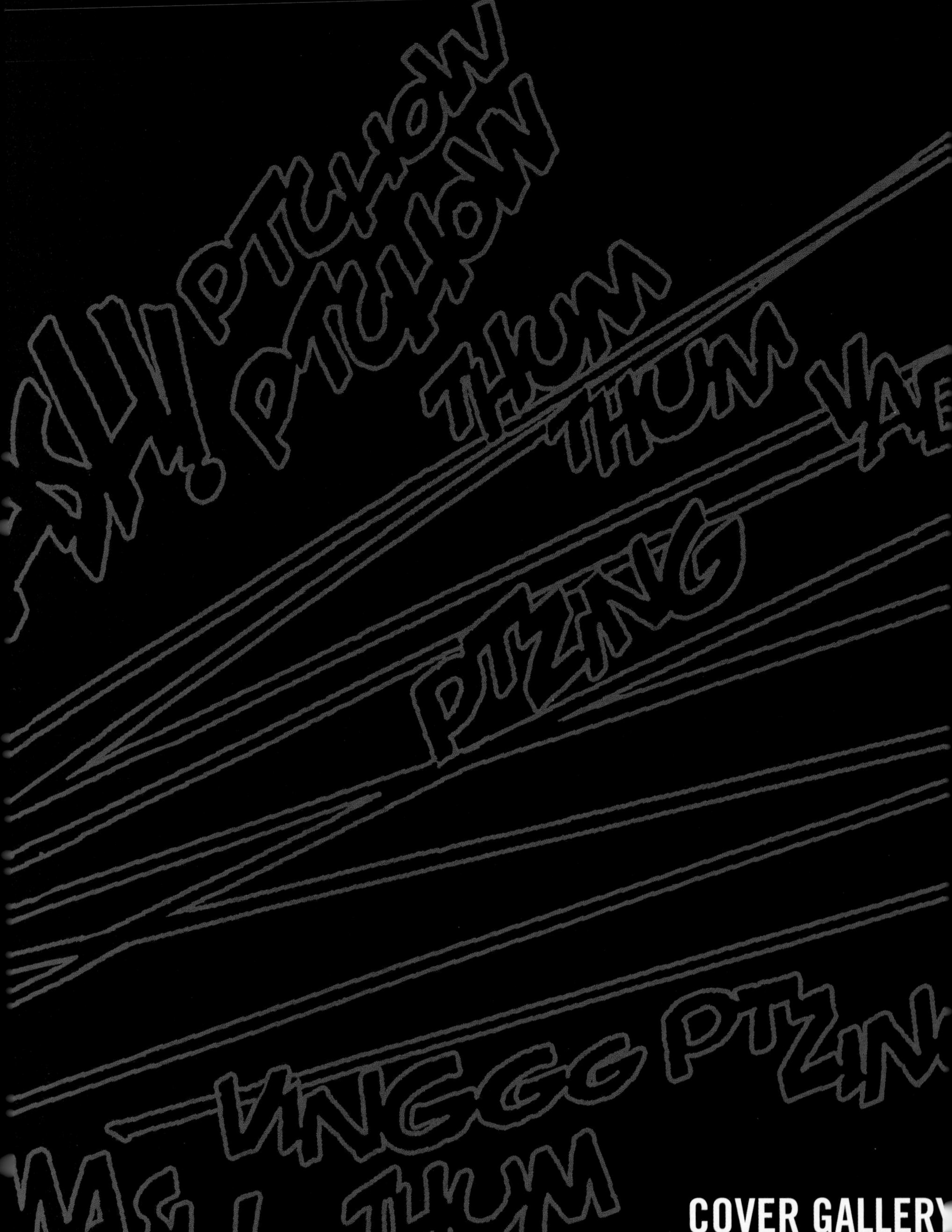
THUM
THUM
PTZING
THUM

COVER GALLERY

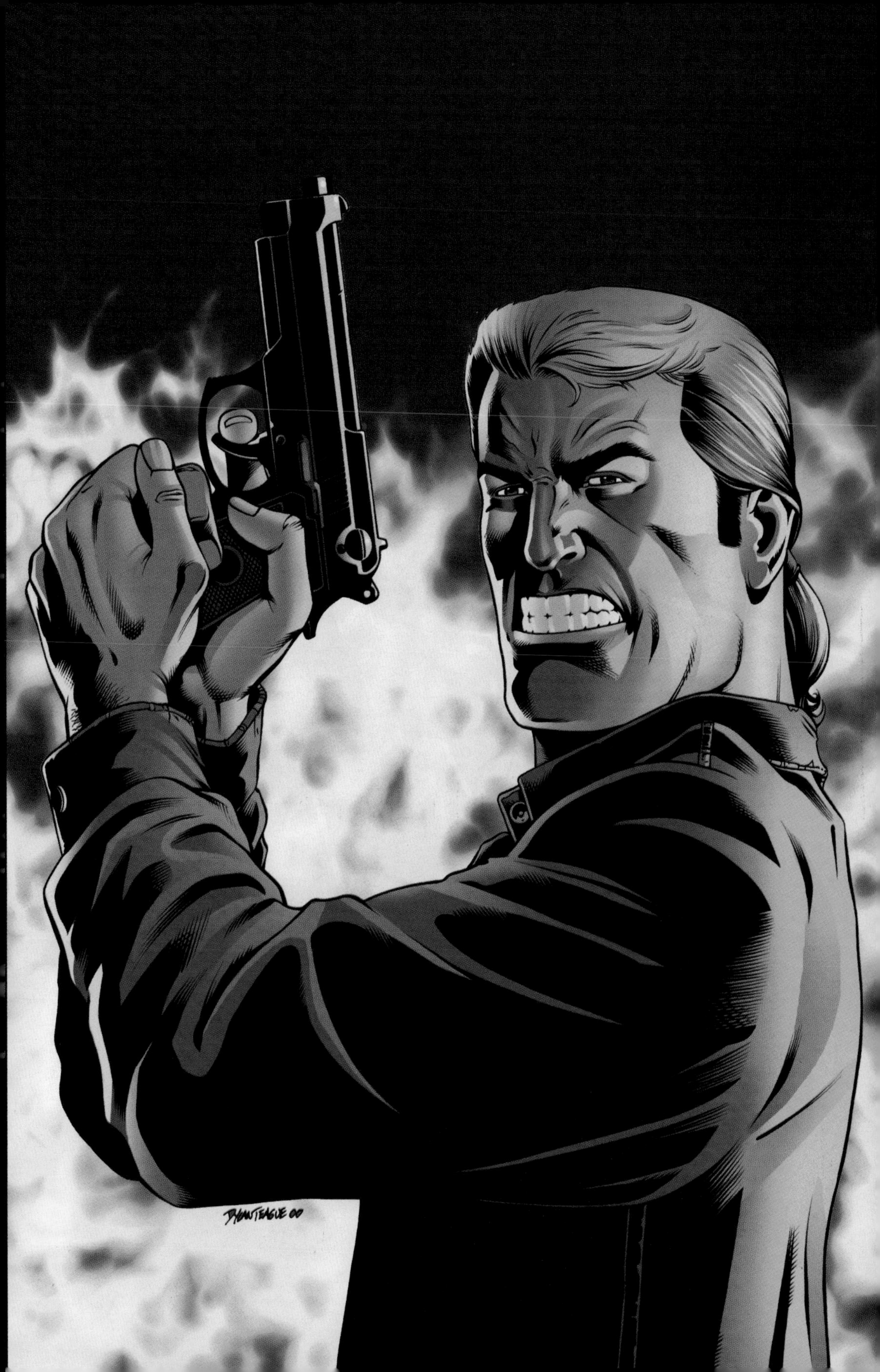
DYLAN TEAGUE 00

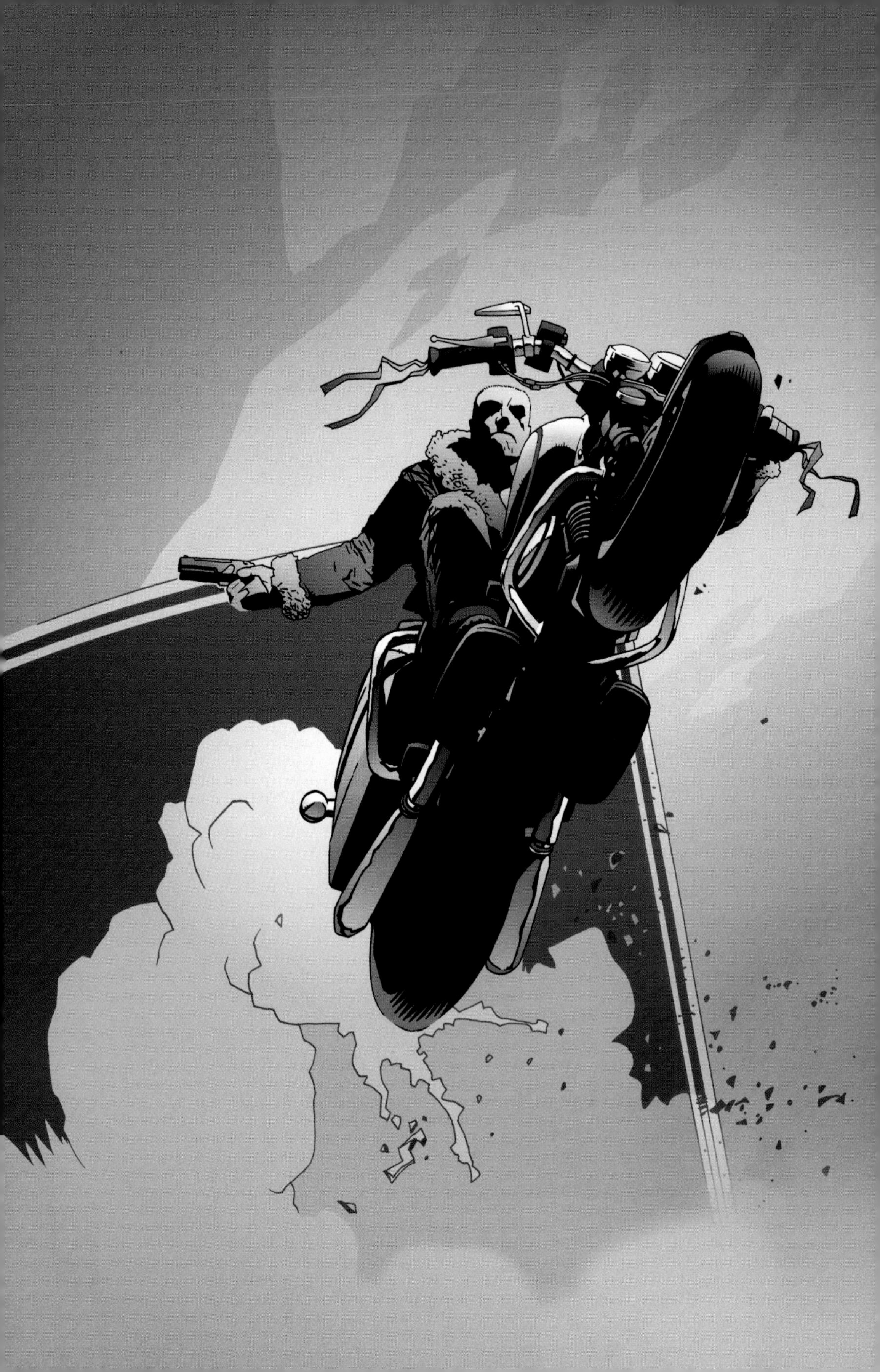

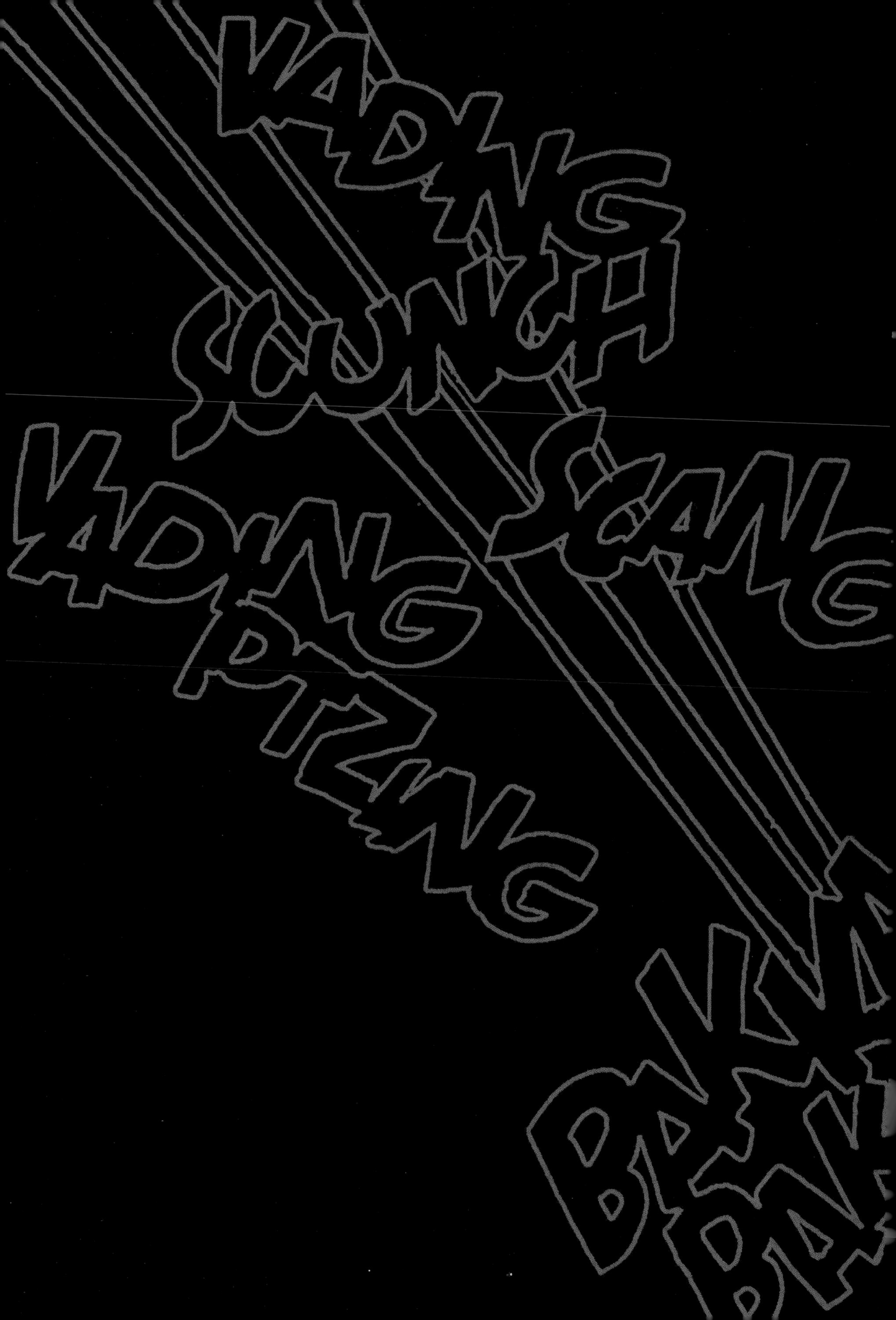

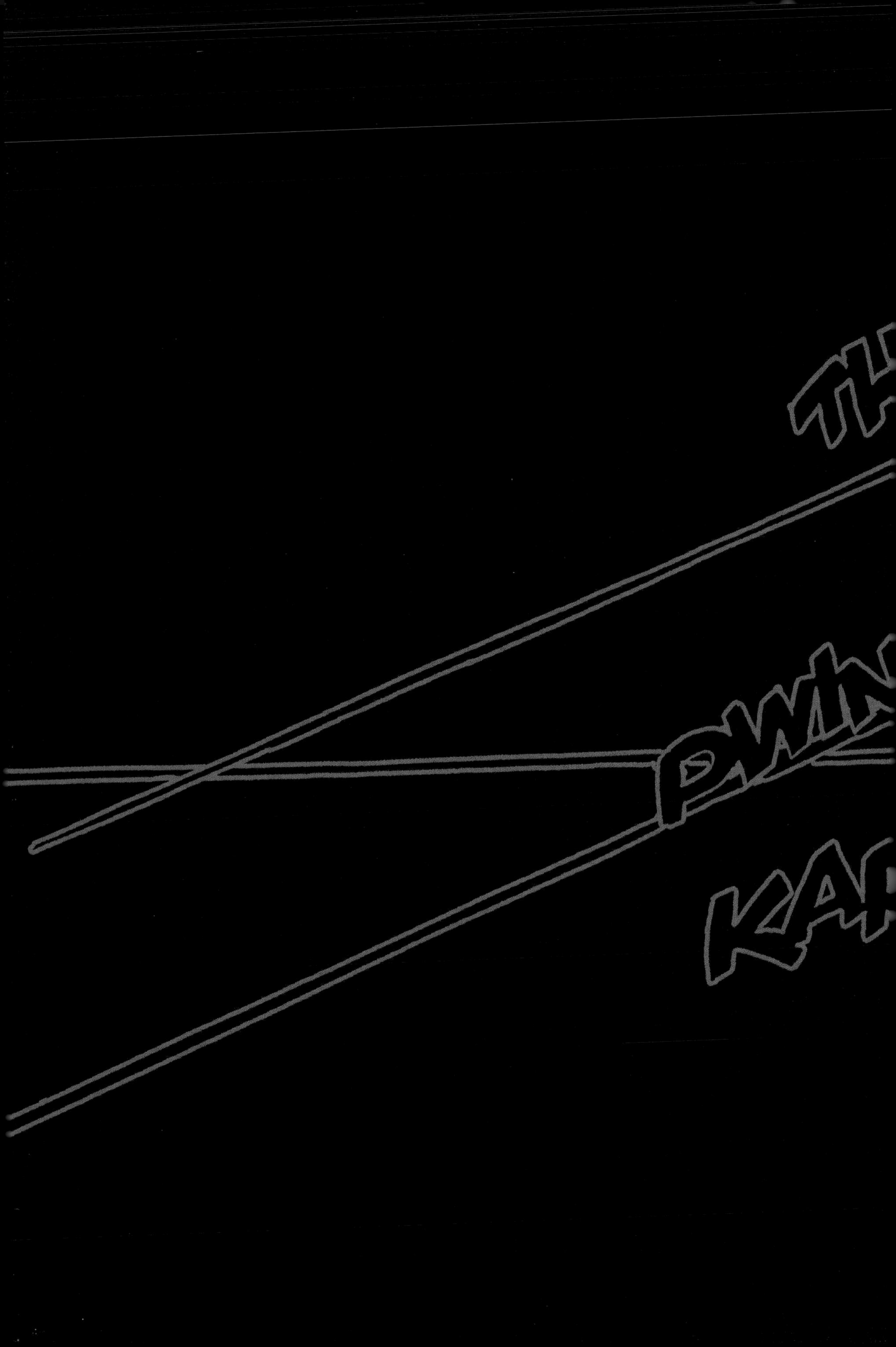

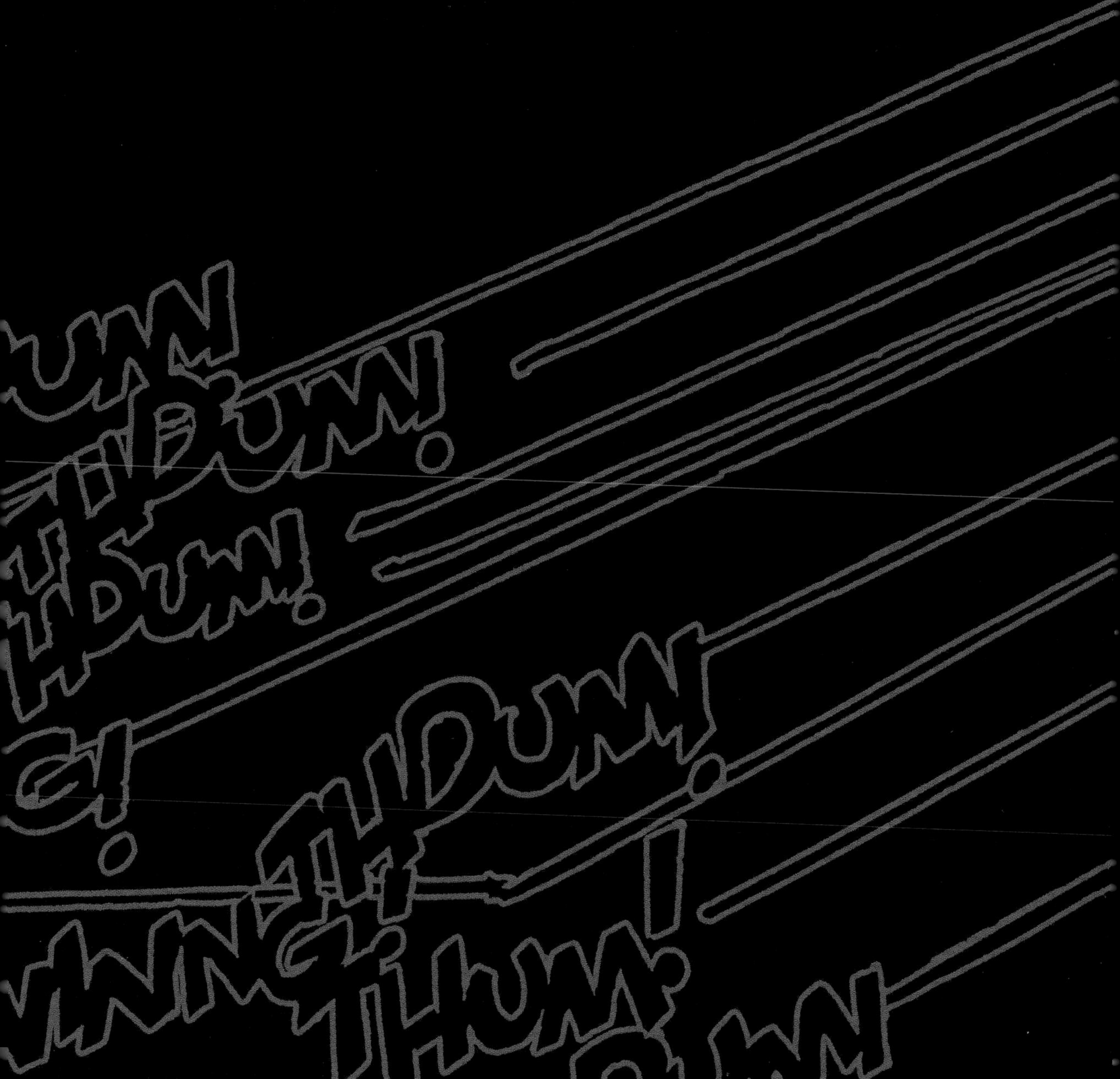
THDUNN!
THDUNN!
THDUNN!
THDUNN!

SKRASH! PTCHOW
PTCHOW

THUM

THUM

PIZING

THWASH! VNGGG PIZING

THWASH THUM

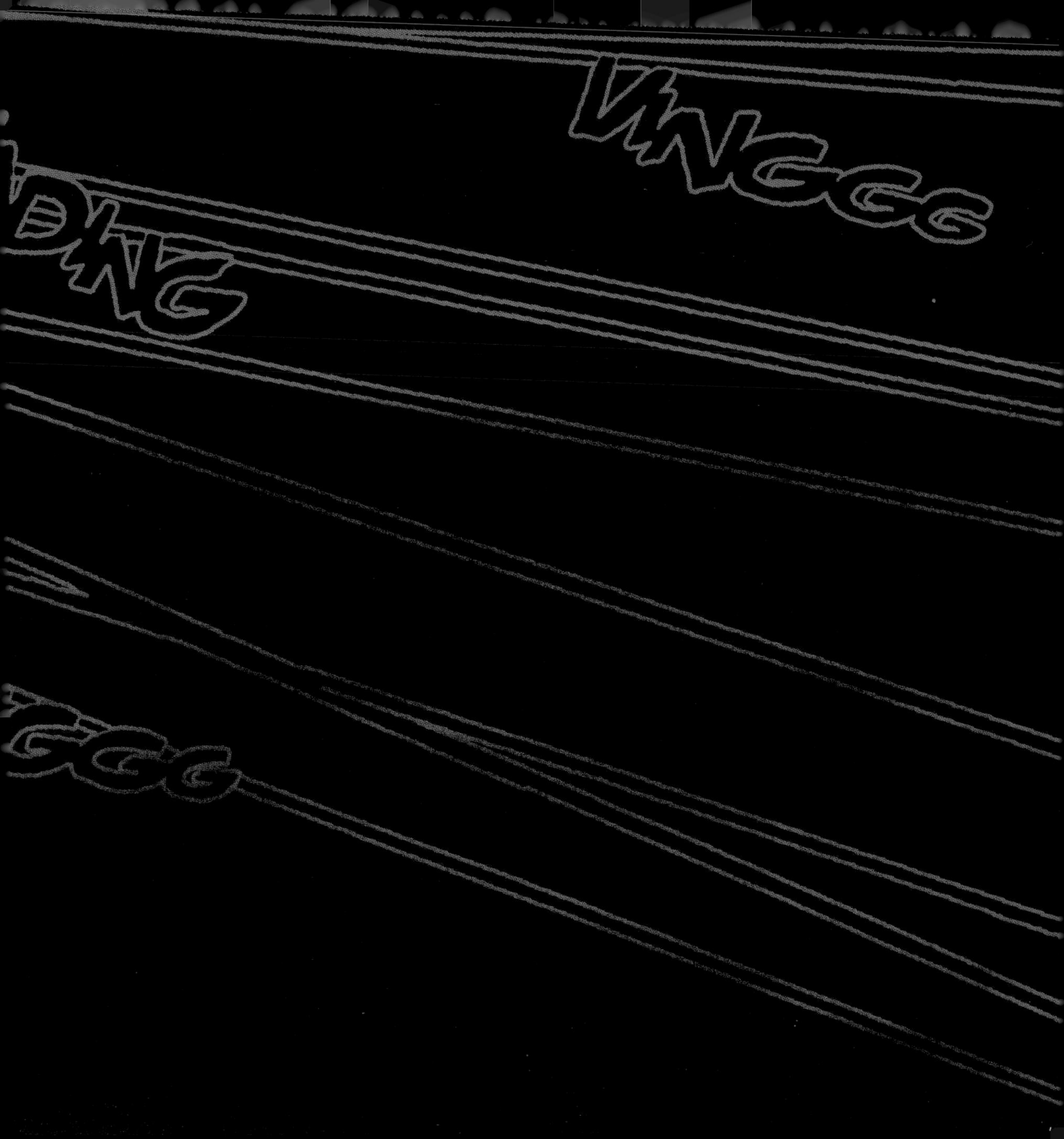
VNGGG
DNG
GGG

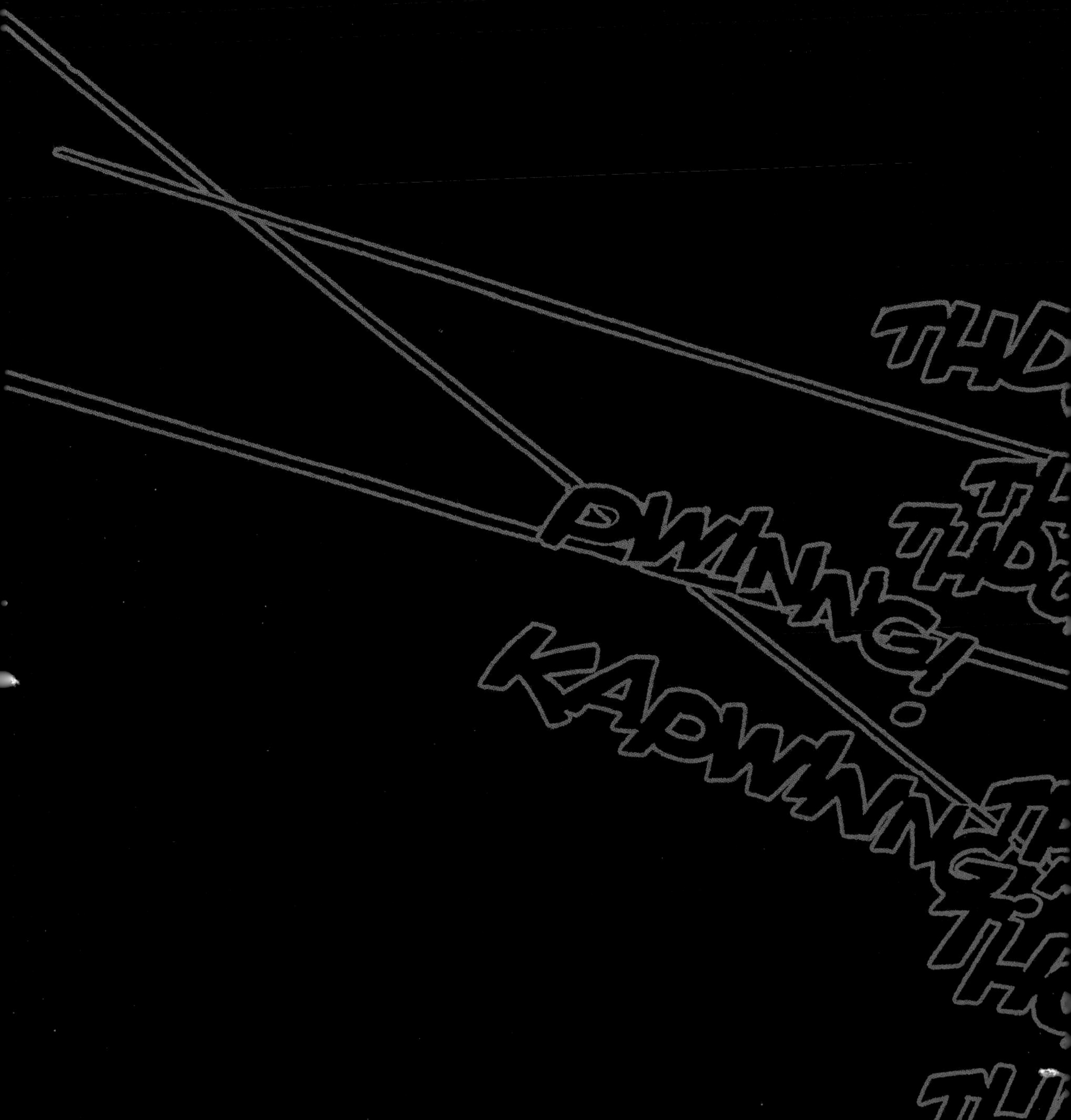

THD

TH
THD
THD

PWNNG!

KADWNNNG!

KADWNNNG!
THS

THS

JOHN WAGNER

John Wagner has been scripting for *2000 AD* for more years than he cares to remember. His creations include *Judge Dredd, Strontium Dog, Ace Trucking, Al's Baby, Button Man* and *Mean Machine*. Outside of *2000 AD* his credits include *Star Wars, Lobo, The Punisher* and the critically acclaimed *A History of Violence*.

ARTHUR RANSON

Arthur Ranson has long been one of *2000 AD*'s most popular artists; having made his initial impact working on *Judge Anderson*, he teamed up with John Wagner to create the highly acclaimed *Button Man* series, and later with Alan Grant for *Mazeworld*. He has also co-created the character of pyrokinetic Mega-City One citizen *Juliet November*, and illustrated both *Judge Dredd* and several *Future Shocks*. Ranson's most recent non-*2000 AD* work has been for Marvel Comics on *X-Factor* and latterly *X-Treme X-Men X-Posé*.